Teaching Success Guide for the Advanced Placement Classroom

King Lear

Advanced Placement Classroom

Advanced Placement Classroom

R. Brigham Lampert

PRUFROCK PRESS INC.
WACO, TEXAS

Library of Congress Cataloging-in-Publication Data

Lampert, R. Brigham.
  King Lear / by R. Brigham Lampert.
       p. cm. -- (Teaching success guide for the advanced placement classroom)
  At head of title: Advanced placement classroom
  Includes bibliographical references.
  ISBN 978-1-59363-835-1 (pbk.)
 1. Shakespeare, William, 1564-1616. King Lear. 2. Shakespeare, William, 1564-1616--Study and teaching (Higher) 3. Lear, King (Legendary character), in literature. I. Title. II. Title: Advanced placement classroom.
  PR2819.L28 2011
  822.3'3--dc23
                       2011029584

Copyright ©2012 Prufrock Press Inc.

Edited by Lacy Compton

ISBN-13: 978-1-59363-835-1

No part of this book may be reproduced, translated, stored in a retrieval system, or transmitted, in any form or by any means, electronic, mechanical, photocopying, microfilming, recording, or otherwise, without written permission from the publisher.

Prufrock Press grants the individual purchasing this book permission to photocopy original activity pages for single classroom use. This permission does not include electronic reproduction rights. Should you wish to make copies of materials we sourced or licensed from others, request permission from the original publisher before reproducing that material.

For more information about our copyright policy or to request reprint permissions, visit http://www.prufrock.com/permissions.

At the time of this book's publication, all facts and figures cited are the most current available. All telephone numbers, addresses, and website URLs are accurate and active. All publications, organizations, websites, and other resources exist as described in the book, and all have been verified. The author and Prufrock Press Inc. make no warranty or guarantee concerning the information and materials given out by organizations or content found at websites, and we are not responsible for any changes that occur after this book's publication. If you find an error, please contact Prufrock Press Inc.

•AP and Advanced Placement Program are registered trademarks of the College Entrance Examination Board, which was not involved in the production of, and does not endorse, this book.

Prufrock Press Inc.
P.O. Box 8813
Waco, TX 76714-8813
Phone: (800) 998-2208
Fax: (800) 240-0333
http://www.prufrock.com

Dedication

I dedicate this book to my parents, the Rev. Dr. Richard and Molly Ann Lampert, whom I greatly admire and whose provision of excellent educational opportunities throughout my life has been unceasing.

Contents

Acknowledgments... xi

Chapter 1
Introduction 1

Chapter 2
Why Teach *King Lear*? 9

Chapter 3
Reading *King Lear* 19

Chapter 4
Understanding *King Lear* 61

Chapter 5
Performing *King Lear* 105

Chapter 6
Talking About *King Lear* 131

Chapter 7
Writing About *King Lear* 157

Glossary 187

Appendix A
Notations on *King Lear*'s Literary Devices 201

References 215
Resources for Further Study 219
About the Author 223
Common Core State Standards Alignment 225

Acknowledgments

Once again, my authorship of this book has been aided in many ways by numerous persons to whom I am greatly indebted. Particularly, I want to offer thanks to my wife Jennifer for her constant encouragement and aid; to Dr. Joyce VanTassel-Baska for giving me a start in professional curriculum writing; to Mrs. Ann Shaver, my teaching partner, who directly inspired the included lesson plan mimicking social media; and to Lacy Compton and the staff at Prufrock Press, without whom this text would not exist.

Chapter 1

Introduction

I do not intend this book as a work of Shakespearean scholarship, criticism, or analysis; neither have I written it as any kind of strictly academic exercise. Instead, I have aimed at producing an extremely classroom-ready, teacher-friendly resource for those of us who wish to enhance our students' experiences and expand their successes, both in the Pre-AP and/or Advanced Placement classroom and on the summative AP English Literature examination, by tackling *King Lear* as a powerful, influential addition to the language arts curriculum. To this end, I have targeted the population of gifted and talented students who potentially benefit so very much from the rigors and joys of Shakespearean study, although the activities and assignments contained herein are likewise appropriate for nongifted classroom populations. Nevertheless, I have assumed in writing this text that its intended population is one able not only to succeed, but also to thrive in such a rigorous course of study. Please note that the material included within this book does not constitute an official College Board curriculum, nor is it officially endorsed by the College Board. It is meant as a curricular supplement for use in Advanced Placement, Pre-AP, International Baccalaureate, honors, gifted, and other similarly denoted advanced English and literature courses.

Scholarship and Standards

As a reader and thinker, I am an unapologetic Shakespearean and have been since high school. As a teacher, I have been fortunate enough to write contractually and publish Shakespearean curricula for much of my career. Prior to penning both this text and *Advanced Placement Classroom: Romeo and Juliet*, also available from Prufrock Press, my work in designing these curricula for gifted students began nearly a decade ago at the Center for Gifted Education at The College of William and Mary, in Williamsburg, VA. Over the course of several years, I designed *Navigator* teachers' guides for six Shakespearean plays, all based on the Center's—and particularly its director and my former academic advisor, Dr. Joyce VanTassel-Baska's—curricular model. Two years ago, I once again wrote curriculum for the Center for Gifted Education, utilizing its model while incorporating *The Merchant of Venice* as part of a more comprehensive, year-long language arts curriculum. The curricular mechanism underlying all of the above was first proposed by Dr. VanTassel-Baska in 1986, and this Integrated Curriculum Model (ICM) has since gained widespread acceptance and use; I myself am a firm believer in its utility.

Emphasizing academic traditionalism, the ICM aims to provide gifted and talented students with (1) advanced content knowledge of a given scholastic discipline or subject, (2) opportunities to employ higher order thinking and processing skills in the acquisition and utilization or reinforcement of that content knowledge, and (3) applications to or considerations of major issues, themes, or ideas that are centrally or peripherally relevant to the given content, yet also applicable to the real world and/or otherwise interdisciplinary. These three dimensions of the ICM—the advanced content dimension, the process-product dimension, and the issues/themes dimension—compose the model upon which I designed many of the individual activities, as well as the full pedagogical scope, included in this book.

Moreover, I have designed this book's contents to accord with national standards for English language arts instruction at the secondary level, both in a general sense and, more particularly, in AP Literature and Composition classes. In this way, I chose two additional pedagogical compasses, the first of which was the National Council of Teachers of English (NCTE) and International Reading Association's (IRA) Standards for the English Language Arts (1996). Table 1 demonstrates the ways in which activities and assignments located within the five major chapters of this book accord with the NCTE's 12 standards.

As I have aimed specifically to produce a resource for AP and Pre-AP teachers of *King Lear*, the second pedagogical compass that I adopted was the College Board's (2007) AP English Literature and Composition course description, a document outlining what is expected and/or desired of AP English Literature teachers, students, and syllabi nationwide. Although the course description does not numerate instructional standards, á la NCTE, it does propose and outline numerous goals and requirements for instruction, according to which I have likewise designed my activities and assignments, as demonstrated in Table 2.

TABLE 1
Alignment With NCTE/IRA Standards for the English Language Arts

Standard	Ch. 3 Reading *King Lear*	Ch. 4 Understanding *King Lear*	Ch. 5 Performing *King Lear*	Ch. 6 Talking About *King Lear*	Ch. 7 Writing About *King Lear*
1. Read a wide range of texts for both intrapersonal and societal/cultural understanding, for the acquirement of new information, for response to society's needs, and for personal fulfillment.	✗	✗	✗	✗	✗
2. Read a wide range of literature to build an understanding of the universal human condition.	✗	✗		✗	✗
3. Apply various active linguistic strategies to comprehend, interpret, evaluate, and appreciate texts.	✗	✗	✗	✗	✗
4. Adjust spoken, written, and visual language methods to communicate effectively with various audiences for different purposes.			✗	✗	✗
5. Employ a wide range of writing strategies and elements to communicate effectively with different audiences for various purposes.		✗			✗
6. Apply knowledge of language structure, conventions, techniques, figurative elements, and genre to create, critique, and discuss texts.	✗	✗	✗	✗	✗
7. Conduct self-directed investigative research by gathering, evaluating, and synthesizing data from a variety of sources, then communicate their findings to an audience.					✗
8. Use various technological and information resources to gather and synthesize information and to create and communicate knowledge.	✗				✗
9. Develop an understanding of and respect for diversity in human language use.	✗	✗	✗	✗	✗
10. Non-native English speakers use their first languages to develop competency and understanding in the English language arts and curricula.					
11. Participate as knowledgeable, reflective, creative, and critical members of a variety of literacy communities.	✗	✗	✗	✗	✗
12. Use spoken, written, and visual language to accomplish a variety of their own purposes.	✗	✗	✗	✗	✗

TABLE 2
Alignment With AP English Literature and Composition Goals/Curricular Requirements

Standard	Ch. 3 Reading *King Lear*	Ch. 4 Understanding *King Lear*	Ch. 5 Performing *King Lear*	Ch. 6 Talking About *King Lear*	Ch. 7 Writing About *King Lear*
1. Intensive study of representative works by canonical Western authors from various time periods, engendering careful, deliberative reading and multiple interpretations.	✗	✗	✗	✗	✗
2. Interpretive, textually based analysis that considers a work of literature's structure, styles, and themes.	✗	✗	✗	✗	✗
3. Interpretive, textually based analysis that considers the social and historical values that a work of literature reflects and embodies.	✗	✗	✗	✗	✗
4. Interpretive, textually based analysis that considers a work of literature's use of such elements as figurative language, imagery, symbolism, and tone.	✗	✗	✗	✗	✗
5. Opportunities to develop understanding of a work of literature, enabling students to discover what they think about their reading via informal, exploratory analytical activities.	✗	✗	✗	✗	✗
6. Opportunities to explain a work of literature via expository analyses that utilize textual details to develop and support interpretations of a text's meaning.	✗	✗	✗	✗	✗
7. Opportunities to evaluate a work of literature's artistry and quality, and its social and cultural values, via argumentative analyses that draw upon textual details.	✗	✗	✗	✗	✗
8. Instruction and feedback that help students develop a wide-ranging vocabulary used appropriately and effectively.	✗	✗	✗	✗	✗
9. Instruction and feedback that help students develop a variety of sentence structures, including appropriate use of subordination and coordination, in their writing.	✗				✗
10. Instruction and feedback that help students develop logical, coherent organization in analysis and writing, including specific techniques such as repetition, transitions, and emphasis.	✗				✗
11. Instruction and feedback that help students develop a balance of generalization and specific, illustrative detail in their analysis.	✗	✗	✗	✗	✗
12. Instruction and feedback that help students develop an effective use of rhetoric in writing and analysis, including such features as tone, voice, and appropriate emphasis in diction and syntax.			✗	✗	✗

Please note that the AP English Literature and Composition course description lists three separate elements that are intrinsic to the close reading and study of a work of literature: (1) the experience of literature, (2) the interpretation of literature, and (3) the evaluation of literature. The College Board ties these three elements to particular approaches to reading and writing activities, and I have also focused on them in producing this book's chapters and activities. Please consider these elements as distinct from the actual goals and curricular requirements outlined in Table 2, yet inherently imbedded within them.

Organization of This Text

At its core, this book includes five chapters of activities and assignments designed to enliven and enhance your classroom instruction of *King Lear*. I recognize and admit that to deliver all of the lesson plans, assign all of the activities, and administer all of the assessments contained within these five chapters would take far longer than the time that most teachers—including myself—allot for one curricular unit of literary study. Nevertheless, as any practiced instructor will admit, it is far better to overplan than to underplan. Thus, I am providing an overabundance of material from which any teacher of the play may cull as he or she sees fit.

Fronting these core pedagogical chapters is a more academic analysis of *King Lear* as a literary work of art. As with *Advanced Placement Classroom: Romeo and Juliet*, I here assume a readership already quite familiar with the play's background, setting, themes, characters, and the like; thus, please consider Chapter 2 a synoptic overview of these aspects of *King Lear*, albeit one from which I hope that you pull a few previously unlearned nuggets of insight. Finally, the five core chapters are followed by a glossary of common literary terminology, an appendix (Appendix A) that effectively annotates the first 400 lines of the play, and lists of references and resources for the further study of Shakespeare, his most powerful and darkest play, and the education of the gifted and talented. Following are brief descriptions of the five core pedagogical chapters' contents.

Reading *King Lear*

Unlike the other four central chapters, this one is organized chronologically according to the play's events. I have organized it thusly because it contains assignments and assessments tied to particular moments and sections of the plot; additionally, as the chapter's focus is on students' initial reading of *King Lear*, it seems sensible to me that it be organized via the way in which all of us first encounter a literary work, from the front cover to the back.

The contents of this chapter are of four main pedagogical types: ideas for teaching higher level vocabulary through *King Lear*; independent journaling questions for each of the play's scenes, each of which may be assigned for homework as a way to differentiate students' conception and interpretation of the drama; brief quizzes formatted to mirror the multiple choice portion of the AP English Literature and Composition exam; and worksheets asking students to perform myriad tasks and respond to various questions, all structured hierarchically according to a generalized taxonomy of cognitive processes. Finally, a "ready-to-roll" lesson plan at the end of the chapter asks students to reframe the events, characters, and dialogue of *King Lear* in modern terms: those of popular, computerized social media.

Understanding *King Lear*

This second central chapter is somewhat dichotomous, containing two distinct approaches to appreciating *King Lear* beyond a simple read-through of its action. The first half of the chapter breaks down several common difficulties that students face when reading Shakespeare's language, particularly its difficult syntax and figurative language. In identifying and analyzing many syntactical difficulties that young readers encounter, addressing head-on their apparent impenetrability, I ultimately hope to illuminate ways that you can help students to overcome these linguistic trials. I also briefly discuss Shakespeare's omnipresent use of figurative and otherwise difficult literary devices; this discussion is augmented by your consideration of the Glossary and Appendix A, in which I define, explain, and locate within *King Lear* itself a plethora of those devices used by Shakespeare.

In the chapter's second portion, I propose several mechanisms by which you can help your students to personalize their understandings of the play's drama, conflict, themes, and characters. To that end, writing prompts meant to engender bibliotherapy are followed by numerous worksheets that consider and require that students analyze, emotionally and otherwise, several of the most famous and/or most poignant quotations found in the text. Finally, two lesson plans are included: one that requires students to consider their own conceptions of the play in light of the visions and products of classical composers, and a second that outlines a variety of ways in which *King Lear*'s themes, characters, and conflicts parallel elements found in the relatively modern poetry of Robert Frost, providing a methodology by which you and your students can interpret those similarities and their importance to the experience of reading *Lear*.

Performing *King Lear*

This chapter is devoted to the physical and oral enactment of *King Lear* and its major characters. As such, it delineates and defines various aspects of stagecraft generally, highlighting key terms that students require an understanding of in order to engage "professionally" in the performance-based activities that follow. In addition to suggestions for spurring your students to perform pieces (or the entirety) of the drama successfully, this chapter concludes with a lesson plan that juxtaposes Nahum Tate's (historically popular, critically demonized) revision of *Lear* against Shakespeare's original.

Talking About *King Lear*

This chapter includes two separate methodologies for engaging students in dialogue concerning the play: both Socratic seminar discussions and inter-student debates. For each of these two dialogic types, I include detailed explanations of their particular procedures, original mechanisms (e.g., rubrics) for assessing students' participation and success, and various topics for discussion from which you can choose. One additional lesson plan also spurs classroom discussion by examining *King Lear* relative to a famous painting and two related poems, while another lesson plan engages students in the consideration, analysis, and verbal presentation of critical theorists' thoughts on *Lear*.

Writing About *King Lear*

I organized this last of the core chapters on the simple fact that not all essay questions are equivalently aimed, formatted, or administered. The chapter highlights five distinct types of writing assignments: 25-minute-long argumentative essays resembling the writing section of the SAT; 40-minute-long analytical essays mirroring the essay section of the AP English Literature and Composition exam; extended, college-length analyses of complex issues related to *King Lear*; independent research projects that ultimately result in student presentations of their findings; and original creative-interpretive projects inviting students to personalize their reflections upon the play. For each of these types of assignments, I include several writing prompts and/or questions, plus evaluative rubrics and related ideas to maximize students' learning during their engagement in the writing process.

Notes on Citations

I have utilized, in writing this book, the traditional method of noting Shakespearean divisions into acts via capitalized Roman numerals, scenes via lowercased Roman numerals, and lines via standard numerals. The final couplet of *King Lear*, then, is by this calculus denoted as Act V, scene iii, lines 394–395. When parenthetically citing quotations from this or other Shakespearean plays, however, I have adopted the American Psychological Association's (APA) consistent usage of standard numerals; hence, the same couplet is cited parenthetically as (5.3.394–395). Additionally, breaks between lines of metrical verse are noted within quotations by my use of slashes.

All excerpts from *King Lear* that I quote in my text are taken from the Folger Shakespeare Library's revised paperback edition of the play (ISBN 978-0-7434-8495-4), edited by Barbara A. Mowat and Paul Werstine. All line numbers cited for these in-text quotations likewise correspond to the Folger edition's numeration, with the exception of excerpts contained on reproducible pages of this book, the lines of which are numbered independently.

Additionally, although my parenthetical citations generally follow APA guidelines, I have retained the literary tradition of citing lines of poetry not according to the pages of text on which they appear, but by the numbers of the quoted lines themselves. Therefore, although a poem's entry in my list of references lists the pages on which that poem appears in its text (e.g., pp. 10–11), I instead cite parenthetically within this book only the lines quoted (e.g., ll. 1–2). As such, any parenthetical citation following a quotation from a poem refers solely to the individual lines that I quote.

CHAPTER 2

Why Teach *King Lear*?

Three years ago, I opened *Advanced Placement Classroom: Romeo and Juliet* with the question, "Why teach Shakespeare?" The answer, of course, is multifaceted, including these highlights: He is the most quoted and alluded to dramatist or author in the Western world, he helped invent the modern English language by (among other things) coining approximately 1,600 words, he recreated the popularly accepted histories of various kings and historical world leaders, his plays are treasure troves of thematic and dramatic effectiveness, and, perhaps most importantly, his cultural import will never disappear. Students who study and—not always the same thing—actually think about Shakespeare's words can augment their vocabularies, syntactical fluencies, understanding of literary devices, thematic comprehension, philosophical reasoning, understanding of human history and human emotion, and on and on.

A more reasonable question to be asked is probably "Why teach *King Lear*?" On this one, many teachers are perhaps stumped. After all, educational common sense holds that *Romeo and Juliet* is the most frequently taught Shakespearean play in high school, *Macbeth* is the most politically enlightening and is therefore especially good during election years, *Hamlet* is the one taught in most senior English classes, *A Midsummer Night's Dream* is the lone comedy of choice ... but *Lear*? *Lear* you don't read until college, right?

According to the College Board, the answer is no; *King Lear* absolutely should be taught in high school. Evidence of this view is clear in reviewing past Advanced Placement English Literature and Composition examinations, the test toward which this book is in large part aimed. Between 1971 and 2011, the College Board listed *King Lear* as a proposed work of choice for students to consider on the open-ended free response question 15 times: in 1977, '78, '82, '88, '89, '90, '96, 2001, '03, '04, '05, '06, '08,'10, and '11 (Effinger, 2011). That's almost twice as many times as *Othello* was listed (8), 10 times more than both *Hamlet* and *Macbeth* were offered, and 11 times more than *Romeo and Juliet* was suggested. In fact, over the last 40 years, *King Lear* has been the Shakespearean play most often recommended by the College Board to answer its AP free response questions; clearly, the governing body of the Advanced Placement (AP) program finds the play more than just a suitable choice for high school students to read.

This number crunching is a simple statistical exercise, but what about the content of the play? Might not *King Lear* be too dark, deep, powerful, and downright depressing for high schoolers to grasp and potentially enjoy? I myself have struggled with this question. In 2006, an AP student of mine named James, anticipating what was to come in the course, commented to me approximately a week before we began the play. "I have a sister who is an English major," he began, "and I asked her what she thought of *King Lear*. She said, 'It's the single most depressing thing I've ever read.'" What could I say to James? *Lear* does have a reputation as dark, perhaps as nihilistic. Why not read *Macbeth* instead? At least it has some fun witches, ghosts, riddles, and whatnot.

I taught *King Lear* regardless, and in retrospect I think that I may have taught it more effectively that year than I did in any year before or since. In my opinion, *Lear* is a perfect play to teach high-achieving students in high school, especially those gifted and talented students with emotional and intellectual overexcitabilities who really might connect with what Shakespeare is trying in his text to communicate. *Hamlet* is really intriguing, and *Romeo and Juliet* is very relatable, but *King Lear*, in my opinion, is simply the most purely and enduringly human of the Bard's works. Every sibling has felt rivalry. Every child has elders. Many young people are close with aging relatives who are perhaps exhibiting signs of Alzheimer's disease or dementia. All humans, at some point, have to move on from something. Everyone has felt betrayed at some point, just as all people have felt vengeful or covetous or sorrowful; loyalty is something that we as a species admire and to which we collectively aspire. As I introduce the play to my own AP students, *Hamlet* definitely makes you think, but *King Lear* makes you feel. This, at least for me, is its chief educative value.

In 2003, before I had ever taught the play in school, several colleagues and I were sitting around the lunch table one day when the discussion turned to just this topic. I professed not a love, but an affinity for *King Lear* (in truth, I don't think very many people do actually *love* this play, but rather respect it). A fellow English teacher professed her own distaste for the play, calling it "pathetic." The conversation continued and we eventually moved on to other topics, but that small comment stuck with me, probably because *Lear* is my favorite. For fun, and apropos of the topic itself, I responded to my colleague in verse. Here is the poem that I wrote, originally published in *Möbius, the Poetry Magazine* (2003):

"In Response to a Colleague's Description of *Lear* as Pathetic"

"It's rage on rage," she said seriously,
"The plot is uninvolving and obtuse,
 Unrealistic situationally,
 And torpid as a dilatory moose.
 No characters induce Falstaff's rapture,
 And none evince Prince Hamlet's nimble mind,
 No Scottish twists of plot nor loves as pure
 As Juliet's or Desdemona's kind."
 Neglecting thus its merit distinctive,
 This summative assay misjudges worst
 From an insouciant, restive perspective
 The most substantive work in English verse:
  A wailed, undiluted, cyclonic blast
  Of what befalls and binds us all at last.

Though somewhat uncouthly self-aware and quite unworthy of its Shakespearean form, that sonnet, in my mind, pretty well sums it up. *King Lear* is powerful in a fatalistic, inevitable, and therefore very sincere and solemn way. Although we all read *Romeo and Juliet*, not all of us actually get to experience that kind of love, and nobody truthfully is as intelligent as Hamlet. Every person living, however, will someday be King Lear, including me. In the meantime, however, as I likewise tell my own students, I want and strive to be Cordelia... oh, and when you go off to college, avoid the Edmunds. *Macbeth* is a play of imagination and fancy; *King Lear* is real. It is absolutely worth teaching.

Shakespeare's England

Although students who have never researched Elizabethan England may believe otherwise, the image of Shakespeare as some historical anomaly, an enlightened genius sprung unexpectedly from the darkness of an uncivilized people, is quite incorrect. By the reign of Queen Elizabeth in England, Johannes Gutenberg had long since invented the movable-type printing press, new translations of foreign literature, both contemporary and classical, were streaming into the British Isles, and the educated upper crust of Tudor society, no longer composed exclusively of nobles, attended Cambridge and Oxford in droves. David

Harris Willson (1972) described Elizabethan Englanders as "a young and vigorous people emerging from the Middle Ages into the warmer and more intense life of the Renaissance," the intellectual and artistic waves that had saturated European, not to mention English, society: "very much alive, alert to the world around them, not merely to grasp the main chance in a material way and to rise in the social scale, but to respond to intellectual and artistic impulses" (p. 314). In what many historians label a golden age of English literature, an abundance of poems, dramas, and essays helped to popularize the very language itself as acceptable among even the wealthiest, most erudite members of society, those who had previously preferred French, considering English as the language of commoners.

Despite an apparent regard for matters of the Church, most of English society was secularly focused: on the obtainment of wealth, on finery and social class, and on overseas expansion. The spread of philosophical humanism and skepticism butted heads with a well-recorded societal infatuation with shows, parades, colorful costumes, and bizarre monstrosities, natural and otherwise.

It was an age of pageantry and of enlightenment, and into that vivacious England, on April 23, 1564, William Shakespeare was born in Stratford, a small town on the Avon River in central England. His parents, John and Mary Shakespeare, were financially stable, if not outright successful, but largely uneducated; John was of the yeoman class, a farmer and glove maker by trade, and Mary, as a female member of the gentry, was never privileged with formal education. It is presumable that young William attended the free Stratford Grammar School, principally studying Latin works by Ovid and Virgil, among others. As children generally left school at the age of 15, William probably took a job or apprenticeship of some kind in 1579, 3 years before his impregnation of Anne Hathaway, a local farmer's daughter 8 years his senior, led to their rushed matrimony and, 6 months later, 18-year-old William's fatherhood to his eldest daughter, Susanna.

Other than the christening of Shakespeare's second and third children, twins Hamnet and Judith, in 1585, no further record of his life until 1592 survives. This period of roughly 10 years, from his marriage to a public slander of Shakespeare by writer Robert Greene, is commonly referred to as the "dark" or "lost" period of the Bard's life. Some scholars contend that he left Anne and their children and moved to London, crafting a career as both an actor and a playwright; after all, Greene's criticism explicates William's public reputation by at least 1592. Other scholars believe that he joined the Royal Navy and traveled to Italy, among other destinations; why else would Shakespeare, they argue, have such an apparent firsthand knowledge of so many of his plays' Italian settings? Another plausible theory is that young William joined a traveling troupe of players and hit the road, journeying wherever the muse and money led, much as the company of players in *Hamlet* does. A rumor popularized shortly after his death claimed that Shakespeare was, during at least some of these years, a butcher of cattle! We may perhaps never

find out exactly where the man went or what he did during this decade, but it is clear that by 1592, when he reappeared fully entrenched in London's theatrical world, he had become a rather respected playwright of six or seven works, probably including *Richard III* and *The Taming of the Shrew*.

During William Shakespeare's youth, actors and playwrights were not regarded in English society as any kind of trustworthy, respectable, or even hygienic class of people. They performed either in traveling troupes, many of which are recorded as having passed through Stratford, or in large spaces such as private inn yards or public squares. No such troupe had its own permanent theater, and the most popular edifice for public entertainment was London's gallows, erected in 1571. It was not until 1576 that the first permanent performance theater, called simply the Theatre, was built by James Burbage in Shoreditch, a suburb of London. Other similar playhouses, most notably the Rose, soon followed, and the reputations, earnings, and lifestyles of theatrical professionals likewise improved as a result.

By 1592, when William Shakespeare resurfaced in written records, theater was a popular and potentially lucrative business. Certainly there were opponents, most notably Puritans, to the immoral behavior and lifestyles of playwrights, actors, and theatergoers, but Queen Elizabeth herself was a patron and fan, and it has been estimated that one in eight Londoners attended theatrical performances at least once weekly. It was illegal for women to act on stage, and playwrights, who aimed to sell several plays per year to acting companies or other theatrical producers, generally received no attendance royalties whatsoever for productions of their works; due to monetary constraints, actors almost never received full scripts of their productions, but were instead forced to work from lists of only their own cues and lines, remaining oblivious to other aspects of a given drama's complete scope. Moreover, these actors generally played multiple roles not only in one play, but in several plays simultaneously. Special effects were nearly impossible to create, and props were scanty. An easy professional life it was not. Nevertheless, careers based in the theater had become, at least in certain social circles, popular and appealing. Shortly following Shakespeare's reemergence in 1592, however, two major events occurred that transformed London's theatrical life permanently: An outbreak of plague forced the closing of all theaters for 2 years, and Christopher Marlowe, Shakespeare's major competitor as a popular dramatist, was murdered at the age of 29.

Following the plague's decreed containment, in June 1594, Shakespeare joined the Chamberlain's Men, with which company he performed for Queen Elizabeth herself numerous times, and began churning out plays at an incredible rate; *Romeo and Juliet* and *A Midsummer Night's Dream* are dated as having been written during this period. By the time he purchased a familial coat of arms in 1596 and a mansion in Stratford in 1597, young William had become a wealthy and powerful man. During that same period, however, death struck the Shakespeare family

Why Teach King Lear?

repeatedly—that of his 11-year-old son Hamnet in 1596 and his father in 1601—and the Bard began penning his most profound and darkest works, the great tragedies of *Hamlet*, *Macbeth*, and *King Lear*, among others. A movement in 1608 from the famed Globe Theatre to the more intimate, indoor Blackfriars Theatre likewise introduced the final period of Shakespeare's literary development, as well as provided him with inventive new possibilities for scene setting and a higher class clientele. By 1612, he was a retired and wealthy resident of Stratford, but in 1616 he died of still-unknown causes, ironically on his birthday.

Lear's England

According to legend, there really was a Lear, or Leir, who was King of Britain millennia ago ... or one millennium ... or some indistinct number of hundreds of years ago, depending upon whom you read and believe. Geoffrey of Monmouth's was probably the most famous and/or widespread of any early commentaries on Lear, and he dated the regent's reign as slightly more modern than the time of the Biblical prophet Elijah. The most prolific version of the Lear story during Shakespeare's own life was certainly Raphael Holinshed's *Chronicles* (1587), which stated that "Leir the sonne of Baldud was admitted ruler over the Britaines, in the yeare of the world 3105, at what time Joas reigned in Juda" (p. 12). These two accounts place Leir's reign over Britain in the Neolithic Age, although isolated and different (but still credible) versions claim that he lived during the more recent Bronze Age, when archaeologists believe that Stonehenge was erected. Regardless, it was a very long time ago.

During that Neolithic Age, farming as sustainable practice had recently arrived in England from mainland Europe, and land clearing and animal herding were just coming into vogue (or physical possibility). Logic indicates, therefore, that Lear's rule over a supposedly unified Britain should be dated later, perhaps during the Bronze or Iron Ages, but nevertheless a quick review of the prehistoric structures still extant in England demonstrates over just what sort of a world Lear reigned; I particularly recommend the sites by Martin J. Powell and Dr. Francis Pryor, listed in the Internet Resources section at the back of this book. Lear's knights were not quite hunting woolly mammoths, but they very well might have been wearing furs!

Archaeologists presume that British inhabitants at that time were illiterate, largely agricultural, and ritualistically religious. They were communally organized, grew grains, kept domesticated animals, used stone tools, and constructed massive burial mounds and monuments relative to lunar and solar alignments. Dover, with its grand white cliffs and beating waves, probably seemed to these people like the literal end of the Earth.

Why then did William Shakespeare, a successful, learned, intelligent, and increasingly wealthy thespian from the enlightened Elizabethan era, choose to write about this time period, about which we know little and people in 1600 knew even less? Its ambiguity probably made it appealing, just as it does today. Additionally, Lear's tale, as related in Holinshed and otherwise, is simply a very dramatic story. Shakespeare, in the wakes of his son's and father's deaths, was probably thinking much about genealogy, and some of the writings of King James I, particularly the *Basilikon Doron* (1603/2008), echo and reframe in political language parts of Lear's legend in what for Shakespeare might have been profound and relevant ways. *King Lear*'s power, after all, arises in part from its timeless relevance; the mysteriousness of its setting only adds to the play's universality. Moreover, and from a theatrical perspective most importantly, "with a setting so far back in time," as Northrop Frye (1986) commented, "the sense of the historical blurs into the sense of the mythical and legendary. The main characters expand into a gigantic, even titanic, dimension that simply wouldn't be possible in a historical context like that of *Henry IV*" (p. 102). *Lear*, we must conclude, could just as well take place anywhere and at any time, but actually gains that universality in large part from its prehistoric setting; it is certain that Shakespeare recognized as much.

Perspectives on the Play

Surely a large part of *King Lear*'s relevance is attributable to its universally recognizable and relatable characters. As I noted above, we are all destined to some degree to be Lear himself, just as we all know (or believe that we know) persons quite like Edmund. Cordelia might be less a real person than an embodied virtue, and the Fool likewise represents some part of ourselves and of human potential that we wish to emulate, but we nevertheless *know* these people fully and somehow easily. There are three sisters, so *of course* the youngest is the sympathetic one; the betrayed brother has escaped and hidden his identity, but *of course* he shall return to claim his vengeance and rightful title. Perhaps another reason why this story, with its once-upon-a-time setting, appealed to Shakespeare was that it essentially amounts to a fairy tale for grown-ups; its characters, representing their archetypal selves as clearly and recognizably as anyone from Grimm's, certainly fit this mold.

As with all Shakespearean plays, however, there is more to *King Lear* than just its persons and its plot. One of the many reasons for Shakespeare's supreme position in the English literary canon is his constant incorporation of philosophy into his dramas; we don't just attend a performance of *Macbeth*, for example, to witness a story concerning the fall of a powerful, overly ambitious nobleman, but also to consider, right alongside the Bard himself, the very natures of power, ambition, guilt, and loyalty as they truly exist within our world and ourselves. Though rarely overtly didactic with his themes, Shakespeare consistently incorporated these philosophical and sociological statements about human life into his plays, a rule to which *King Lear*, our fairy tale for grown-ups, is no exception.

Many critics see in *Lear*, for example, an overt religious allegory. In addition to the play's numerous apostrophized and commented references to the (sometimes named, sometimes ambiguously aggregated) gods, it contains a number of apparent parallels to Biblical characters, parables, and stories. Considering the loss of his family, title, possessions, and health, Lear himself resembles the Biblical Job, while Cordelia's honesty, purity of character, benevolence, forgiving disposition, and innocent death have been portrayed by some scholars as Christ-like characteristics. Both stories' narrative arcs begin with the separation of parent and child, later to conclude with their reunion, paralleling the Bible in various ways. Shakespeare's constant subversion of the light-sight, darkness-blindness relationship echoes Chapter 9 of the Gospel of John, and the Edmund-Edgar-Gloucester story in some ways resembles the parable of the Prodigal Son. Quite simply, moreover, the play's apparent moral tendencies—against greed, narcissism, and pride; for loyalty, ethical perseverance, and compassion—are Christian, if not inclusively religious, in nature. This interpretation of the play is of course complicated by the fact that *King Lear* takes place in a pre-Christian world and a pre-Judaic Britain, so its pagan characters are oblivious to their Biblical representations and ineligible in a strictly orthodox sense for heavenly salvation; nevertheless, as the play was first performed on the festive day after Christmas, for the royal court no less, we can safely assume that Shakespeare at least had in mind some theological or otherwise religious aspirations.

On the other hand, many commentators have read *King Lear* as an extremely nihilistic work, stemming immediately from Lear and Cordelia's early emphasis on "Nothing" as an emotional gauge and Shakespeare's continuous emphasis of the word throughout the play (1.1.96–99). Humans' misconceptions of wisdom, insight, and observation are also constantly iterated (as in the Fool's paradoxical wisdom, the power and ease of deception throughout the play, and the repetitive inability of eyes to see truly), implying that the world as we know it is in fact backward, if not entirely senseless. Perhaps most powerful of all, in this nihilistic vein, is the utter tragedy of the story's denouement, all without cause and clearly without divine intervention; King Lear in fact represents quite the opposite of a traditional (and perhaps wished-for) *deus ex machina*, and as Harold Bloom (1998) so succinctly wrote, "For those who believe that divine justice somehow prevails in this world, *King Lear* ought to be offensive" (p. 493). On this point, nihilistic interpreters discern emptiness and meaninglessness where moralist critics see religious didacticism, but no matter—Shakespeare, as was his wont, left us with no clear answers either way.

What *is* clear, however, is the Bard's political leaning on matters of the rising bourgeoisie at the expense of the established English aristocracy, which in Shakespeare's 17th century was a social issue of much concern. Two of the play's most despicable characters, Edmund and Oswald, are caricatures of bourgeois social climbers, demonstrating disregard for tradition and chivalric "manners," but clear concern for self-advancement at the expense of the upper class. Kent's haughty statements to Oswald and Cornwall in Act II, scene ii perhaps paraphrase (or satirize) common aristocratic perspectives on the ascending gentry, and the ultimate failings of the evil plots within the self-serving nobility (represented by Goneril, Regan, et al.) and the French invasion of England underscore Shakespeare's highlighting of or hope for civil authority and peace. *King Lear* is thus perceivable as social and/or political commentary, from an interpretive perspective just as valid as any other.

Finally, and this may be hard to credit at face value, an outlying critical theory holds that the play itself is comedic—if not in a humorous sense, then in a strictly traditional one. As Charles Boyce (1990) noted, like Dante's *Divine Comedy*, this play's "principal action can hardly be called a plot at all; it is simply a progression, taking the central character from vanity and folly through deepening madness to a recovered consciousness and ultimate collapse" (p. 349). Just as Dante the pilgrim is led in verse through the Inferno, Purgatory, and celestial spheres, so King Lear travels discursively through landscapes both emotional and physical during his play's five acts. Traditional comedies, Greek and otherwise, also parallel *King Lear* in their common inclusions of choral (i.e., observationally verbal) fools, their incorporation of disguise as a plot device, their juxtaposition of older and younger generations, their usages of parallel and concurrent plots, and their progressions of setting from city/court to wilderness/country and ultimately back to city/court. Considering all of these elements, *King Lear* may as well be the "evil twin" of *A Midsummer Night's Dream*!

No matter how one chooses to read, view, and/or interpret the play, there is no denying its power, at once both truthful and unsettling. *All's Well That Ends Well* it definitely isn't, but *King Lear* nevertheless remains a work, as it has been for four centuries, that challenges readers, audience members, scholars, directors, and actors alike; certainly its wealth of virtues is worth wrestling with in your language arts classroom, too.

Conclusion

While this chapter has outlined briefly the thematic and symbolic depth of this wonderful play, the next five chapters detail various techniques for engaging your students in a demanding, differentiated, and ultimately enjoyable study of *King Lear*, beginning with Chapter 3, which concerns students' initial experience of reading the drama.

Chapter 3

Reading *King Lear*

This chapter contains activities and assignments to guide students through the initial process of reading *King Lear*. Unlike others to come, this chapter is organized according to the play's five acts, through which students' reading will proceed. For each act, I have included assignments, quizzes, and worksheets that aim both to enhance students' understanding of the plot and characters and to require engagement with the text and higher level thinking, and thus to prepare them for the type of in-depth observation and analysis required by the AP Literature and Composition exam. Specifically, I have provided teachers with the following components for each of the five acts: vocabulary analysis, journaling questions, taxonomical worksheets, and AP-style quizzes.

Vocabulary Analysis

One of the major difficulties that inexperienced students of Shakespeare face arises from his sometimes admittedly difficult diction (syntax is another common cause of difficulty, but I consider it separately in the next chapter). In the whole of his works, Shakespeare utilized more than 20,000 different words, many of which are archaic or otherwise unorthodox for even the most well-read of modern adolescents. Thus, encountering and deeply studying Shakespeare in school offers students the opportunity to improve their own vocabularies by leaps and bounds, as well as their understanding of the ways in which words and languages are formed and evolve.

I believe that linguistic instruction, especially when focused on building vocabulary, is maximized when it is both student-directed and contextualized in taught curricula, so I here include a vocabulary network—Figure 1—that students can use as a template for their investigations of diction.

As students proceed through *King Lear*, they should identify and collect words that they find either puzzling or interesting, then utilize this organizational network as a mechanism for further research. For each of the five acts, I have compiled a list of words that students commonly find confusing; you may wish to divide these words among your students and require their analyses prior to reading the acts and scenes in which they occur, thereby preempting difficulties in reading comprehension.

Additionally, there are many creative ways in which classroom teachers can "publicize" students' vocabulary products, helping the entirety of a class to benefit from the scholarship of individual learners. Bulletin boards, simple pair-and-shares, collected linguistic folios or mini-dictionaries, and oral presentations to one's own or other classes are all highly feasible options for spreading the edification (like "pair and share," "spread the ed." is a simple and memorable classroom phrase with which to direct pupils) that students garner through their own use of this vocabulary network.

Vocabulary lists for each of the five acts are included in Table 3. The list provides reference points to where each word occurs in the text.

Journaling Questions

When I teach Shakespeare to my own AP Literature students, I always ask them to complete journaling assignments on nights when they read for homework. Daily reading quizzes following such homework assignments are of course useful, but do not by themselves necessarily ensure that students engage with each night's assignment attentively and fully. Asking students to respond analytically to their readings, on the other hand, requires that they collect particularly important facets of Shakespeare's scenes as they read. The simple act of reading a scene or two for homework thus becomes an exercise in interpreting characters' motivations, tones, and actions; paying close attention to symbolism and literary devices; mining the text for important details; and ultimately reporting one's findings in organized, supported mini-essays. Such journal entries prove to be exceptional practice for the kinds of quick thinking and analytical writing that students are required to produce on the AP Literature and Composition exam.

I do not grade these sorts of journal entries using any extraneous rubric, but instead simply and swiftly evaluate students' responses based upon three simple criteria: length and depth, their utilization of textual support, and the "correct-

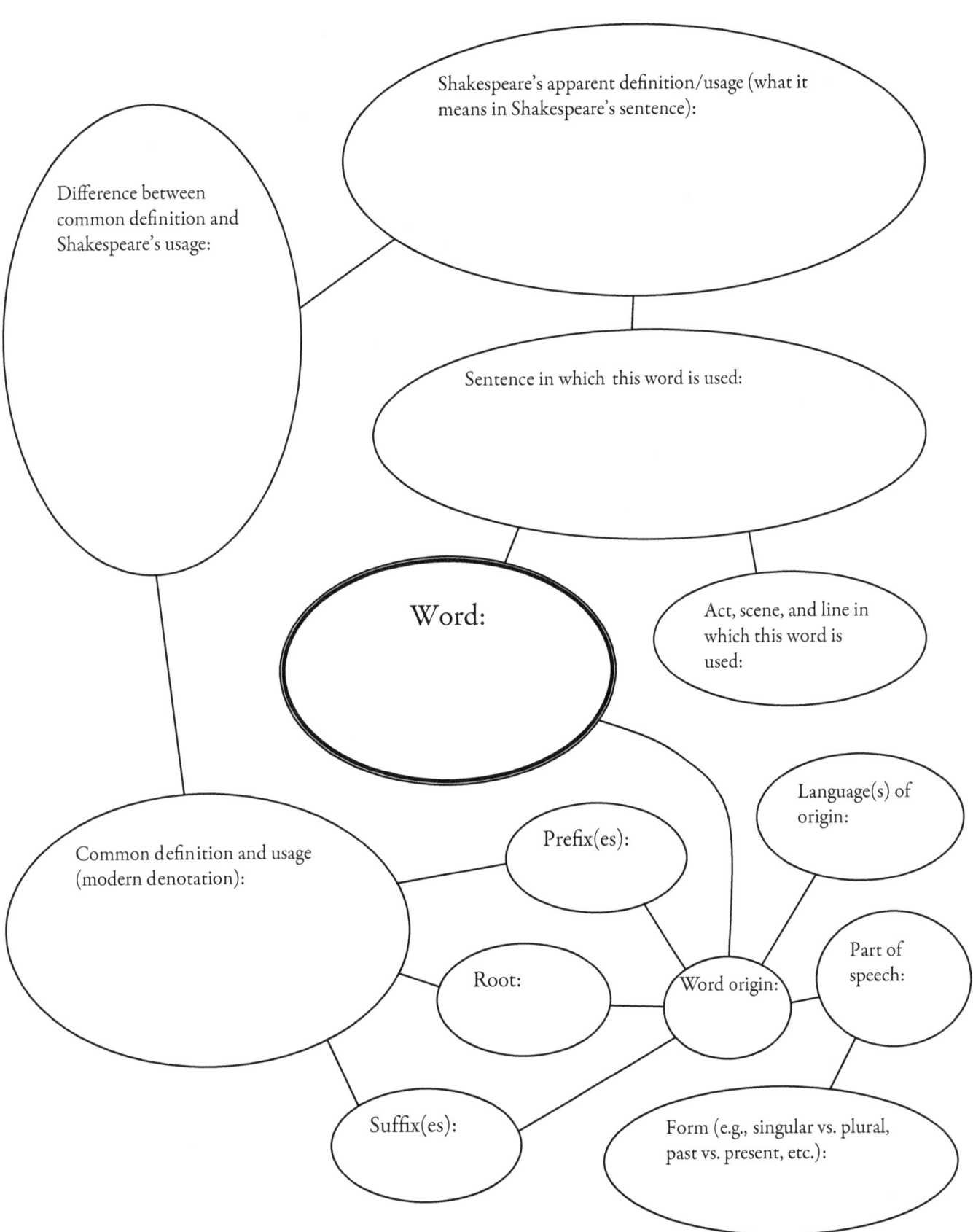

Figure 1. Vocabulary network.

TABLE 3
Vocabulary Lists for *King Lear*

Act I

conferring (1.1.42)	potency (1.1.196)	auricular (1.2.97)	pestilent (1.4.118)
amorous (1.1.51)	provision (1.1.197)	machinations (1.2.119)	insolent (1.4.207)
sojourn (1.1.51)	dominions (1.1.201)	evasion (1.2.134)	retinue (1.4.207)
divest (1.1.54)	beseech (1.1.241)	lecherous (1.2.138)	discreet (1.4.219)
champains (1.1.70)	forevouched (1.1.253)	firmament (1.2.140)	dispositions (1.4.227)
hereditary (1.1.88)	soliciting (1.1.266)	catastrophe (1.2.141)	lethargied (1.4.235)
opulent (1.1.95)	dowerless (1.1.297)	melancholy (1.2.142)	debauched (1.4.249)
begot (1.1.106)	scanted (1.1.323)	maledictions (1.2.154)	disquantity (1.4.256)
propinquity (1.1.126)	therewithal (1.1.344)	dissipation (1.2.155)	degenerate (1.4.263)
barbarous (1.1.128)	choleric (1.1.345)	nuptial (1.2.156)	ingratitude (1.4.270)
preeminence (1.1.147)	legitimate (1.2.19)	countenance (1.2.164)	disnatured (1.4.297)
abode (1.1.150)	prescribed (1.2.25)	forbearance (1.2.174)	dotage (1.4.346)
revenue (1.1.153)	perused (1.2.40)	credulous (1.2.187)	diligence (1.5.4)
unmannerly (1.1.162)	reverence (1.2.49)	negligence (1.3.13)	perforce (1.5.39)
reverb (1.1.173)	casement (1.2.63)	diligence (1.4.36)	
miscreant (1.1.185)	abominable (1.2.82)	ceremonious (1.4.59)	
recreant (1.1.191)	indignation (1.2.85)	abatement (1.4.60)	

Act II

endeavor (2.1.37)	varlet (2.2.28)	benediction (2.2.176)	abated (2.4.180)
conjuring (2.1.44)	carbonado (2.2.39)	obscured (2.2.183)	varlet (2.4.214)
auspicious (2.1.45)	bestirred (2.2.54)	vantage (2.2.186)	indiscretion (2.4.226)
parricides (2.1.55)	disclaims (2.2.55)	vigilance (2.3.4)	dotage (2.4.227)
manifold (2.1.56)	ruffian (2.2.63)	precedent (2.3.13)	provision (2.4.238)
unprovided (2.1.61)	reverence (2.2.71)	mortified (2.3.15)	enmity (2.4.242)
dissuaded (2.1.74)	halcyon (2.2.82)	salutations (2.4.37)	dowerless (2.4.245)
unpossessing (2.1.77)	antipathy (2.2.91)	intermission (2.4.38)	embossed (2.4.258)
reposal (2.1.78)	perchance (2.2.95)	meiny (2.4.40)	carbuncle (2.4.258)
dullard (2.1.85)	radiant (2.2.113)	dolors (2.4.60)	amity (2.4.278)
hither (2.1.100)	discommend (2.2.116)	infirmity (2.4.120)	superfluous (2.4.306)
riotous (2.1.110)	beguiled (2.2.118)	indisposed (2.4.125)	whither (2.4.341)
revenues (2.1.116)	entreat (2.2.120)	remotion (2.4.129)	incense (2.4.351)
needful (2.1.148)	reverent (2.2.136)	sepulchering (2.4.148)	
pinfold (2.2.9)	beseech (2.2.153)	vouchsafe (2.4.176)	
brazen (2.2.28)	pilferings (2.2.157)	raiment (2.4.176)	

Act III

unquietly (3.1.2)	couriers (3.2.6)	heretics (3.2.91)	superflux (3.4.40)
fretful (3.1.4)	rotundity (3.2.9)	usurers (3.2.96)	pendulous (3.4.73)
impetuous (3.1.9)	servile (3.2.23)	perpetual (3.3.4)	judicious (3.4.80)
unbonneted (3.1.16)	pernicious (3.2.24)	privily (3.3.14)	contriving (3.4.96)
outjest (3.1.19)	wrathful (3.2.45)	tyranny (3.4.2)	paramoured (3.4.98)
speculations (3.1.28)	affliction (3.2.51)	contentious (3.4.8)	extremity (3.4.109)
whereof (3.1.33)	undivulged (3.2.55)	malady (3.4.10)	importune (3.4.169)
negligence (3.1.36)	perjured (3.2.57)	tempest (3.4.15)	censured (3.5.3)
bemadding (3.1.42)	incestuous (3.2.58)	filial (3.4.17)	reprovable (3.5.8)
cataracts (3.2.2)	courtesan (3.2.86)	ingratitude (3.4.17)	malicious (3.5.10)

Act III, continued			
apprehension (3.5.20)	anatomize (3.6.80)	pinion (3.7.26)	enkindle (3.7.105)
equity (3.6.40)	provision (3.6.102)	ignobly (3.7.43)	overture (3.7.109)
minikin (3.6.47)	sufferance (3.6.115)	confederacy (3.7.53)	roguish (3.7.126)
counterfeiting (3.6.64)	questrists (3.7.18)	anointed (3.7.71)	

Act IV			
lamentable (4.1.5)	pantingly (4.3.31)	diminished (4.6.24)	cozener (4.6.179)
unsubstantial (4.1.7)	clamor (4.3.36)	deficient (4.6.28)	impertinency (4.6.192)
mutations (4.1.11)	sovereign (4.3.51)	precipitating (4.6.62)	stratagem (4.6.202)
commodities (4.1.22)	benediction (4.3.53)	perpendicularly (4.6.68)	proclaimed (4.6.253)
wanton (4.1.41)	venomously (4.3.56)	henceforth (4.6.93)	duteous (4.6.281)
contemns (4.2.41)	aright (4.3.64)	accommodate (4.6.100)	reciprocal (4.6.291)
disbranch (4.2.43)	fumiter (4.4.3)	gauntlet (4.6.109)	indistinguished (4.6.300)
reverence (4.2.51)	bereaved (4.4.10)	marjoram (4.6.112)	unsanctified (4.6.303)
barbarous (4.2.53)	aidant (4.4.19)	ague (4.6.124)	hovel (4.7.45)
degenerate (4.2.53)	remediate (4.4.19)	presages (4.6.137)	benediction (4.7.66)
discerning (4.2.64)	hitherward (4.4.24)	sulphurous (4.6.143)	apace (4.7.108)
deformity (4.2.74)	importuned (4.4.29)	consumption (4.6.144)	arbitrament (4.7.109)
bemonster (4.2.78)	descry (4.5.15)	apothecary (4.6.145)	
dislocate (4.2.80)	eliads (4.5.29)	usurer (4.6.178)	
ample (4.3.14)	preferment (4.5.42)		

Act V			
alteration (5.1.3)	incurred (5.3.5)	manifold (5.3.135)	disdained (5.3.224)
forfended (5.1.13)	devour (5.3.27)	adversary (5.3.147)	pilgrimage (5.3.232)
conjunct (5.1.15)	valiant (5.3.46)	eminence (5.3.159)	woeful (5.3.239)
bemet (5.1.23)	retention (5.3.54)	conspirant (5.3.163)	abhorred (5.3.248)
rigor (5.1.25)	compeers (5.3.81)	illustrious (5.3.163)	puissant (5.3.254)
avouched (5.1.50)	asquint (5.3.85)	cozened (5.3.184)	contracted (5.3.270)
diligent (5.1.60)	patrimony (5.3.89)	beguiled (5.3.184)	falchion (5.3.333)
exasperates (5.1.68)	subcontracted (5.3.103)	proclamation (5.3.219)	prithee (5.3.378)
censure (5.3.3)	heinous (5.3.110)	semblance (5.3.223)	

ness" of their analyses. Each entry is awarded numerical scores for "L/D," "TS," and "C," which together make up a single homework grade. The last criterion—"correctness"—is by necessity subjective, especially because the journaling questions themselves generally are open-ended, but my inclusion of this criterion allows me to discount responses that are simply deficient in terms of their sensibility and supportability. Over the course of one unit of Shakespearean study, entries accumulate within students' journals, wholly demonstrating learners' substantive engagement with text, far beyond what traditional reading quizzes allow.

Lists of potential questions for each of the five acts are included below.

Act I, scene i: As the play opens, the audience is introduced to Lear's three daughters: Goneril, Regan, and Cordelia. Focus on Shakespeare's characterization of them, as demonstrated in their actions, their own speech, and the speaking of other characters *about* them. How are these three young women different than and similar to one another in terms of their personalities, emotions, motivations, and personas?

- *Act I, scene ii:* In this scene, Edmund, the bastard son of Gloucester, is allowed the freedom to soliloquize and thus to express his true thoughts. Compare his statements and actions in scene ii to the persona that he exhibits at the beginning of scene i. Compose a journal entry considering Edmund's characterization (i.e., what and why the young man seems to think, feel, believe, and do).

- *Act I, scene iii:* Goneril implies in this brief scene that Lear in the past (i.e., even before the opening of the play) has acted in ways to frustrate her. Analyze her insinuations to suppose what things Lear might or must have done; what does Goneril's portrayal of her father imply about his past behavior and their relationship?

- *Act I, scene iv:* We here see the erstwhile king for the first time since renouncing his title; based upon this first "civilian" encounter with Lear, what is *your* impression of the man and his personality? How do you respond to him, either emotionally or intellectually? On a related note, what is your response to the way in which Goneril treats him in this scene?

- *Act I, scene v:* Among the most entertaining, and also the most puzzling, of characters in the play is Lear's Fool. Whenever present in this drama, the Fool—ironically and paradoxically—says some pretty wise things. Based on his commentary and dialogue in this scene, analyze the apparent insight and intelligence of the Fool.

- *Act II, scene i:* As the play's second act opens, Edmund seems successful in pulling the proverbial wool over everyone else's eyes. Consider his methods for doing so, then evaluate the scene's various characters in that light: Does the fact that his ruses are successful say more about Edmund or about the other persons with whom he interacts? What exactly does it imply about each of them?

- *Act II, scene ii:* Rather than being a unified literary device or circumstance, irony exists in multiple forms: verbal, dramatic, and situational. Mine this scene for examples of all three types. Where and how do the three forms of irony exist here, and what does their existence at this point of the plot suggest about the world of the play?

- *Act II, scene iii:* Edgar's soliloquy, comprising the entirety of this scene, both echoes and differs from earlier speeches—namely Lear's and Edmund's—in its suggestion of the malleability of character. By this point of the script, Shakespeare seems to be implying something about the relationship between identity (i.e., who someone really is) and personal choice.

What does Edgar's soliloquy suggest about this relationship, and how does it echo earlier implications by both his brother and his former king?

- *Act II, scene iv:* Many students often mistake the difference between tone and atmosphere in writing, but this conclusive scene of Act II largely demonstrates their distinctness. Compose a journal entry in which you analyze how characters' tones (i.e., the diction and syntax that they choose) create and impact the atmosphere of the scene as a whole. How do your findings mirror, differ from, augment, or comment upon your conclusion in the previous journal entry concerning scene iii?

- *Act III, scene i:* To some large extent, *King Lear* is a play about one's loss of control, about humans' inability to create and/or maintain order as they see fit. How does this theme arise in this scene? Tally and analyze several examples from scene i of a person's incompetence to control things beyond his or her self.

- *Act III, scene ii:* Among iconic images from *King Lear*, the portrayal of Lear in this scene, an elderly isolate angrily and determinedly shaking his fist at the heavens, is certainly the most famous. Why? Think thematically and deeply: What is it about Lear's monologue and portrayal in this scene that has so spoken to generations of readers and playgoers, making it among the most recognizable scenes in all of Shakespeare?

- *Act III, scene iii:* When we first meet him in Act I, scene i, Gloucester is certainly a rather distasteful character. In your estimation, has he remained so? Compose a journal entry regarding this scene in which you consider your reaction at this point to the hoodwinked Earl. Has he become for you a sympathetic character? Why or why not?

- *Act III, scene iv:* In several ways, Shakespeare's motivation for penning this scene as he did seems to have included a desire to engender emotional responses from his audience. What aspects of scene iv elicit this response from you? Compose a journal entry in which you consider dialogic elements and circumstances of the plot that provoke both sympathy and empathy.

- *Act III, scene v:* Though totaling fewer than 30 lines, this brief scene is a pivotal one in the play. Why? What is the impact of scene v on both plot development and characterization? In the latter vein, consider characters that both do and do not actually appear in the scene.

- *Act III, scene vi:* Falsity and fantasy here make a profound return as motifs in *King Lear*. The play itself, of course, opens with an emphasis on lies and pretense, and in scene vi of this act, the concepts of falseness and illusion—of things not truly being as they appear to be, by choice or otherwise—constitute a substantial portion of the characters' focus. Where do you find examples of this motif of untruth, and why do you think Shakespeare suddenly includes them in such abundance here?

- *Act III, scene vii:* Although scholars and critics often use the terms interchangeably, differences do exist among persons who are described as parallel characters, mirror images, and foils. I think of these three terms as existing on a continuum of similarity: parallel characters are alike in most, if not all, ways; foils are alike in some ways, but different than each other in several critical other ways; and mirror-image characters actually have a somewhat oppositional relationship, as their attributes and circumstances are to a degree inverted or reversed, as is one's own image when reflected in a mirror. At the conclusion of Act III, consider Lear and Gloucester. Are they best described as parallel characters, foils, or mirror images? Justify your answer with evidence from scene vii and the rest of the play thus far.

- *Act IV, scene i:* Despite the circumstances of Gloucester's blindness and Edgar's pretense as Poor Tom, this scene ironically focuses upon, or at least includes numerous examples of, the concept of perspective. At several points in scene i, characters take stock of their situation, consider it relative to other circumstances that they either have gone through or might potentially go through, and evaluate their present condition in that regard. Where do you find evidence of this perspective-taking, and why do you believe that Shakespeare included it abundantly at this point of the play?

- *Act IV, scene ii:* In a very general sense, every scene of a given play's script is written for one of two purposes: to enhance and deepen characterization and/or theme, or to move its plot forward. There can be a middle ground, of course, but the basic purpose of any literary scene can be viewed as either plot development or "depth development." For which of these two purposes—or for a mixture of both—do you think Shakespeare wrote this scene? Justify your answer with supporting details from the text.

- *Act IV, scene iii:* Consider Kent. At this point of the play, he is the only member of Lear's retinue who has not deserted the erstwhile king; after all, even the Fool has vanished by Act IV. Ironically, Kent himself is the one that Lear has most mistreated. Why does Kent so doggedly follow Lear? What does it say about his character, and how is your answer to some degree exhibited in this brief scene?

- *Act IV, scene iv:* Among the most commonly cited motifs in *King Lear* is Shakespeare's focus on eyes and sight, concretized thematically in the suggestion that ocular faculties are misleading and foolish. Within the 32 lines of scene iv, characters mention eyes and things related to them at least five different times. Why? What is Shakespeare's apparent purpose in so emphasizing the motif of eyesight at the moment of Cordelia's return to the stage?

- *Act IV, scene v:* In your estimation, who is the most villainous character at this point of the play: Edmund, Regan, Goneril, or Oswald? How does the dialogue of scene v strengthen or shift your conception of the "bad guys" in *King Lear*?

- *Act IV, scene vi:* If any scene in this terribly sad, powerful play is capable of being criticized as "laughable," it is probably this one, which has been considered by generations of readers, theatergoers, and scholars to be quite incredible. In one portion of your journal entry, consider what elements of ridiculousness or infeasibility exist in this scene; in another portion, suppose why Shakespeare might have included them in his grand tragedy despite their incredibility. After all, the Bard was a master dramatist in every sense of the phrase; especially at the point of his career when *King Lear* was written, Shakespeare simply did not make mistakes. What might he have been going for in this scene, beyond theatrical legitimacy on stage?

- *Act IV, scene vii:* We get a definite portrayal of Lear's mindset in scene vii, as he conveys in dialogue with Cordelia his own self-image both in the moment and, we can assume, in previous scenes. Based on evidence from this scene, consider Lear's mental state; what does he apparently think, believe, and feel about himself, about others, and potentially about life or the cosmos in general? How do your answers to this question indicate that Lear has changed throughout the play?

- *Act V, scene i:* Juxtaposed against the previous scene full of bittersweetness, sympathy, and hope, the opening scene of Act V fairly radiates evil, disloyalty, and potential chaos. Consider here the play's villains, and compare and contrast their individual motivations. Why is each intent on his or her actions and goals? How are they all alike and different than one another in these respects?

- *Act V, scene ii:* Edgar, in lines 10–11 of this scene, utters one of the play's most memorable statements: "Men must endure / Their going hence even as their coming hither." In what ways do these famous lines perhaps summarize a theme of *King Lear*?

- *Act V, scene iii:* In all Shakespearean dramas, final lines—of speeches, of scenes, of acts, and of entire plays themselves—are often important in focusing on philosophical or thematic points at which the Bard is aiming. Consider several final lines in this scene: The final statements made by characters in monologues or in their entire lives, and the final statements of the tragedy as a whole. In what ways are these final lines poignant or otherwise important relative to *King Lear* as a unified work of art?

Taxonomical Worksheets

It is my experience that, in general, worksheets as an instructional device have a poor reputation among teachers of the gifted, who perhaps see them as prepackaged busywork for instructors lacking the creativity or energy to design their own assessments or engage their classes interpersonally. Although I too generally distrust "prepackaged busywork," I find this stereotypical view of worksheets as a genre rather reductive, for instruments that eschew tediously repetitive exercises in order to stretch students' intellectual reasoning, practices of scholarship, and creative faculties can actually be wonderful formative devices. To this end, I have designed and included five worksheets—one for each act of *King Lear*—that reward students for engaging in cognitively and creatively demanding tasks at particular levels of cognitive difficulty. Having built these worksheets upon the concept of taxonomically organized intellectual processes, I believe that the more challenging the task that a student completes, the more he or she should be rewarded in the grade book.

Please note that these worksheets are not based strictly upon any single taxonomy of cognitive processes, although they resemble them all in their requirement of academic tasks that escalate in incremental difficulty. Students who wish to earn the highest marks on these worksheets are obligated to complete not only the task attached to the grade that he or she desires, but also those assignments "below" it on the worksheet. Overall, then, highly motivated students who successfully complete these worksheets in their entireties and thereby earn "A" grades interpret and respond to *King Lear* in a myriad of ways, demonstrating everything from their comprehension of basic plot events to their ability to formulate and defend judgmental hierarchies concerning entirely subjective topics.

Although every task required of students who wish to earn a D- calls for textual details in response to a simple fact-based question or prompt, there certainly are any number of legitimate ways in which students can answer every other question or complete each task on these worksheets; in these cases, there is almost never a singular "right answer." Thus, teachers should regard each student's answers and responses individually, considering their legitimacy in relation to the text itself, not in relation solely to other students' answers and responses.

When assessing students' answers and products, pay attention to tasks and questions that require the consideration of multiple parts (e.g., the fulfillment of a given task *plus* the provision of textual support for that task). Students who complete only half of a given task's requirements should not receive credit for the full completion of that task. Moreover, students should be required to complete all of the tasks and answer all of the questions listed below the one for which they wish to earn the highest grade; do not just award a student an A for completing the A assignment, but make him or her complete the rest of the worksheet to get that grade. In this way, you can not only ensure that learners experience and engage in a number of differing cognitive processes, but also direct students to consider multiple areas and details of the act in question, rather than just one isolated scene or event.

The taxonomical worksheets can be found at the end of this chapter, on pages 33–42.

AP-Style Quizzes

On the multiple-choice portion of the AP Literature and Composition Exam, students read short passages of prose and poetry in order to answer questions demanding precise understanding and excellent analysis of the pieces' literary devices, tones, purposes, overarching themes, and formal structures. This section of the examination puts students under tremendous pressure to manage time effectively, for it involves approximately the same number of multiple-choice questions as it allows students minutes in which to answer them (usually something akin to 60 questions in 60 minutes). If students spend one minute on each question, then no time is left for them to read, annotate, and analyze the excerpts themselves, which is of course necessary. Needless to say, this multiple-choice section is not one that AP Literature students should approach cold; practicing on instruments that mimic the section's format and level of difficulty helps students to develop time- and stress-management techniques, test-taking strategies, interpretive skills, a strong knowledge base, and general comfort and confidence with the demanding assessment.

I designed these AP-style quizzes with this kind of mimicry (and ultimate test-taking benefit) in mind. They are *not* reading quizzes that effectively assess students' understanding of assigned homework, but rather pop quizzes to be administered after students have fully digested each of the play's acts. Suggested time limits for all quizzes are included, and if followed, they should similarly help students to develop coolness under the pressure of the AP exam.

These AP-style quizzes are included at the end of this chapter, on pages 43–52. Detailed answers to the quizzes are included on pages 53–56.

Lesson Plan: Social Media Mockup

The activity in this lesson plan allows students to use technology to create individualized and reformulated versions of characters and plot points in *King Lear*. The lesson aims to help students identify readily with the circumstances and persons of the play, to review the entirety of *King Lear*'s action, and to reframe the entire tragedy as if it were a modern and very visible cyber-drama.

The complete lesson plan for this activity is included on pages 57–59.

Conclusion

This chapter concludes with the reproducible pages for each of the acts' taxonomical activities and the AP-style quizzes. The following chapter provides various activities for understanding *King Lear* as a meaningful and important work of art and as a philosophical statement, helping learners to move beyond basic comprehension and identification of key themes and elements into a deeper, more personal ownership of the play as a timelessly human work.

Chapter Materials

Name: _____   Date: _____

Taxonomical Worksheet for Act I of *King Lear*

Please use only the space provided to the right of each task/question.

To get an **A** on this assignment, you must accomplish this task, plus all of the ones below.	Among the major human issues considered in this play is love—familial, obsequious, and otherwise. Consider the public demonstrations, as well as the private thoughts and words, of Lear's three daughters. Please judge, based on muttered asides, spoken monologues, and written communiqués, whether you think the three daughters do—or ever have—truly love their kingly father, as well as to what degree. In the space to the right, justify your evaluation.	
To get a **B+** on this assignment, you must complete this task, plus all of the ones below.	In the first scene, Lear entices his daughters' flattery, promising inherited wealth if they proclaim publicly their love for him. Cordelia refuses, introducing a major conflict. At that moment, Lear is forced by Cordelia to balance in his response several different duties: that of a father, that of a political ruler, and that of a public servant. His words and actions demonstrate his handling of these conflicting roles, but what he says and feels may be quite different. Please compose for Lear an interior monologue—what he thinks and feels, rather than says—in response to Cordelia's "Nothing." Justify your choice of prose or verse.	

Reading King Lear

Name: _____ Date: _____

To get a **B-** on this assignment, you must complete this task, plus all of the ones below.	Edmund's soliloquy to open scene ii of Act I is among the most famous in all of Shakespeare. In this speech, Edmund essentially communicates who he is, where he has been, what he believes, and what he plans for his future; it demonstrates outstandingly clear characterization. Please analyze this soliloquy, outlining exactly what it is that we should think and feel about Edmund because of it.	
To get a **C** on this assignment, you must accomplish this task, plus the ones below.	In Act I of this play, Shakespeare's characters speak in a variety of forms: prose, iambic pentameter, iambic trimeter, and so on. Consider why Shakespeare might have written in this way, having various characters speak in different forms at distinct moments of the play. In your estimation, what was he trying to accomplish? Justify your answer(s).	
To get a **D+** on this assignment, you must complete this task, plus the one below.	Among the most entertaining characters in a well-staged production of *King Lear* is the Fool. In Act I, he says some things that seem to have "method to their madness." Please interpret several of the Fool's aphorisms, rhymes, and/or jokes, deciphering why they are paradoxically both sensible and nonsensical.	
To get a **D-** on this assignment, you must accomplish this task.	The play opens with the dissolution of a united kingdom, the fragmenting of something that is whole. Please explain Lear's plan for both resigning his royal position and living the rest of his life.	

Name: _____   Date: _____

Taxonomical Worksheet for Act II of *King Lear*

Please use only the space provided to the right of each task/question.

To get an **A** on this assignment, you must accomplish this task, plus all of the ones below.	Human beings have always told stories in archetypal ways, involving plots, motifs, themes, and character types that are common among all cultures. A simplistic, yet valuable, way to analyze any kind of archetypal story is to distinguish among its laudable characters and its evil ones, its dichotomous "good guys" and "bad guys." Please determine, based on the entireties of Acts I and II, whether each major character in this play is essentially, archetypically "good" or "bad." In the space to the right, justify your judgments based on characters' autonomous presences and their decisions and actions relative to one another.	
To get a **B+** on this assignment, you must complete this task, plus all of the ones below.	In the final scene of this act, when confronted with his two eldest daughters' solidarity against him, Lear threatens, "I will have such revenges on you both / That all the world shall—I will do such things— / What they are yet I know not, but they shall be / The terrors of the earth!" (2.4.321–324). Finding himself without a home, without compassionate care, and without a large retinue, what options does Lear really have? Please consider and describe what you think his best option is at this moment. It can be anywhere on a spectrum from acquiescence to revenge, but make sure to justify your choice with sound logic.	

Reading King Lear

Name: _____ Date: _____

To get a **B-** on this assignment, you must complete this task, plus all of the ones below.	By the end of Act II, just whose side the Fool is truly on seems ambiguous. His speeches and comments appear both to insult Lear and to express sympathy, as well as to shed light on his own motivations and place in the "new royalty." What do you think the Fool's motivation and loyalties are? Please analyze his speeches in this act to answer the question, paying particular attention to tone and circumstance.	
To get a **C** on this assignment, you must accomplish this task, plus the ones below.	Edgar, the legitimate son of Gloucester, finds himself outlawed and hunted in this act. In scene iii, he plans to disguise himself in order to escape. Consider other ways in which Edgar might overcome his betrayal and sudden reputation; Rather than run and hide, what could Edgar do? Justify your answer logically, referring specifically to characters and circumstances in the play.	
To get a **D+** on this assignment, you must complete this task, plus the one below.	In their reactions to Kent and Oswald's quarrel in scene ii, there seem to be some differences between Cornwall and Gloucester, despite their similar social status. Based on this scene and others in Acts I and II, please describe their similarities and differences, justifying your ideas with references to the play.	
To get a **D-** on this assignment, you must accomplish this task.	When placed in the stocks at the end of scene ii, Kent inspects a letter that he has received and carried. What can we infer are the contents of the letter, based upon what he says about it?	

King Lear

Name: _____ Date: _____

Taxonomical Worksheet for Act III of *King Lear*

Please use only the space provided to the right of each task/question.

To get an **A** on this assignment, you must accomplish this task, plus all of the ones below.	In the middle of this act, Lear, Kent, the Fool, Edgar, and Gloucester all meet in a rugged hovel in the wilderness. Depending upon one's definition, all five of these characters can potentially be labeled mad. The meaning of the words "mad" and "insane" are ambiguous and debatable, of course, but please try to formulate a legitimate definition of madness in the space provided. Then, rank each of these five characters based on their relative levels of sanity or insanity, according to your definition. Take into account not only dialogue, but also such considerations as their motivation, cognition, loyalty, and potential to go elsewhere.	
To get a **B+** on this assignment, you must complete this task, plus all of the ones below.	Imagine that Edmund, Goneril, and Regan are captured by some moral arbiter at the end of Act III. They are all three accused of and tried for various crimes. Create a list of these charges, separating them into crimes committed equally by all three and offenses made by only one or two of them. Please be aware that because the arbiter in question is a moral judge, rather than one concerned with "the letter of the written law," the accusations against Edmund, Goneril, and Regan should consist of ethical contraventions (i.e., violations of human rights and dignity).	

Reading King Lear

Name: _____   Date: _____

To get a **B-** on this assignment, you must complete this task, plus all of the ones below.	Lear's wrathful monologue to open scene ii is hugely famous among Shakespearean critics, actors, and readers. In it, he addresses not so much other characters, be they present or absent, but rather nature itself. Please analyze why this monologue, as well as the speeches that Lear continues to make until he moves toward shelter, is so famous. What about these words makes them so powerful? Consider tone, theme, and circumstance.	
To get a **C** on this assignment, you must accomplish this task, plus the ones below.	In scene iv, Edgar disguises himself partly through dialogue. To modern readers, however, some of the allusions that he uses for that purpose seem arcane and thus ineffective. Consider Edgar's goals in communicating with the wanderers in scene iv, then rewrite his dialogue using modern equivalents that are more understandable to most 21st-century readers.	
To get a **D+** on this assignment, you must complete this task, plus the one below.	To even the most patient and careful readers, scene vi of this act can be confusing. Please interpret what actually occurs in scene vi, both in the characters' minds and in reality, prior to Lear's falling asleep.	
To get a **D-** on this assignment, you must accomplish this task.	Is Edmund simply and pointlessly evil, or is there something that he hopes to gain through his insidiousness? Citing particular lines of dialogue, analyze Edmund's true motivation or lack thereof.	

Name: _____ Date: _____

Taxonomical Worksheet for Act IV of *King Lear*

Please use only the space provided to the right of each task/question.

To get an **A** on this assignment, you must accomplish this task, plus all of the ones below.	For various reasons, some critics and theatergoers over the centuries have seen the events of scene vi to be relatively implausible. In addition to the action of this scene, Gloucester's apparently total credulity perhaps contributes to playgoers' take on scene vi as far-fetched. Nevertheless, it occurs just as Shakespeare intended and set it down, so there must be a reason why. Please defend the perhaps ridiculous events and oversights of scene vi. In your estimation, what makes Gloucester's sincere credulity actually plausible?	
To get a **B+** on this assignment, you must complete this task, plus all of the ones below.	What do you suppose Cordelia might say if given the chance to confront her two sisters? Imagine that Goneril, Regan, and Cordelia are reunited at the end of Act IV, able to speak to each other in both secrecy and safety. Compose what you think Cordelia's speech might be, then a rebuttal or other response by one of the other sisters. Be sure to model your interaction on the actual dialogic patterns that the sisters establish in the text of Act IV, including meter and rhyme.	

Reading King Lear

Name: _____ Date: _____

To get a **B-** on this assignment, you must complete this task, plus all of the ones below.	Many critics have read this play as a cycle of separation and reunion. Cordelia and her father Lear finally reunite in the final scene of Act IV. Consider their different reactions upon seeing each other and, in Lear's case, realizing who the other is. What do these reactions demonstrate about the two characters' emotions and beliefs, the deeper truths of their persons? Justify your answer with textual support.	
To get a **C** on this assignment, you must accomplish this task, plus the ones below.	In scene v, Oswald admits to carrying a letter from Goneril to Edmund. Based on your understanding of the play thus far and its characters, what might the contents of this note be? In the space to the right, please compose what you imagine this note might say. Be sure to write not only plausibly, but also in both iambic pentameter and rhyming couplets.	
To get a **D+** on this assignment, you must complete this task, plus the one below.	In scene vi of this act, Edgar leads his father, Gloucester, to Dover. Interpret what else happens, both physically and emotionally, in this scene's first half, until Lear's arrival. What do the characters do, and how are they changed by these events?	
To get a **D-** on this assignment, you must accomplish this task.	What is the relationship among Goneril, Regan, and Edmund? Are they principally allies against a common foe or enemies of each other? Please determine, based on Act IV, how these three characters seem to view each other.	

King Lear

Name: _____ Date: _____

Taxonomical Worksheet for Act V of *King Lear*

Please use only the space provided to the right of each task/question.

To get an **A** on this assignment, you must accomplish this task, plus all of the ones below.	Regardless of their particular ethical beliefs, actions, disloyalties, or honesty, which of the play's major characters actually accomplishes the most between Acts I and V? Please rank the drama's participants not based on goodness, badness, honesty, or any other personality trait, but strictly on the degrees to which they achieve their respective goals throughout the course of the play. Which of the characters proves to be the most or least productive and effective in this way? At the bottom, please interpret your hierarchy. Does it imply to you any final conclusion concerning this drama's ultimate meaning or themes?	
To get a **B+** on this assignment, you must complete this task, plus all of the ones below.	Perhaps lost amid the personal conflicts and struggles of this play's individual characters is the fact that England, the country once unified under King Lear's sovereignty, remains fragmented and susceptible to attack by the vengeful French or others at the conclusion of Act V. If you were the Duke of Albany, rightful ruler of only half of Lear's divided kingdom, then how would you proceed after the play's conclusion, both politically and socially? What is a legitimate plan for reestablishing English strength in the wake of such a sudden, unnerving loss of leadership?	

Name: _____ Date: _____

To get a **B-** on this assignment, you must complete this task, plus all of the ones below.	What are we to make of Edgar's concluding quatrain, the last words of the play? As a general rule in Shakespeare, the final lines—of monologues, of scenes, and of acts—are extremely important for a reader's determination of meaning. Edgar's final speech, constituting the finale of the entire play, must be equally important. Considering tone, theme, and circumstance, analyze why this final quatrain is or is not an appropriate ending to this drama.	
To get a **C** on this assignment, you must accomplish this task, plus the ones below.	Although many characters in the play—Edmund, Cordelia, Goneril, and Regan—demonstrate clearly and consistently malevolent or benevolent personal characteristics, both Gloucester and Lear himself are morally somewhat ambiguous. Compose an "ethical obituary" for either of these characters, emphasizing his affective personal traits more than his political statuses or accomplishments.	
To get a **D+** on this assignment, you must complete this task, plus the one below.	Of what cause does Lear himself die? Unlike in the cases of Edmund, Cordelia, Goneril, and Regan, there is no physical ailment afflicting Lear at the end of Act V. In fact, he is strong enough to carry the slain Cordelia onstage in his arms. Please analyze a probable and plausible cause of his death.	
To get a **D-** on this assignment, you must accomplish this task.	How and why does Cordelia die? Previously, at the conclusion of Act IV, she and her father have been reunited and she is leading a French military force to oppose her sisters. What has happened by the end of Act V to so cause her undoing?	

Name: _____ Date: _____

AP-Style Multiple Choice Quiz
King Lear, Act I

Directions: This quiz consists of a selection from *King Lear* and questions regarding its content, form, and style. After reading the excerpt, choose and circle the best answer to each question.

Read the following excerpt carefully before choosing your answers. **Suggested time–8 minutes.**

	Fool:	[*to Kent*] Sirrah, you were best take my coxcomb.
	Lear:	Why, my boy?
	Fool:	Why? For taking one's part that's out of favor. [*to Kent*] Nay, an thou canst not smile
Line		as the wind sits, thou'lt catch cold shortly. There, take my coxcomb. Why, this fellow
5		has banished two on 's daughters and did the third a blessing against his will. If thou
		follow him, thou must needs wear my coxcomb.— How now, nuncle? Would I had two
		coxcombs and two daughters.
	Lear:	Why, my boy?
	Fool:	If I gave them all my living, I'd keep my coxcombs myself. There's mine. Beg another
10		of thy daughters.
	Lear:	Take heed, sirrah—the whip.
	Fool:	Truth's a dog must to kennel; he must be whipped out, when the Lady Brach may stand
		by th' fire and stink.
	Lear:	A pestilent gall to me!
15	**Fool**:	Sirrah, I'll teach thee a speech.
	Lear:	Do.
	Fool:	Mark it, nuncle:
		Have more than thou showest,
		Speak less than thou knowest,
20		Lend less than thou owest,
		Ride more than thou goest,
		Learn more than thou trowest,
		Set less than thou throwest,
		Leave thy drink and thy whore
25		And keep in-a-door,
		And thou shalt have more
		Than two tens to a score.
	Kent:	This is nothing, Fool.
	Fool:	Then 'tis like the breath of an unfee'd lawyer. You gave me nothing for 't.—Can you
30		make use of nothing, nuncle?
	Lear:	Why no, boy. Nothing can be made out of nothing.
	Fool:	[*to Kent*] Prithee tell him, so much the rent of his land comes to. He will not believe a
		Fool.
	Lear:	A bitter Fool!
35	**Fool**:	Dost know the difference, my boy, between a bitter fool and a sweet one?
	Lear:	No, lad, teach me.
	Fool:	That lord that counseled thee
		To give away thy land,
		Come place him here by me;
40		Do thou for him stand.
		The sweet and bitter fool
		Will presently appear:
		The one in motley here,
		The other found out there.
45	**Lear**:	Dost thou call me "fool," boy?
	Fool:	All thy other titles thou hast given away. That thou wast born with.

Reading King Lear

Name: _____ Date: _____

1. In this excerpt, the coxcomb functions as a symbol of
   (A) success
   (B) nature
   (C) youth
   (D) foolishness
   (E) hierarchy

2. In lines 12–13, the Fool comments upon people's reaction to truth by utilizing
   (A) a simile
   (B) a metaphor
   (C) a prologue
   (D) an anachronism
   (E) epistrophe

3. Lines 18–23 incorporate
   (A) masculine rhyme
   (B) feminine rhyme
   (C) internal rhyme
   (D) slant rhyme
   (E) approximate rhyme

4. The Fool's words on lines 32–33 imply that
   (A) Kent is unable to communicate clearly with Lear
   (B) Lear has neither land nor money available to him
   (C) Kent resembles the "unfee'd lawyer" of line 29
   (D) humans' belief in truth depends upon wealth
   (E) Kent and the Fool are pleased with Lear's situation

5. The versified speech found on lines 37–44 is written in
   (A) iambic trimeter
   (B) iambic tetrameter
   (C) iambic pentameter
   (D) trochaic trimeter
   (E) trochaic pentameter

6. The Fool's tone throughout this excerpt is
   (A) angry
   (B) despondent
   (C) apathetic
   (D) playful
   (E) frustrated

King Lear

Name: _____   Date: _____

AP-Style Multiple Choice Quiz
King Lear, Act II

Directions: This quiz consists of a selection from *King Lear* and questions regarding its content, form, and style. After reading the excerpt, choose and circle the best answer to each question.
Note: Pay particular attention to the requirement of questions that contain the word EXCEPT.

Read the following excerpt carefully before choosing your answers. **Suggested time—8 minutes.**

Edgar:	I heard myself proclaimed,
	And by the happy hollow of a tree
	Escaped the hunt. No port is free; no place
Line	That guard and most unusual vigilance
5	Does not attend my taking. Whiles I may 'scape
	I will preserve myself, and am bethought
	To take the basest and most poorest shape
	That ever penury in contempt of man
	Brought near to beast. My face I'll grime with filth,
10	Blanket my loins, elf all my hairs in knots,
	And with presented nakedness outface
	The winds and persecutions of the sky.
	The country gives me proof and precedent
	Of Bedlam beggars who with roaring voices
15	Strike in their numbed and mortifièd arms
	Pins, wooden pricks, nails, sprigs of rosemary,
	And, with this horrible object, from low farms,
	Poor pelting villages, sheepcotes, and mills,
	Sometime with lunatic bans, sometime with prayers,
20	Enforce their charity. "Poor Turlygod! Poor Tom!"
	That's something yet. "Edgar" I nothing am.
	[*He exits.*]

1. All of the following lines in this selection are written in perfect iambic pentameter EXCEPT
    (A) line 7
    (B) line 11
    (C) line 17
    (D) line 18
    (E) line 21

2. Edgar's tone at the beginning of this selection can best be described as
    (A) affable
    (B) fearful
    (C) resigned
    (D) saddened
    (E) perplexed

3. The word "proclaimed" in line 1 can be understood as meaning
    (A) celebrated
    (B) identified
    (C) ignored
    (D) reflected
    (E) created

Reading King Lear   **45**

Name: _____ Date: _____

4. Both lines 13 and 14 contain
   (A) onomatopoeia
   (B) jargon
   (C) verbal irony
   (D) alliteration
   (E) prose

5. Lines 16–19 utilize multiple examples of
   (A) allusion
   (B) internal rhyme
   (C) parallelism
   (D) antagonism
   (E) allegory

6. Lines 20–21 are best understood as communicating
   (A) Edgar's decision to misidentify himself
   (B) the contrast between wealth and beggary
   (C) the sensibility of speech rather than silence
   (D) Edgar's statements to three distinct persons
   (E) an emotional appeal to Fate as a cosmic force

7. Wholly, this soliloquy communicates Edgar's plan to
   (A) strike out against local beggars and villagers
   (B) construct physical shelter for the benefit of others
   (C) search the countryside for supernatural occurrences
   (D) protect his property from animals and natural disasters
   (E) disguise himself in order to assume a beggarly persona

Name: _____ Date: _____

AP-Style Multiple Choice Quiz
King Lear, Act III

Directions: This quiz consists of a selection from *King Lear* and questions regarding its content, form, and style. After reading the excerpt, choose and circle the best answer to each question.

Read the following excerpt carefully before choosing your answers. **Suggested time—8 minutes.**

Kent:	Alas, sir, are you here? Things that love night
	Love not such nights as these. The wrathful skies
	Gallow the very wanderers of the dark
Line	And make them keep their caves. Since I was man,
5	Such sheets of fire, such bursts of horrid thunder,
	Such groans of roaring wind and rain I never
	Remember to have heard. Man's nature cannot carry
	Th' affliction nor the fear.
Lear:	Let the great gods
	That keep this dreadful pudder o'er our heads
10	Find out their enemies now. Tremble, thou wretch,
	That hast within thee undivulgèd crimes.
	Unwhipped of justice. Hide thee, thou bloody hand,
	Thou perjured, and thou similar of virtue
	That art incestuous. Caitiff, to pieces shake,
15	That under covert and convenient seeming
	Has practiced on man's life. Close pent-up guilts,
	Rive your concealing continents and cry
	These dreadful summoners grace. I am a man
	More sinned against than sinning.
Kent:	Alack, bareheaded?
20	Gracious my lord, hard by here is a hovel.
	Some friendship will it lend you 'gainst the tempest.
	Repose you there while I to this hard house—
	More harder than the stones whereof 'tis raised,
	Which even but now, demanding after you,
25	Denied me to come in—return and force
	Their scanted courtesy.
Lear:	My wits begin to turn.—
	Come on, my boy. How dost, my boy? Art cold?
	I am cold myself.—Where is this straw, my fellow?
	The art of our necessities is strange
30	And can make vile things precious. Come, your hovel.—

1. Kent's statements on line 1–7 are best understood as establishing
   (A) distrust
   (B) anaphora
   (C) atmosphere
   (D) apostrophe
   (E) motivation

2. The word "Gallow" on line 3 is best understood as meaning
   (A) unhitch
   (B) construct
   (C) propose
   (D) frighten
   (E) eradicate

3. Lines 7–8 are best understood as communicating
   (A) humans' essential opposition to nature's strong wrath
   (B) the inherent fearfulness of bearing large responsibilities
   (C) a natural contrast between emotion and the auditory sense
   (D) the release of memory caused by difficult circumstances
   (E) people's natural aversion to burdensome illnesses

4. Lear apostrophizes on lines
   I. 10
   II. 12
   III. 16

   (A) I only
   (B) II only
   (C) I and III only
   (D) II and III only
   (E) I, II, and III

5. On lines 20–21, Kent indicates
   (A) potential shelter from the storm
   (B) his inability to find welcome safety
   (C) the transitory fierceness of nature
   (D) difficulty in confronting mortality
   (E) that loyalty is a temporary condition

6. Wholly, this excerpt concerns
   (A) the retributive actions of a wronged deity
   (B) an unexplained absence of startled companions
   (C) paradoxical occurrences in natural circumstances
   (D) the characters' movement to a sheltering structure
   (E) human disloyalty as a product of natural, inherent wrath

Name: _____   Date: _____

AP-Style Multiple Choice Quiz
King Lear, Act IV

Directions: This quiz consists of a selection from *King Lear* and questions regarding its content, form, and style. After reading the excerpt, choose and circle the best answer to each question.

Read the following excerpt carefully before choosing your answers. **Suggested time—7 minutes.**

	Kent:	Why the King of France is so suddenly gone back know you no reason?
	Gentleman:	Something he left imperfect in the state, which since his coming forth is thought of, which imports to the kingdom so much fear and danger that
Line		his personal return was most required and necessary.
5	**Kent:**	Who hath he left behind him general?
	Gentleman:	The Marshal of France, Monsieur La Far.
	Kent:	Did your letters pierce the Queen to any demonstration of grief?
	Gentleman:	Ay, sir, she took them, read them in my presence, And now and then an ample tear trilled down
10		Her delicate cheek. It seemed she was a queen Over her passion, who, most rebel-like, Fought to be king o'er her.
	Kent:	O, then it moved her.
	Gentleman:	Not to a rage. Patience and sorrow strove Who should express her goodliest. You have seen
15		Sunshine and rain at once; her smiles and tears Were like a better way. Those happy smilets That played on her ripe lip seemed not to know What guests were in her eyes, which parted thence As pearls from diamonds dropped. In brief,
20		Sorrow would be a rarity most beloved If all could so become it.
	Kent:	Made she no verbal question?
	Gentleman:	Faith, once or twice she heaved the name of "father" Pantingly forth, as if it pressed her heart;
25		Cried "Sisters, sisters, shame of ladies, sisters! Kent, father, sisters! What, i' th' storm, i' th' night? Let pity not be believed!" There she took The holy water from her heavenly eyes, And clamor moistened. Then away she started,
30		To deal with grief alone.
	Kent:	It is the stars. The stars above us govern our conditions, Else one self mate and make could not beget Such different issues.

1. Lines 10–12 communicate Cordelia's
    (A) emotional self-control
    (B) rebellious activities
    (C) distinct verbal qualities
    (D) conflict with her father
    (E) characteristic intelligence

Reading King Lear

Name: _____   Date: _____

2. The Gentleman, on lines 14–16, verbalizes
    I.   a paradox
    II. an analogy
    III. personification

   (A) I only
   (B) II only
   (C) I and II only
   (D) I and III only
   (E) II and III only

3. On lines 18–19, the Gentleman uses figurative language to express
   (A) his admiration for Cordelia's character
   (B) his disbelief in the importance of sympathy
   (C) the relative values of pearls and diamonds
   (D) an impassioned plea for vengeful action
   (E) the importance to victory of accumulating allies

4. Shakespeare's shift in focus from the absent King to Cordelia is here accompanied by
    I.   the usage of rhetorical questions
    II. a shift from prose text to verse
    III. strictly unemotional atmosphere

   (A) I only
   (B) II only
   (C) I and III only
   (D) I and III only
   (E) I, II, and III

5. Shakespeare establishes the tone of lines 23–27 particularly through the use of
    I.   punctuation
    II. concise syntax
    III. repetitive diction

   (A) I only
   (B) II only
   (C) I and II only
   (D) II and III only
   (E) I, II, and III

6. Kent's statement on lines 30–33 is best understood as conveying
   (A) a theory that siblings' differences are caused by supernatural forces
   (B) the belief that human beings' belief in free will is erroneous
   (C) the idea that singular persons harbor multiple selves within
   (D) the point that rule of a kingdom is best handled by a higher power
   (E) a concept concerning the way in which human beings fall in love

King Lear

Name: _____ Date: _____

AP-Style Multiple Choice Quiz
King Lear, Act V

Directions: This quiz consists of a selection from *King Lear* and questions regarding its content, form, and style. After reading the excerpt, choose and circle the best answer to each question.

Read the following excerpt carefully before choosing your answers. **Suggested time—7 minutes.**

	Albany:	Where have you hid yourself?
		How have you known the miseries of your father?
	Edgar:	By nursing them, my lord. List a brief tale,
Line		And when 'tis told, O, that my heart would burst!
5		The bloody proclamation to escape
		That followed me so near—O, our lives' sweetness,
		That we the pain of death would hourly die
		Rather than die at once!—taught me to shift
		Into a madman's rags, t' assume a semblance
10		That very dogs disdained, and in this habit
		Met I my father with his bleeding rings,
		Their precious stones now lost; became his guide,
		Led him, begged for him, saved him from despair.
		Never—O fault!—revealed myself unto him
15		Until some half hour past, when I was armed.
		Not sure, though hoping of this good success,
		I asked his blessing, and from first to last
		Told him our pilgrimage. But his flawed heart
		(Alack, too weak to conflict to support)
20		'Twixt two extremes of passion, joy and grief,
		Burst smilingly.
	Edmund:	This speech of yours hath moved me,
		And shall perchance do good. But speak you on.
		You look as you had something more to say.
	Albany:	If there be more, more woeful, hold it in,
25		For I am almost ready to dissolve,
		Hearing of this.
	Edgar:	This would have seemed a period
		To such as love not sorrow; but another,
		To amplify too much, would make much more
		And top extremity. Whilst I
30		Was big in clamor, came there in a man
		Who, having seen me in my worst estate,
		Shunned my abhorred society; but then, finding
		Who 'twas that so endured, with his strong arms
		He fastened on my neck and bellowed out
35		As he'd burst heaven, threw him on my father,
		Told the most piteous tale of Lear and him
		That ever ear received, which, in recounting,
		His grief grew puissant, and the strings of life
		Began to crack. Twice then the trumpets sounded,
40		And there I left him tranced.
	Albany:	But who was this?
	Edgar:	Kent, sir, the banished Kent, who in disguise
		Followed his enemy king and did him service
		Improper for a slave.

Name: _____ Date: _____

1. On line 3, the word "List" is best understood as
   (A) a noun meaning "a compilation of"
   (B) a directive meaning "Listen to"
   (C) a category of anecdotal tales
   (D) a comparison between two reports
   (E) an independent interrogative word

2. Lines 18–21 describe
   (A) an apostrophe
   (B) an anachronism
   (C) a paradox
   (D) an analogy
   (E) a simile

3. Based strictly on information found in this excerpt, Edgar and Kent are similar in that
   I. both men have been caretakers of an elder
   II. both men disguised their true identities
   III. both men revealed themselves to their elders

   (A) I only
   (B) III only
   (C) I and II only
   (D) II and III only
   (E) I, II, and III

4. Lines 33–40 portray Kent as
   (A) emotional
   (B) laconic
   (C) apathetic
   (D) furious
   (E) confused

5. Edmund's response to Edgar's report of his own father's death is
   I. more grief-stricken than Albany's response
   II. more encouraging than Albany's response
   III. more hopeful than Albany's response

   (A) III only
   (B) I and II only
   (C) I and III only
   (D) II and III only
   (E) I, II, and III

Quiz Answers

Act I

1. D. The coxcomb is a symbol of foolishness here not only because it is worn by the Fool, but also because it is associated with imprudent actions, such as "taking one's part that's out of favor," giving away one's wealth, and following a man who has disowned his daughters (l. 3).
2. B. The Fool's statement on line 12 that "Truth's a dog [that] must [go] to kennel" is a clear metaphor, portraying an intangible virtue as an animal without using the directness of "like" or "as."
3. B. Lines 18–23 utilize feminine (i.e., multisyllabic) end rhyme.
4. B. An understanding of the Fool's comment to Kent depends upon the recognition that it responds to Lear's utterance that "Nothing can be made out of nothing" (l. 31). On lines 32–33, the Fool essentially notes to Kent that "nothing" is now what Lear can charge for renting his land, which has of course been passed into other hands.
5. A. With the overlooked exception of line 40, each line of this speech contains six syllables that alternate high and low emphases/stresses. In other words, each line contains three iambs, so the speech is written in iambic trimeter.
6. D. The Fool is clearly playful here, lightheartedly mocking Lear for his foolishness. Were his tone any of the other choices, then the Fool's diction would be more forceful and less amusing, and the Fool himself would probably not be hanging around with the erstwhile King anyhow.

Act II

1. C. Line 17 contains 11 total syllables, and thus it cannot be *perfect* iambic pentameter.
2. B. Edgar's comments that he "heard [him]self proclaimed" (l. 1) and "Escaped the hunt" (l. 3), as well as that "most unusual vigilance" (l. 4) might prevent him "Whiles [he] may 'scape," are clearly fearful (l. 5). Although it is probable that he is also perplexed or saddened by this circumstance, he does not voice these emotions at the beginning of this soliloquy, where the question directs readers.
3. B. Edgar is here saying that he heard others—presumably Edmund or guards—identifying him as a villain who must be hunted and caught; hence, he ran away.
4. D. This question's phrasing requires that students find a literary device that is used twice, both on line 13 and on line 14. The only one of the

choices that works is alliteration, as evidenced by "proof and precedent" (l. 13) and "Bedlam beggars" (l. 14).

5. C. Lines 16–19 effectively constitute a series of three lists: "Pins, wooden pricks, nails, sprigs of rosemary" (l. 16); "low farms, / Poor pelting villages, sheepcotes, and mills" (ll. 17–18); and "Sometime with lunatic bans, sometime with prayers" (l. 19). Each list is constructed in a parallel fashion, and the question itself requires students to identify a literary device that is evidenced in "multiple" places, rather than in one.

6. A. Edgar here implies that in order to escape capture, he will have to assume the persona of Poor Tom, assumedly a "Turlygod," rather than reveal his own (l. 20). His statement that "'Edgar' I nothing am" is a syntactically roundabout way of communicating that he no longer plans to identify himself (l. 21).

7. E. This question is related to the previous one, requiring of students basic reading comprehension. From this selection, we learn that Edgar is aware of his own outlaw status and that he plans to assume a different persona, going so far as to "grime [his face] with filth, / Blanket [his] loins, [and] elf all [his] hairs in knots" (ll. 9–10) in order to travel as a Bedlam beggar, of whom "The country gives [common] proof and precedent" (l. 13). In this way, he hopes to escape capture.

Act III

1. C. In this monologue, Kent describes "wrathful skies" (l. 1), "sheets of fire [and] bursts of horrid thunder" (l. 5), and "groans of roaring wind and rain" (l. 6) that "Man's nature cannot carry" (l. 7). Thus, the archetypal dark-and-stormy-night atmosphere is immediately established.

2. D. Perhaps a difficult question for students to answer, this problem requires that readers understand the word's meaning in the context of its full sentence that "The wrathful [i.e., stormy] skies / [Frighten] the very wanderers of the dark / And make them keep their caves" (ll. 2–4). A potentially distracting, albeit incorrect, answer is "eradicate," although its denotation of complete elimination or extermination simply goes too far for Kent's statement; after all, nocturnal creatures are not destroyed by the storm, just encouraged not to come out in it.

3. A. This question is also a potential trouble spot for students, as Kent's use of the words "carry," "affliction," and "fear" can all be misconstrued and lead quiz-takers astray (ll. 7–8). In this case, "carry[ing an] affliction" implies neither a physical burden nor an illness, and it is not to be understood literally as a responsibility. In fact, examining the words individually is probably more misleading than interpreting the sentence as a whole

in context, which essentially communicates that humans by nature do not like being outside in big storms.

4. E. In all three of these cases, Lear addresses something absent or intangible: a guilty "wretch" (l. 10), a "bloody hand" referred to as "thee" (l. 12), and "pent-up guilts" addressed with the possessive pronoun "your" (ll. 16–17).

5. A. In order to answer this question, students need know what a hovel is, that its identification as "hard by here" means "nearby" (l. 20), and that the "friendship" that it can "lend [Lear] 'gainst the tempest" is shelter (l. 21).

6. D. At the selection's end, Lear's direction, "Come, your hovel," indicates that he wishes to go to it (l. 30). Thus, the characters move from openness to shelter.

Act IV

1. A. Describing Cordelia as "a queen / Over her passion, who . . . / Fought to be king o'er her," the Gentleman is stating that Cordelia did not succumb to passion (i.e., emotion), but rather controlled it (ll. 10–12).

2. C. The coexistence of sunshine and rain constitute a paradox; using the comparative "like," the Gentleman analogically compares that paradox to Cordelia's smiles and tears (l. 16). However, although his statement describes both natural phenomena and signs of human emotion, he does not quite personify (i.e., portray) the natural phenomena as humanlike; he simply compares them.

3. A. In his simile, the Gentleman values Cordelia's tears "As pearls from diamonds dropped" (l. 19). In other words, Cordelia is like a diamond, and her dropped tears are as valuable as pearls; the Gentleman obviously respects Cordelia greatly. Students might be thrown off by potential answer C, as the Gentleman does imply here that pearls are less valuable than the diamonds from which they drop; which one is worth more, however, is really not the point for which he makes the statement, and the strongest answer choice thus remains A.

4. B. The questions asked by Kent are not rhetorical, but rather inquire of answers from the Gentleman, whose description of Cordelia certainly qualifies as emotional. Students should note, though, that the prose used to discuss Lear shifts to iambic verse as soon as the Gentleman describes Cordelia.

5. E. Shakespeare uses all three of these elements to portray Cordelia as emotionally distraught, repeating words in short, exclamatory bursts.

6. A. This question is probably the most difficult one on this quiz because of Kent's citing of "The stars above us [that] govern" humans (l. 31). In isola-

tion, this statement echoes *Romeo and Juliet* in suggesting that human behavior is potentially led by a higher power; however, when students read the rest of Kent's statement, it becomes clear that he is describing not behavior, but the "issu[ance]" (l. 33) forth of differences from "one self" (l. 32). This statement is potentially construable as describing multiple personalities, once again misleading students, but the recollection that it is spoken in response to the Gentleman's description of Cordelia's anger at her own sisters indicates that A is the correct choice.

Act V
1. B. As "list" is etymologically similar and related to "listen," and as Edgar is obviously giving Albany a direction, this question's correct answer should be clear.
2. C. Edgar describes Gloucester's heart failure as "'Twixt . . . joy and grief," which demonstrates contradictory emotions (l. 20). Furthermore, the fact that his heart "Burst smilingly" is clearly paradoxical (l. 21).
3. C. The key to answering this question correctly is its condition that students are to evaluate the possibilities based "strictly on information found in this excerpt," which does not describe Kent's revelation of his true identity to Lear. Option III is thus incorrect.
4. A. Kent is not described by Edgar as confused, laconic, or apathetic. It is construable that Kent is furious, but whether he be angry, happy, overjoyed, relieved, anxious, fearful, or whatever else, it is clear from Edgar's portrayal that Kent is emotional in some way. Thus, choice A is a stronger and clearer answer than D.
5. D. Upon hearing Edgar's description of Gloucester's bittersweet passage onwards, Edmund—usually delivered as an aside—encourages his brother to continue in the hope of it doing some good, while Albany wishes Edgar to cease talking because he cannot take more sadness. Option I contradicts the other two, which are definitely extant, so D is the correct choice.

Lesson Plan 1
Social Media Mockup

Purpose/Objective

This activity is designed to help students comprehend aspects of *King Lear*'s plot, characterization, motifs, and themes by creating mock social media webpages using desktop publishing software. Additionally, in designing their pages, students can try their hand at writing their own versions of some of Shakespeare's language (e.g., puns, songs, proverbs, figurative language).

Placement

This lesson can be delivered in two ways. As an overarching project designed to last the entirety of students' study of the play, it can be assigned to them as early as Act I, the expectation being that students shall add details to their social media pages as the plot progresses. On the other hand, the lesson can be delivered to students after the play's conclusion, allowing the class to engage in the creation of social media pages all at once.

Materials Required

You will require computers on which students can work, as well as desktop publishing software such as Microsoft Publisher.

Duration

This lesson can be stretched out over the course of the play or accomplished in one approximately 90-minute class period, at the teacher's discretion.

Lesson Plan

1. *Anticipatory Set:* Use of social media websites (e.g., Facebook, MySpace, Twitter) is so common among tech-savvy adolescents that the great majority of your class probably will have experience with using or viewing them. Thus, a brief discussion about their common format and purpose should be easily broached. Ask students why such sites are popular, what people can accomplish by using them, and what kinds of details they are useful

for when advertising or publishing information online. This discussion should last between 2 and 5 minutes.

2. *Communication of Objective:* Inform students that this lesson allows them to create mock social networking pages for characters from King Lear. On these pages, students should "post" aspects of their respective characters' lives, personalities, emotions, and involvement in the drama's plot that are relevant, or that might prove interesting to other characters, and each mock page should be designed to resemble an actual web-based social medium. Thus, this activity will help students not only to get more comfortable with the world and persons of *King Lear*, but also to play—in a very legitimate sense—with creative computer software.

3. *Preparation:* Students should choose or be assigned individual characters from *King Lear*. Students who are paired with even relatively minor characters, such as Oswald, should be able to complete this lesson both successfully and enjoyably, so do not confine your class to the two central families, per sé. Students should be given some initial guidance and time to experiment with your desktop publishing program of choice, as well. You should at this point communicate to your class whether this lesson will be completed in one or two class periods or over a significantly longer span of time.

4. *Computer Work:* In designing their mock social pages, students should consider creating various details and content, relevant to their respective characters, that aligns with information found on modern social media. Particularly, students should consider adding the following elements:
   - Aesthetically, students' mock social pages can either mimic existing websites or be variations on a common social media template; an example of the latter approach might be to create a series of blog entries from the Dover Druidic Police Bureau, monitoring the local appearances of seemingly lunatic wandering vagabonds, as well as two oppositional armies.
   - Students can describe and update their characters' qualities in a Personal Information section, including information such as likes, dislikes, favorite sayings, relationship statuses, and the like. This aspect of a mock social page would aid students' understanding of Shakespeare's characterization.
   - A running log of the play's plot can be maintained in a commentary "wall," on which events can be communicated in succinct bursts to mimic status updates (e.g., "Cornwall has captured Gloucester . . . Regan interrogates violently . . . Gloucester suddenly can't see straight . . . Edmund and Gloucester are no longer friends . . ."). This particular

aspect of the assignment will help students to comprehend the plot, including its parallel narratives.

- Students could also try their hand at composing Shakespearean dialogue, perhaps writing their excerpts in Elizabethan prose or attempting to paraphrase or update famous speeches from the play (e.g., a 21st-century version of Lear's "Blow, winds, and crack your cheeks" monologue).
- Perhaps most amusing of all might be running Internet-based conversations between a student's assigned character and other people in the play. Act I, scene i, for instance, would probably be much more lighthearted if paraphrased as a series of concise, back-and-forth text messages among members of the royal family! This aspect of the pages might be accomplished either by allowing individual students to create their own comments, ostensibly made by characters in the play, or by empowering groups of students to comment on each other's pages via the use of collaborative wiki media. In the latter instance, students might be assigned particular roles from the drama and asked to comment, using the personae of their respective characters, on classmates' wiki-made social pages; this interactivity would certainly add a more collaborative, potentially more entertaining ingredient to the assignment.

Closure

Having spent time constructing their mock social pages, students will of course want to share and compare them. Thus, students should be allowed to "publish" and present their products either on secure network sites or, via LCD projectors, on a whiteboard at the front of the class. Either way, the resultant social media will of course provide your class with an entertaining mechanism with which to digest one of the Bard's most ponderously philosophical plays.

Chapter 4

Understanding *King Lear*

Simply because a student reads a Shakespearean play, of course, does not necessarily mean that he or she really "gets" it. Especially in preparation for the AP English Literature exam, it obviously does students little good simply to read the words on the page, but not to understand what they signify or demonstrate, especially in a play as powerfully philosophical as *Lear*. Much overlap exists, therefore, between the content of the previous chapter, "Reading *King Lear*," and this one; many of the activities in Chapter 3 could logically be placed in Chapter 4, and vice versa. Nevertheless, I have attempted to distinguish between activities and assignments highlighting the play's events and artistry at an introductory "surface" level and, in this chapter, at a deeper, more cognitively demanding one. Moreover, while the previous chapter was organized according to the play's five chronological acts, this one, as well as all subsequent chapters, is organized by topic of inquiry.

This chapter contains more thorough approaches to and analyses of some of *King Lear*'s linguistically difficult and artistically creative aspects, in addition to writing prompts requiring students not only to comprehend and interpret what characters say and do, but also to relate such utterances and actions to their own lives, synthesizing Shakespeare's play with elements of the proverbial "real world." Thus, if the contents of the previous chapter required students to absorb the play's dramatic action (i.e., its plot), then this chapter's activities will focus their interpretive lenses more sharply, addressing the potentially personal questions, "So what? Why is this play relevant to my life?" Through an examination firstly of Shakespeare's demanding, but certainly worthwhile-to-master, syntactical patterns and creative linguistic devices, and secondly of his timeless emotional, social, and political relevancies, I hope to help you provide your students with answers to these important questions.

Difficulties With Shakespeare's Syntax

Dealing with Shakespeare's huge and sometimes unusual vocabulary is one problem facing many modern readers, but interpreting his similarly challenging syntax, the way in which he uses and combines the words that he chooses, proves a different difficulty altogether. Consider, for example, this statement to Kent by King Lear, taken from Act I, scene i, spoken in response to Kent's statement that Lear "dost evil" (l. 190):

> That thou hast sought to make us break our vows—
> Which we durst never yet—and with strained pride
> To come betwixt our sentence and our power,
> Which nor our nature nor our place can bear,
> Our potency made good, take thy reward:
> Five days we do allot thee for provision
> To shield thee from disasters of the world,
> And on the sixth to turn thy hated back
> Upon our kingdom. (ll. 192–200)

Technically, that's one English sentence, spread over nine lines of verse. Perhaps the most common difficulty that young readers and students of Shakespeare encounter results from an inexperience with dramatic verse; I find that students who are not directed otherwise often read the text line-to-line, in small units of 10 syllables each, expecting each given line somehow to make sense by itself, independent of neighboring lines. If read in this way, then much of Shakespeare's writings will not make sense.

Line 195 above, for example, simply reads, "Which nor our nature nor our place can bear"; it is composed of a relative pronoun, a dichotomous possessive subject seemingly compounded by reusing the same correlative conjunction twice, and a concluding modal verb. Moreover, four of the line's 10 syllables—"nor" and "our," both repeated twice—sound alike and serve confusingly similar syntactic purposes, and the phrase containing them—"nor our nature nor our"—is effectively an alliterative tongue twister, signifying nothing by itself. The relative pronoun that opens the line is here separated from any kind of referent, and the correlative conjunction "nor" is used in an archaic sense, at least the first time. Any reader who simply takes line 195 at face value, independent of its dramatic and syntactical context, would probably construe a meaning either close to nothingness or, at most, misleadingly incorrect; after all, the most understandable words in this line are "nature," "place," and "bear," so perhaps Lear is directing Kent to be careful when camping.

The pitfalls of line-to-line interpretation are obvious, and students should be directed to struggle against their perhaps natural inclination to read Shakespeare in this way, looking instead for the often unusually long sentence structures of which his text is constructed. Line 195 makes much more sense, of course, if encountered in the context of the entire sentence spanning lines 192–200.

Once students do get into the habit of reading Shakespeare sentence-to-sentence rather than line-to-line, however, he still presents them with numerous syntactical and otherwise creative difficulties that, although common within his own literary corpus, are quite problematic for speakers and writers of modern English. Syntactical inversion and word omission are almost certainly the trickiest.

Syntactical Inversion

Standard English syntax generally requires that, in most clauses, nouns be placed before verbs, which are placed before their direct objects (e.g., "Bob ate oranges"). Shakespeare often inverts this order, engendering consternation among readers who cannot easily or do not naturally follow the flow of "inverted" sentences. In line 197 above, for example, Shakespeare writes, "Five days we do allot thee for provision." AP English students should certainly recognize "allot" as a verb, distinguishing it from its adjectival homophone, but they are still liable to get tripped up by this unorthodoxly inverted syntax, although today we would say to Kent, "I, the King, allot you five days for provision," Shakespeare here separates the direct and indirect objects, using them to bookend the clause's subject and verb. Of course, Lear's use of the royal "we" and archaic "thee" are other potential pitfalls for aspiring, but inexperienced, Shakespearean interpreters.

He commonly inverts the order of nouns and verbs, too. Consider the beginning of Act IV, scene iii. In the scene's opening sentence, Kent asks a Gentleman, "Why the King of France is so suddenly gone back know you no reason?" (ll. 1–2). Today, we would ask, "Do you know the reason why the King of France has so suddenly gone back?" Shakespeare omits the auxiliary "do," and once again the direct and indirect objects are split, bookending the sentence's subject and its verb; moreover, the verb "know" *precedes* its subject, "you," setting up another latent booby trap. Analogously, instead of asking, "Can you call on the telephone to order a pizza?" this example is equivalent to structuring the question syntactically, "Order a pizza call you on the telephone?" Continue this kind of syntax throughout the play, throw in some archaic diction, omit a referent or modal verb here and there ... no wonder Elizabethan English is so troublesome to read!

Word Omission

Considering a different example, we find another Shakespearean syntactical oddity that puzzles inexperienced readers. Edmund closes Act III, scene iii by stating,

> This courtesy forbid thee shall the Duke
> Instantly know, and of that letter too.
> This seems a fair deserving, and must draw me
> That which my father loses—no less than all.
> The younger rises when the old doth fall. (ll. 21–25)

In the first sentence, we again recognize an example of the inverted syntax previously described, but the phrase "and of that letter too" presents a new puzzle (l. 22). Shakespeare is here utilizing zeugma in establishing "shall the Duke / Instantly know" as an antecedent to two different objects: "This courtesy forbid thee" and "of that letter too" (ll. 21–22). The parallelism is not recognizable, however, because the preposition "of" is omitted from the initial object "This courtesy forbid thee." In modern, standard English syntax, this sentence would read, "The Duke shall instantly know *of* this courtesy forbid *to* thee and *of* that letter too." Obviously, the prepositions—neglected, we assume, for metrical reasons—make a large difference in terms of this sentence's decipherability.

The second sentence of this selection introduces another puzzling omission, or rather substitution. The demonstrative pronouns "This" (l. 23) and "That" (l. 24) here substitute for entire syntactical structures: respectively, the preceding clause, outlining the Duke's impending knowledge, and the phrase that follows, "no less than all," explaining what Gloucester will soon lose to Edmund (l. 24). Whether Shakespeare chose to make such omissions for metrical purposes or with the assumption that his audience would recognize the pronouns' import is debatable. What is clear, however, is that their exclusion makes this passage harder to understand. Such omissions are not uncommon in Shakespeare's language, so helping students to spot, accept, and bypass them when reading is a critical step toward building their understanding and appreciation of his artistry.

Figurative Language and Other Artistic Devices

Perhaps more difficult for young Shakespearean readers to decipher than his syntactical "traps," however, is the Bard's consistent usage of figurative language to convey important points. Returning to Kent's conversation with the Gentleman in Act IV, scene iii, we find a potentially confusing report of Cordelia:

> It seemed she was a queen
> Over her passion, who, most rebel-like,
> Fought to be king o'er her.
> [...] You have seen
> Sunshine and rain at once; her smiles and tears
> Were like a better way. Those happy smilets
> That played on her ripe lip seemed not to know
> What guests were in her eyes, which parted thence
> As pearls from diamonds dropped. (ll. 15–25)

Without at least a cursory understanding of metaphor, we here find that ambivalent Queen Cordelia is fighting passionate and kingly rebels, seemingly in the sunshine after a rain, and that something has invaded her eyes and lips, causing her jewelry to fall. This interpretation's misconstrual is perhaps exaggerated, but rather than saying outright something along the lines of, "Cordelia struggled to maintain her emotional composure," which is actually all that these lines denotatively communicate, the Gentleman creates a complicated series of analogies and other figures of speech. For students coming to maturity in the age of blogs and text messaging, this kind of writing is simply difficult.

Anyone who has ever taught Shakespeare to such students has surely been asked the very legitimate question, "Why doesn't he just say what he means?" The sincerest answers to this question, that he is being either "dramatic" or "artistic" with his language, are definitely true, but probably as reductive and unsatisfying to us as teachers as to our students. Nevertheless, Shakespeare's incorporation of artistic literary devices into his characters' dialogue absolutely heightens both their own and the audience's emotions, paints more vivid imagery and creates meaningful dramatic subtext, and allows the Bard to "say" much more than he is actually "saying." The audience's difficulty—our *responsibility*, if you will—lies in the interpretation of such devices, of course; yes, we get a much clearer picture of just how Cordelia looks and apparently feels via the Gentleman's description of her in lines 15–25 than we would were he simply to say, "She had emotional difficulty," but unless we actively pore over these figurative lines to interpret and grasp their meaning, we are liable to lose our way and simply miss the noble characterization of Cordelia here communicated.

In order to understand how such literary devices and elements enhance the play's drama, depth, and action, we must understand them independent of the text itself. As such, I include on pages 187–200 a glossary of literary terminology describing and demonstrating such devices and elements.

Additionally, although it is useful for students to understand and be able to define these literary devices and elements in isolation, their true analytical value arises when they are contextualized in and used during studies of actual literature.

If students can find examples of hyperbole in Gloucester's dialogue, for example, then they are more liable to understand the purpose of the device as a mechanism for portraying intense emotion.

It is unfeasible to pick out every occurrence in *King Lear* of each of these literary devices. Nevertheless, I have culled many of the clearest examples of them from the first 400 lines of the play, found in Appendix A on pages 201–214. In this appendix, I have also outlined important developmental points at the beginnings of both parallel plots—that involving Lear's family and that involving Gloucester's family—hoping to help you identify them for your students as you proceed through the drama's beginning together. There is certainly more of importance waiting to be mined from the play's opening, but this appendix should provide you and your students with an excellent foundation upon which to build your contextualized understanding of Shakespeare's literary devices and dramatic structure.

Lesson Plan: Robert Frost, the American Shakespeare

It has surprised many of my own AP students over the years how many similarities there are between the 20th-century poetry of Robert Frost and the quasi-Druidic world of *King Lear*; of course, such a realization in class is preceded by the teacher actually choosing the right poems to share. In order to augment your class's comprehension of and relationship with this darkest of Shakespearean plays, you can incorporate the lesson plan on pages 72–81. This activity requires students to compare and contrast with *King Lear* a variety of poetry by Frost, proceeding through their sequence in parallel with Shakespeare's drama.

Self-Reflective Prompts

I personally feel that any work of literature, regardless of its historical and/or aesthetic reputation, truly does students little permanent good to read or understand unless it contributes in some meaningful way to their own understandings of themselves and their lives. Questions regarding a narrative's plot, characters, conflicts, or symbolism pale, I believe, in comparative importance to the most important inquiry posed by teenagers encountering any book, play, or poem in English class: "What does this have to do with me?" If a teacher can help his or her students to answer this question meaningfully and sincerely for themselves, then that teacher does those students the largest educational service possible by helping them to understand the *personal* value of a literary education.

Thus, it is always important to allow students a chance to reflect upon their literary studies not just as artifacts from bygone eras and places, disengaged from the modern teenage world, but as mirrors to be considered honestly and individually, capable of demonstrating just how connected to the larger human family any adolescent truly is, no matter how disconnected from it he or she may feel.

The following questions offer students that opportunity to examine themselves and their families in the mirror of *King Lear*. I do not feel that students should be evaluated when asked to consider these topics—perhaps the responses will not even be collected or read by the teacher at all; privacy, after all, engenders honesty. You might wish to ask students to spread out around their classroom or other quiet place, writing individually and silently upon a given topic for 10 minutes or so, after which time they could pack their responses away and move on to something else. On the other hand, you could assign these self-reflections for homework just as easily. Regardless of your approach to administering these prompts, I advise you to create a safe environment for students' self-reflection and metacognition, one in which they do not feel threatened by evaluative grades, the imminent critiques of their peers, or perhaps even the promise of you, the teacher, reading their personal statements. Especially for gifted teenagers full of rampant emotional overexcitabilities, a place to write sincerely and safely is a very valuable place, and certainly worth protecting.

- Which of the play's characters do you feel that you understand best and/or can connect with most easily? Explain why.

- What or whom do you personally feel is to blame for the downfall of a unified England in this play? On whom or what is the lion's share of culpability to be placed?

- For many people, *King Lear* is an extremely powerful downer of a play, a work utterly depressing in its thematic message. When viewed in a different light, however, this play can actually be taken as powerfully beautiful or even hopeful. After all, both parallel plots center around the initial separation and, in their denouements, ultimate reunion of a parent and his beloved child. In this way, *King Lear* can be viewed in its essence as a play emphasizing love, loyalty, and trust. Which of these two perspectives on the play do you think is most accurate or legitimate, and why?

- Some people find in *King Lear* a depiction of the dangers that arise from social or political practices common in the early Western world (e.g., primogeniture, arranged marriages). Have you personally ever felt trapped, betrayed, or threatened by a custom from the past from which you could not escape? If so, then what were the circumstances, and how did you ultimately deal with the situation?

Understanding King Lear

> This play is a consideration, among other topics, of relationships between the old and the young. Its greatest emotional power perhaps comes from its portrayal of a once-powerful man losing his autonomy and his mind, deserted by the safety of his family and his past. Have you ever lost, either physically or otherwise, an aged family member? What were the circumstances? Do the events of *King Lear* parallel that experience in any way?

Lesson Plan: Musical Interpretations of *King Lear*

This lesson plan requires students to engage with the play using both their linguistic and nonlinguistic intelligences, comparing Shakespeare's text of *King Lear* with their own mental conceptions of the play, and then with several classical composers' interpretations of the play. Wholly, the lesson will both enhance students' study of *King Lear* and reinforce their understanding of tone and atmosphere.

The complete lesson plan for this activity is included on pages 82–84.

Quotation Identification and Analysis

For centuries past, and for good reason, scholarly recognition of philosophical and otherwise famous quotations from Shakespeare's plays has been a form of cultural currency in academia. In some sense, to recognize the origin and import of "Nothing will come of nothing" (1.1.99) has long been to signify one's learnedness, and piecemeal though they are, the ideological statements imbedded in the Bard's plays should therefore not be ignored as curricula in and of themselves.

The following worksheets provide teachers with a mechanism for helping students to build personal caches of such famous quotes' significances and probable usages, focusing upon their logistical importance, dramatic or emotional substance, philosophical implications, and relevancy to contemporary culture. Overall, students' consideration of these quotes from *King Lear* should help them to develop a deeper understanding of the play's significance to their own lives and their worlds, perhaps causing them to see the drama not as an Elizabethan relic, nor simply as a dramatic tragedy, but as a truthful, poignant commentary upon human natures bad and good, and the world in which they hold sway.

The worksheets on pages 85–103 may be assigned collectively, perhaps in a packet required for submission at the conclusion of students' study of the drama, or individually, providing an opportunity for students to reflect and interact in traditional jigsaw activities or via oral presentations. Regardless of how you choose to assign or issue these analytical worksheets, I advise that you distribute to all students the completed sample sheet, modeling for them both an appropriate length of response and the type of answer suitable for each reflective question. As with most analytical activities included in this book, students should recognize that there is no singular "right way" to complete these worksheets; certainly some responses are potentially more reasonable and supportable than others, but students should feel free to interpret and extrapolate quotations' significances as they individually wish. You therefore may wish to assess them based on completeness and legitimacy, rather than on "correctness."

Conclusion

The following materials include the various lesson plans and quotation worksheets for this chapter. These and the other activities found here will aid your students in preparing for activities found in later chapters, where they will be asked to apply their understanding of the play in various ways.

Chapter Materials

Lesson Plan 2
Robert Frost, the American Shakespeare

Purpose/Objective

The purpose of these discussions is to consider the events, themes, and characters of *King Lear* in light of a series of more modern, more simply written, and perhaps more relatable American poems by Robert Frost. These discussions will both augment students' understanding of the play itself and help them to articulate the difficult issues prevalent in what is perhaps Shakespeare's truest human drama.

Placement

This lesson is not a singular activity, per sé, but rather a series of successive discussions that should help you to humanize and make more recognizable the events of a play that takes place more than 1,000 years ago and is written in difficult and, in some sense, archaic language. Each poem by Robert Frost, as explicated below, should be shared with the class at a particular point of the play, for it illumines an aspect of the drama's plot or character development that is probably best discussed in light of specific dramatic circumstances. Thus, your student's encounter with Robert Frost—the "American Shakespeare"—should last throughout their experience of reading *King Lear*.

Materials Required

You will require copies of all of the poems listed below. They are all by Robert Frost and thus are probably accessible online, in which case Internet access is also required, or in a tangible collection of his poetry, one of which is recommended in the Resources for Further Study section of this book, found on pp. 219–222.

Duration

As stated above, this lesson consists of a series of short readings and analytical conversations, each of which should last anywhere between 10 and 20 minutes. Moreover, the teacher's option is to conclude this lesson with a full-blown Socratic seminar discussion considering the various ways in which Frost's art, themes, and human understanding mirror or are distinct from Shakespeare's (see pp. 132–138 of this book for further information on Socratic seminars).

LESSON 2

Lesson Plan

1. *Anticipatory Set:* Prior even to beginning your reading of *King Lear*, open your investigation of the text with a discussion of the various reasons why Shakespeare is so difficult for numerous people to comprehend (for your reference, I tackle this issue myself on pp. 62–66 of this book). In response to the question "Why do so many people think that Shakespeare is so hard or so boring?" you are likely to get responses detailing his outdated language, his characters' differentness, the degree to which his settings are unrecognizable relative to modern society, and the like. Rather than disagree with these points, a concession to them will move you toward the focus of this lesson: connecting Shakespeare, with his language of hundreds of years ago and circumstances of thousands of years ago, to (relatively) modern American life.

2. *Communication of Objective:* Inform students that in order to accomplish just that goal, you as a group are going to compare Shakespeare's drama with various short poems by Robert Frost, who has been called the "American Shakespeare" for various reasons, including his essential humanness, his separation from the requirement of particular settings of time and place, and the commonalities of their themes. At various points throughout its reading of *King Lear*, the class will examine a specific poem by Frost that, while not explicitly related to *Lear*, nevertheless represents themes, emotions, and characteristics of the play, the purpose of which is to make Shakespeare's drama simply more understandable.

3. *Approach:* Each of the poems listed below should be considered by the class at the point of the play noted. In my own courses, I have always found—especially after a homework assignment requiring students to read, comprehend, and compose a journal entry regarding *Lear*—that a Frost poem is a fine way to begin a class, offering both a mechanism for students to recall their previous night's reading and a bridge to fine thematic discussion, always a good entrée to a successful class period! After sharing a poem with your students, help them to explore it by approaching the work with a three-step analytical methodology, consisting of three questions at successively higher levels of cognitive engagement: (1) What does it say? (2) What does it mean? (3) Why does it matter? Regarding this particular lesson and series of poems, the first question, "What does it say?" engages students on a literal level, asking them to comprehend lines of text, its circumstance, and the surface-level happenings of a poem. The second question, "What does it mean?" engages students on an interpretive level, requiring them to understand the symbolic or otherwise evocative point of what Frost describes; it is here that students dissect meta-

LESSON 2

phors and whatnot. Finally, the question "Why does it matter?" engages students in a synthesis of theme and meaning with *King Lear*, asking them to conflate the purpose of Frost's verse with the events of last night's reading assignment. Wholly, this analytical calculus should serve you and your classes well as a prescriptively formulaic way to "dig out the human heart" of Shakespeare's elder text. For a more thorough discussion of this three-question interpretive methodology, you may wish to seek out the work of Sheridan Blau (2003) and Kelly Gallagher (2004), both included in the References section of this book.

4. *Series of Poems:*

"Birches" (1916/1969)

When It Should Be Read	At the conclusion of Act I, scene i.
What It Says	The poem describes birch trees that the speaker sees commonly in the woods, bent over permanently from the heavy results of ice storms, although the speaker expresses a preference for imagining that they are bent that way by young boys who use the birches as playthings. Finally, the speaker communicates his wish that he were such a boy, climbing birch trees "toward heaven" until their frailty bent with his weight and gently "set [him] down again" on Earth (ll. 56–57).
What It Means	The speaker communicates his preference for imaginative, playful fancy—"But I was going to say when Truth broke in / With all her matter-of-fact about the ice-storm / I should prefer to have some boy bend them"—over the harsh realities of life (ll. 21–23). Moreover, the constant and positive references to youth in this poem contrast with the somber descriptions of bent, weather-beaten elder trees, communicating a related preference for youth over age. Finally, the speaker's desire to climb a birch tree toward heaven, only to be let down to Earth again before it's too late—"May no fate willfully misunderstand me / And half grant what I wish and snatch me away / Not to return"—symbolizes both a fear of death and a desire for continued living, if not for outright reincarnation (ll. 51–53).
Why It Matters to *King Lear*	In Act I, scene i, the king himself exhibits all three of these psychological conditions: a preference for fanciful untruth over harsh truth in his treatment of his three daughters' flatteries and honesty; the irreversible, and perhaps outright crippling, effects of hard-lived old age, more seen in Lear's temperament than in any other demonstration; and a recognition, probably a fearful one, that death is imminent.

"Hyla Brook" (1916/1969)

When It Should Be Read	In the middle of Act I.
What It Says	This poem describes a woodland brook that by summer has "run out of song and speed," having previously been home to both flowing waters and singing frogs/hylae (l. 1). It contrasts the satisfying brook of memory with the hot, dry, disappeared brook of the present. Rather than conclude, however, that he is disappointed with the current brook's absence (i.e., nothingness), the speaker ends his poem with line 15, disrupting the potential blank verse sonnet: "We love the things we love for what they are."
What It Means	This poem is interpretable as a comment both upon time and its inevitable changes and upon the selflessness of love. In the latter sense, Frost suggests at the end, "real" love is not concerned with what a beloved person, object, place, or idea *used* to be, *will* be, or *could* be, but rather with what it *is*; honest love, Frost implies, requires acceptance, both of a present state and of the changes wrought by time.
Why It Matters to *King Lear*	Three individuals in Act I—Cordelia, Kent, and the Fool—demonstrate through their patience and loyalty to Lear the accepting love described by Frost; France likewise accepts and loves Cordelia for who she is, unlike Burgundy and all other characters in this play, who seem to love their beloveds for who they really are.

"Gathering Leaves" (1923/1969)

When It Should Be Read	In the middle of Act II, when Lear has left Goneril's castle in a rage and it is already clear that Goneril and Regan are allied against him.
What It Says	The speaker of this poem discusses the chore of raking, collecting, and storing fallen leaves, presumably in autumn. The poem's first half considers this process, but the second half shifts to a consideration of its purpose and value, concluding ultimately that the mountainous piles of leaves collected in a shed have negligible weight, no aesthetic value, and no potential use; nevertheless, the speaker resolves, "a crop is a crop," so he shall continue to engage in the acquisitive process (l. 22).

What It Means	The leaves in this poem may symbolize any tangible or immaterial object in the pursuit of which humans spend their time: grades, wealth, success, fame, talent, interpersonal relationships, knowledge, books, shoes, etc. Like Hamlet in Act V's famed graveyard scene, the speaker of "Gathering Leaves" ultimately recognizes, despite the massive expenditure of time and energy that his pursuit has cost, that his final collection is existentially worthless, unable to do anything for him as he continues to move through the cycle of life's seasons.
Why It Matters to *King Lear*	The speaker of this poem may as well be Lear himself as he moves in the play's first half from royalty to spurned father to total outcast. Everything in his life that he has acquired, accomplished, or created is essentially helpless to stop his empowered daughters and uncompensated retinue from turning their backs on him, leaving him to nature alone. As Goneril remarks in Act I, scene i, "he hath ever but slenderly known himself" (ll. 339–340). Yes, Regan concurs, "The best and soundest of his time hath been but rash," spent, we may assume, gathering metaphorical leaves (ll. 341–342).

"Bereft" (1928/1969)

When It Should Be Read	Somewhere between the conclusion of Act II and the beginning of Act III, scene ii, as Lear heads into the storm upon the heath before delivering his famously defiant monologue to the sky.
What It Says	The poem's speaker describes standing on the porch of a home, watching autumnal storm clouds mass in the west and listening to a wind that he recalls hearing somewhere "before / Change like this to a deeper roar" (ll. 1–2). The poem is ripe with the language of menace: the wind deepens; the shore froths, perhaps prior to rising and flooding the house; the floor sags vulnerably; piles of leaves coil, hiss, and strike like a snake; and the tone of the scene communicates that the weather itself is coming after the admittedly solitary speaker.
What It Means	One theme of this poem is the effective helplessness of individual humans against the overwhelming and potentially brutal force of nature. Even more important, however, is the underlying fear inherent in solitude, an admission that having "no one left but God" in one's life is perhaps a frightening place to be, if only because the mass of humanity is simply and clearly not there to help (l. 16).

Why It Matters to *King Lear*	As he confronts the storm on the heath, Lear may as well be, once again, Robert Frost's speaker. He is largely abandoned, he feels alone, and even the forces of nature seem to be coming after him personally. The Lear of Act III, scene ii effectively confronts the storm described in "Bereft," and with it all of the malevolent energy of a world—a cosmos—intent on defeating the already helpless. This poem is thus greatly effective in illuminating Lear's peril, even as his outward appearance still communicates defiant strength.

"Storm Fear" (1913/1969)

When It Should Be Read	At the conclusion of Act III, when Lear and the others are in the hovel.
What It Says	This poem resembles "Bereft" in that it describes the force of nature effectively attacking humankind. In this case, the speaker is awake in his house at night, listening to the windblown snow and marking how the cold encroaches slowly upon the protection of the dying fire inside.
What It Means	Again, nature is portrayed here as malevolent and insidious: "Come out! Come out!" it half-whispers, half-barks (l. 6). Likewise again, the speaker communicates his fear, stating that it "cost no inward struggle not to" acquiesce to the storm's challenge and contrasting the weakness of his small family against the frightening power outside (l. 7). In this case, though, the speaker at the poem's end admits a doubt as to whether he will ultimately live through the experience, effectively acknowledging not only his own fear and abandonment by helpful others beyond his family, but also his own mortality and the potential for a wicked, extraneous "other" to end his life.
Why It Matters to *King Lear*	Lear, by this point, has found shelter in the hovel and companionship among several others, but he has clearly begun to lose his mind and has already acknowledged that he now "feel[s] what wretches feel" (3.4.39), presaging Frost in claiming that we as lone, defenseless humans "wert better in a grave than to answer … [the] extremity of the skies" (3.4.108–109).

"An Old Man's Winter Night" (1916/1969)

When It Should Be Read	In the middle of Act IV.
What It Says	As if looking into an illuminated house through its windows at night, this poem's speaker describes a solitary old man walking into a room, forgetting why he did so, turning and walking out, and ultimately falling asleep by the stove. The speaker concludes that this old man is effectively unable to keep up with his responsibilities, but must be resigned to rest.

What It Means	Almost 90% of this poem establishes sympathy and atmosphere: coldness, solitude, sadness, boredom, perplexity, and resignation. Its interpretable key arises only at the end, in the last three lines: "One aged man—one man—can't keep a house, / A farm, a countryside, or if he can, / It's thus he does it of a winter night" (ll. 26–28). Here, Frost suggests that this one old man's condition is—or will be—*all* men's condition, for age inevitably and inherently accompanies doleful loneliness and waning abilities; no matter what our responsibilities are, he implies, moving from small ("a house") to large ("a countryside"), we at our ends will prove unable to manage them, as is the elder subject of this poem.
Why It Matters to *King Lear*	If read in the midst of Act IV—with Gloucester having lost his eyes and (he believes) his sons, and with Lear having lost his daughters and his mind, instead comforting himself by making garlands of flowers—this poem is perhaps the perfect opening to a discussion of pathos. After all, as written by Harold Bloom (1998), Lear is at the base of it "a startlingly intimate figure, since he is an emblem of fatherhood itself" (p. 493). In my experience as a classroom teacher, this is the point where engaged students truly, finally *feel* this play.

"Fire and Ice" (1923/1969)

When It Should Be Read	At the conclusion of Act IV.
What It Says	Extremely famous among Frost's works, this poem effectively discusses the end of the world, or at least of human life, wondering if it will be caused by fire or by ice. He concludes that he expects a fiery end, but acknowledges that ice is possible as well.
What It Means	The speaker analogically equates fire with desire, but ice with hate. The simple point is clearly made, then, that ambitious longing (i.e., concentration on self) can be as destructive as hate (i.e., concentration on others). Either of these extreme emotions, then, can cause human beings to destroy themselves.
Why It Matters to *King Lear*	Most of these poems by Robert Frost have been interpretable relative to Lear himself, but this one is relevant to the drama's "bad guys": Goneril, Regan, and Edmund. Students can of course pick out examples of each of these three characters demonstrating both desire and hatred, but the simple conclusion to be drawn is that they are all three set on a self-destructive path.

"Reluctance" (1913/1969)

When It Should Be Read	In Act V, prior to the play's final scene.
What It Says	The speaker of the poem describes returning home, presumably on foot, at the onset of winter, having traveled through the previous season(s). He wishes to continue walking, but his feet (i.e., his body) seem unable or unwilling to comply, and he comments at the end that it has probably always been human nature not to accept the ends of enjoyable experiences.
What It Means	As with most of Frost's poetry focused on nature, this poem is not really about nature at its core. The prevalence of deathbed language—"I have come by the highway home" (l. 5), "it is ended" (l. 6), "all dead on the ground" (l. 7), "others are sleeping" (l. 12), "dead leaves lie huddled and still" (l. 13), "last lone aster" (l. 15), "flowers . . . wither" (l. 16)—communicates rather overtly that the speaker recognizes his arrival at the end of his life, though he of course "ach[es] to seek" more (l. 17). Muddling the final rhetorical question suggesting man's stubbornness is the speaker's assertion that "To go with the drift of things" in life and death is "To yield . . . to reason," for the final word suggests the logic of death and the illogic of wanting to stay alive (ll. 21–22). There is something inhuman, Frost seems to assert, about an individual's acceptance of the simple, logical fact that he or she will die. Its atmosphere is solemn and resigned, but this poem in some way appears to applaud the tenacious spirit of human stubbornness, even as it dismisses its folly.
Why It Matters to *King Lear*	At the end of the play, although Lear and Cordelia are reunited, even though Edgar has taken careful charge of his father and is set on avenging his blindness, this is still a Shakespearean tragedy, and the wicked characters still hold official power. It is simply going to end unhappily and the students all know it, but none of them, of course, wishes for it. This poem is thus a good opportunity for metacognitive analysis, a consideration on the students' part of why we as people generally dislike and try to wish away unhappy endings. As Frost suggests, since all lives end in death, to hope for their prolonging is illogical, yet almost all readers do so. Why? In my own courses, I have used this poem as a springboard into a larger discussion concerning why most classic literature (at least those titles that we read in my school) end tragically. I think that it says something about us that we even ask the question, just as it says something about us that we still hope for a happy ending to *King Lear*.

LESSON 2

"The Onset" (1923/1969)

When It Should Be Read	At the conclusion of the play.
What It Says	This atmospherically gentle poem describes the first snow of winter, how the speaker stands alone and watches flakes fall and collect, acquiescent to its inevitability as a guiltless dying man is at the moment of death. The poem continues, moreover, in its observation that snow never overtakes the land permanently, but rather melts each spring in a natural, cyclical way.
What It Means	A poem of hope, this two-stanza piece denies the ultimately destructive power of winter (i.e., of death), in contrast to earlier poems. If all else in nature, the speaker asks, returns cyclically after a season of rest, then why not humans? Rather than being viewed as a poem particularly about reincarnation, this work has been interpreted more convincingly as a Christian poem, marked especially by the transformation of snow into "[baptismal] water of a slender April rill / That flashes tail . . . like a disappearing [demonic] snake," as well as by its emphasis on the everlasting whiteness of a church, the poem's final word (ll. 19–21). If this interpretation is acknowledged and/or accepted, then its hopeful atmosphere is religious in nature, effectively rising from a hope for salvation.
Why It Matters to *King Lear*	Lear, Cordelia, and the rest are pagans, as they themselves indicate in dialogue, so what does this poem have to do with the play? Historically, soon after the age of Lear, Christianity would spread to the British Isles, and Shakespeare, of course, was an ideological product of religious Elizabethan England. Perhaps Shakespeare intended the play's conclusion as a movement away from paganism and toward Christianity; after all, its first recorded performance was on December 26, 1606, the day after Christmas. Even more relevant, though, might be a final discussion of the play's ending in light of this poem, asking whether the ending of the play is at all hopeful. Lear's final words, after all, are "Do you see this? Look on her, look, her lips, / Look there, look there!" as if he sees something in death that no other character does (5.1.374–375). Broaching the subject of a potential afterlife is a dicey proposition, at least in public school, but if nothing else this poem potentially sets a positive spin on an otherwise dreadfully sad denouement.

Closure

Following these short analytical discussions, students could write responses to what they discussed, which, especially because the topics of the afore-outlined conversations include some pretty heavy topics, might be much easier for teenagers to do in writing than out loud. On the other hand, you might select two of these poems and juxtapose them as they might appear on an AP English Literature essay question, asking students to compare and contrast their themes, tones, usage of literary devices, and/or overall effects.

Lesson Plan 3
Musical Interpretations of King Lear

Purpose/Objective

This activity is designed to help students analyze the tone and atmosphere of various points of *King Lear*, comparing them to selected pieces of Aribert Reimann's (Reimann & Albrecht, 1979) operatic setting of Shakespeare's play. Thus, it attempts both to access students' musical intelligence and to allow them an opportunity to synthesize disparate media portrayals of the same dramatic themes, focusing on an aural expression of the emotional undercurrents running throughout Shakespeare's plot.

Placement

This activity should be conducted after students have completely read Act III of *King Lear*.

Materials Required

An audio recording of Aribert Reimann's *Lear* is necessary for this activity, as is the technology required to play it aloud. The most widely available version of this opera is identified in the References section of this book. It is advisable, also, that you procure copies for your students—or one copy to project, additionally requiring an overhead document camera—of Reimann's (1979) libretto for the two excerpts considered in this activity: Part Two, Scene 1, beginning with "*Edmund, wir fingen deinen Vater ein*," and Part One, Scene 3, consisting of the "*Zwischenspiel* [Interlude] *II*" and "*Blast, Winde, sprengt die Backen!*"

Duration

This activity should occur over approximately 30–40 minutes of one class period.

Lesson Plan

1. *Anticipatory Set:* Ask students to answer the following question in their notebooks: How do film producers and directors decide what kinds of

music should be created or compiled in a given movie's soundtrack? After they consider the question and compose an answer, have them pair and share their answers with one another, then ask for volunteers to share aloud with the class. This question well may broach in discussion the issues of popular vs. classical music, previously recorded songs vs. new compositions, vocal vs. instrumental, and the like.

2. *Communication of Objective:* Via a printed biography or orally, introduce your students to Aribert Reimann, a German composer of classical music whose most famous works are musical settings of pieces of literature, including works by Garcia Lorca, Kafka, Euripedes, and of course Shakespeare. Tell your students that they will listen to selected excerpts of his operatic version of *King Lear*, comparing the timbre and approach of Reimann's interpretation with the original's atmosphere.

3. *Prediction:* Informing students that they will first listen to Reimann's version of the famous storm scene in Act III, ask them to predict what the atmosphere of the operatic piece will be; they may do so individually, in pairs, and/or as a class. Share with students several telling quotes from Reimann (1979) concerning his creative process in writing the opera in the late 1970s; for example, "I realize that this must be my starting point. The dark colour, massive brass agglomerations and layering in the lower strings lead me to the character of Lear," or his description of the play's overarching theme, "man's isolation in a state of utter loneliness, exposed to the brutality and utter pointlessness of existence," might provide students some insight into what they are about to hear (pp. 9–10). After sharing a quote or two in this vein, ask students if they wish to revise their predictions.

4. *The Storm Scene:* Play for your students the "*Zwischenspiel* [Interlude] *II*" and Lear's aria that opens Part One, Scene 3, providing them with the textual libretto in order to follow Lear's monologue. Cutting off the excerpt when the Fool and Kent enter the scene, inquire of the class whether the piece heard mirrored their expectations; again, they may discuss this response together or separately, although a whole-class discussion should ultimately arise.

5. *Gloucester's Blinding:* Inform students that they will listen to one other scene, portraying Gloucester's blinding by Regan et al., and ask them to predict what this excerpt will sound like, based on Reimann's version of the storm scene. After a brief discussion, play the opening scene of Part Two ("*Zweiter Teil*") of the opera, beginning with Cornwall's "*Edmund, wir fingen deinen Vater ein*" and ending with Cornwall's death on a darkening stage. Again, inquire of your students whether this piece matched their mental image of what Shakespeare's scene *should* sound like.

6. *Evaluation:* The penultimate questions of this activity invariably will be, "Does this musical version match the tone and atmosphere of Shakespeare's play? Why or why not?" You may ask students to pen answers to these questions in their notebooks or discuss them orally; directions for conducting a Socratic seminar discussion on the topic can be found on pp. 132–138 of this book. On the other hand, you may even wish to expand this final evaluation into a timed 25-minute SAT-style essay, directions for which are found on pp. 158–162. Regardless, judgment of the musical appropriateness of Reimann's interpretation will help students to solidify their own envisionings of the ancient world and powerful circumstances described in Shakespeare's original.

Closure

Your discussion of musical interpretation can be extended by adding a third version of *King Lear* to Shakespeare's and Reimann's versions: Hector Berlioz's symphonic overture based on the play, *Le roi Lear*, Opus 4, debuted in 1833. A discussion considering whether Berlioz's interpretation is more fitting than Reimann's can certainly occur and would allow your students an opportunity both to compare and contrast two nonlinguistic works of art and to concretize further their own imaginings of the play's "proper" atmosphere. A particularly recommended 2010 recording of Berlioz's overture is listed in the Resources for Further study section of this book, found on pp. 219–222.

On the other hand, musically talented or otherwise capable students might wish to compose their own pieces representing atmospheric, thematic, or other elements of *King Lear*. Apple's Garage Band software and similar media allow users to play creatively with various sounds, effects, and compositional techniques, and students enabled to interpret the drama in their own musical ways might accrue many benefits from the process. Less able musicians may wish, however, simply to compile recordings into a *de facto* soundtrack for the play, constructing a playlist or running order of prerecorded songs/movements to symbolize various stages, emotions, themes, or motifs in the drama. In either case, students' consideration of and reflection upon *King Lear* will be strengthened by this personal engagement.

Name: _____ Date: _____

Example Quotation, Including Adequate Student Sample Responses

Quotation: "Nothing will come of nothing."

This quotation is spoken by *King Lear* **in Act** __One__ , **scene** __One__ .

What is the logistical importance of this quotation?

This quote is spoken by King Lear himself during his resignation ceremony. He has already heard flattery from Goneril and Regan, but Cordelia has just refused to say anything but "Nothing" to him; he is threatening to write her out of his will unless she flatters him as well.

What is the dramatic or emotional importance of this quotation?

I think that this quote indicates the introduction of the first major conflict in the play. Up to this point, no character has confronted another (even Edmund ignores his father's public insults), but Cordelia refuses to play along, which signals the drama's inciting incident. I am not really sure what Lear must be feeling as he says these threatening words: maybe disbelief, anger, frustration, or betrayal. The audience, watching the obviously disingenuous Goneril and Regan lie to their father, followed immediately by Cordelia's brave honesty, really has no choice but to side with the youngest daughter against her sisters. We also must feel some kind of scorn for Lear; at least I do.

Who is a cultural figure that might quote this line in response to the events of his or her life?

I am not sure why, but I immediately thought of political ambassadors when I read this line by itself. I picture a dignitary from the United States traveling to a foreign country in order to negotiate some kind of a truce, trade agreement, anti-violence pact, or something. One ambassador in my vision really doesn't want to make concessions, refusing to compromise his position even the smallest bit. As a result, the ambassador who IS trying to compromise tells his counterpart, "Come on, you've got to give a little bit; nothing will come of nothing." This idea/portrayal might be melodramatic, but I see it vividly, and I think it is an interesting political counterpoint to Lear's threatening request for false love from his genuinely loving daughter.

Name: _____ Date: _____

Quotation: "Come not between the dragon and his wrath."

This quotation is spoken by _____ **in Act** _____, **scene** _____.

What is the logistical importance of this quotation?

_____
_____
_____
_____
_____
_____
_____
_____
_____

What is the dramatic or emotional importance of this quotation?

_____
_____
_____
_____
_____
_____
_____
_____
_____

Who is a cultural figure that might quote these lines in response to the events of his or her life?

_____
_____
_____
_____
_____
_____
_____
_____
_____

Name: _____ Date: _____

Quotation: "Love's not love / When it is mingled with regards that stand
Aloof from th' entire point."

This quotation is spoken by _____ **in Act** _____, **scene** _____.

What is the logistical importance of this quotation?

_____
_____
_____
_____
_____
_____
_____
_____
_____

What is the dramatic or emotional importance of this quotation?

_____
_____
_____
_____
_____
_____
_____
_____
_____

Who is a cultural figure that might quote these lines in response to the events of his or her life?

_____
_____
_____
_____
_____
_____
_____

Understanding King Lear

Name: _____ Date: _____

Quotation: "Who is it that can tell me who I am?"

This quotation is spoken by _____ **in Act** _____, **scene** _____.

What is the logistical importance of this quotation?

_____
_____
_____
_____
_____
_____
_____
_____
_____

What is the dramatic or emotional importance of this quotation?

_____
_____
_____
_____
_____
_____
_____
_____
_____

Who is a cultural figure that might quote these lines in response to the events of his or her life?

_____
_____
_____
_____
_____
_____
_____
_____
_____

Name: _____ Date: _____

Quotation: "How sharper than a serpent's tooth it is
To have a thankless child."

This quotation is spoken by _____ **in Act** _____, **scene** _____.

What is the logistical importance of this quotation?

_____
_____
_____
_____
_____
_____
_____
_____

What is the dramatic or emotional importance of this quotation?

_____
_____
_____
_____
_____
_____
_____
_____

Who is a cultural figure that might quote these lines in response to the events of his or her life?

_____
_____
_____
_____
_____
_____
_____

Name: _____ Date: _____

Quotation: "Striving to better, oft we mar what's well."

This quotation is spoken by _____ **in Act** _____ **, scene** _____ .

What is the logistical importance of this quotation?

_____
_____
_____
_____
_____
_____
_____
_____

What is the dramatic or emotional importance of this quotation?

_____
_____
_____
_____
_____
_____
_____
_____

Who is a cultural figure that might quote these lines in response to the events of his or her life?

_____
_____
_____
_____
_____
_____
_____
_____

Name: _____ Date: _____

Quotation: "'Edgar' I nothing am."

This quotation is spoken by _____ **in Act** _____, **scene** _____.

What is the logistical importance of this quotation?

_____
_____
_____
_____
_____
_____
_____
_____

What is the dramatic or emotional importance of this quotation?

_____
_____
_____
_____
_____
_____
_____
_____

Who is a cultural figure that might quote these lines in response to the events of his or her life?

_____
_____
_____
_____
_____
_____
_____
_____

Understanding King Lear

Name: _____ Date: _____

Quotation: "Those wicked creatures yet do look well-favored
When others are more wicked."

This quotation is spoken by _____ in Act _____, scene _____.

What is the logistical importance of this quotation?

_____
_____
_____
_____
_____
_____
_____
_____

What is the dramatic or emotional importance of this quotation?

_____
_____
_____
_____
_____
_____
_____
_____

Who is a cultural figure that might quote these lines in response to the events of his or her life?

_____
_____
_____
_____
_____
_____
_____

Name: _____ Date: _____

Quotation: "O sir, to willful men / The injuries that they themselves procure
Must be their schoolmasters."

This quotation is spoken by _____ **in Act** _____, **scene** _____.

What is the logistical importance of this quotation?

_____
_____
_____
_____
_____
_____
_____
_____
_____

What is the dramatic or emotional importance of this quotation?

_____
_____
_____
_____
_____
_____
_____
_____
_____

Who is a cultural figure that might quote these lines in response to the events of his or her life?

_____
_____
_____
_____
_____
_____
_____
_____

Understanding King Lear

Name: _____ Date: _____

Quotation: "I am a man
More sinned against than sinning."

This quotation is spoken by _____ **in Act** _____, **scene** _____.

What is the logistical importance of this quotation?

_____
_____
_____
_____
_____
_____
_____
_____
_____

What is the dramatic or emotional importance of this quotation?

_____
_____
_____
_____
_____
_____
_____
_____

Who is a cultural figure that might quote these lines in response to the events of his or her life?

_____
_____
_____
_____
_____
_____
_____
_____

Name: _____ Date: _____

Quotation: "Let not the creaking of shoes nor the rustling of silks betray thy poor heart to woman."

This quotation is spoken by _____ in Act _____, scene _____.

What is the logistical importance of this quotation?

_____
_____
_____
_____
_____
_____
_____
_____

What is the dramatic or emotional importance of this quotation?

_____
_____
_____
_____
_____
_____
_____
_____

Who is a cultural figure that might quote these lines in response to the events of his or her life?

_____
_____
_____
_____
_____
_____
_____
_____

Name: _____ Date: _____

Quotation: "When we our betters see bearing our woes,
We scarcely think our miseries our foes."

This quotation is spoken by _____ in Act _____, scene _____.

What is the logistical importance of this quotation?

_____
_____
_____
_____
_____
_____
_____
_____
_____

What is the dramatic or emotional importance of this quotation?

_____
_____
_____
_____
_____
_____
_____
_____
_____

Who is a cultural figure that might quote these lines in response to the events of his or her life?

_____
_____
_____
_____
_____
_____
_____
_____
_____

Name: _____ Date: _____

Quotation: "I have no way and therefore want no eyes.
                  I stumbled when I saw."

This quotation is spoken by _____ **in Act** _____, **scene** _____.

What is the logistical importance of this quotation?

_____
_____
_____
_____
_____
_____
_____
_____
_____

What is the dramatic or emotional importance of this quotation?

_____
_____
_____
_____
_____
_____
_____
_____
_____

Who is a cultural figure that might quote these lines in response to the events of his or her life?

_____
_____
_____
_____
_____
_____
_____
_____

Understanding King Lear

Name: _____ Date: _____

Quotation: "The worst is not
So long as we can say 'This is the worst.'"

This quotation is spoken by _____ **in Act** _____, **scene** _____.

What is the logistical importance of this quotation?

_____
_____
_____
_____
_____
_____
_____
_____
_____

What is the dramatic or emotional importance of this quotation?

_____
_____
_____
_____
_____
_____
_____
_____
_____

Who is a cultural figure that might quote these lines in response to the events of his or her life?

_____
_____
_____
_____
_____
_____
_____
_____

Name: _____ Date: _____

Quotation: "As flies to wanton boys are we to th' gods;
They kill us for their sport."

This quotation is spoken by _____ **in Act** _____, **scene** _____.

What is the logistical importance of this quotation?

_____
_____
_____
_____
_____
_____
_____
_____
_____

What is the dramatic or emotional importance of this quotation?

_____
_____
_____
_____
_____
_____
_____
_____
_____

Who is a cultural figure that might quote these lines in response to the events of his or her life?

_____
_____
_____
_____
_____
_____
_____
_____

Understanding King Lear

Name: _____ Date: _____

Quotation: "Henceforth I'll bear / Affliction till it do cry out itself
'Enough, enough!' and die."

This quotation is spoken by _____ **in Act** _____ **, scene** _____ **.**

What is the logistical importance of this quotation?

_____
_____
_____
_____
_____
_____
_____
_____
_____

What is the dramatic or emotional importance of this quotation?

_____
_____
_____
_____
_____
_____
_____
_____
_____

Who is a cultural figure that might quote these lines in response to the events of his or her life?

_____
_____
_____
_____
_____
_____
_____
_____

Name: _____ Date: _____

Quotation: "... they told me I was everything.
'Tis a lie. I am not ague-proof."

This quotation is spoken by _____ **in Act** _____, **scene** _____.

What is the logistical importance of this quotation?

_____
_____
_____
_____
_____
_____
_____
_____
_____

What is the dramatic or emotional importance of this quotation?

_____
_____
_____
_____
_____
_____
_____
_____
_____

Who is a cultural figure that might quote these lines in response to the events of his or her life?

_____
_____
_____
_____
_____
_____
_____

Understanding King Lear

Name: _____ Date: _____

Quotation: "Men must endure / Their going hence even as their coming hither. Ripeness is all."

This quotation is spoken by _____ **in Act** _____, **scene** _____.

What is the logistical importance of this quotation?

_____
_____
_____
_____
_____
_____
_____
_____
_____

What is the dramatic or emotional importance of this quotation?

_____
_____
_____
_____
_____
_____
_____
_____
_____

Who is a cultural figure that might quote these lines in response to the events of his or her life?

_____
_____
_____
_____
_____
_____
_____
_____

Name: _____ Date: _____

Quotation: "The gods are just, and of our pleasant vices
　　　　　　　　Make instruments to plague us."

This quotation is spoken by _____ **in Act** _____, **scene** _____.

What is the logistical importance of this quotation?

_____
_____
_____
_____
_____
_____
_____
_____
_____

What is the dramatic or emotional importance of this quotation?

_____
_____
_____
_____
_____
_____
_____
_____

Who is a cultural figure that might quote these lines in response to the events of his or her life?

_____
_____
_____
_____
_____
_____
_____

CHAPTER 5

Performing *King Lear*

A solid and complete understanding of *King Lear*—its profound dialogue, its universal characters, its insightful comic relief, its dramatic power—cannot arise solely from reading the play as one would a well-crafted novel or story, which is written largely to be encountered and absorbed alone, to be experienced at least initially by individuals, existing chiefly in the space between the author's words on the printed page and the images created in a reader's imagination. Plays, on the other hand, are envisioned and penned to be performed, to be enacted in "real time and space" both physically and verbally.

In literature classes, therefore, I always prefer that students not only read Shakespeare's plays alone, but also consider, enact, and discuss them collectively, pondering together over the meanings of his verse, stumbling cooperatively over those especially hard-to-pronounce words and lines, debating and ultimately concluding how a given character is "supposed" to feel, to speak, to move. This chapter offers ways in which teachers can initiate such performances by students and induce reflective activities aimed at improving the final quality of their presentations.

Stage Terminology

Before beginning preparations for actual performance, it is important for both students and teachers to understand several key terms that are common among dramatists, terms that are important to the following activities' dramatic authenticity and to students' overall ability to write fluently and learnedly about Shakespeare's stagecraft on the AP Literature and Composition exam. When discussing with your students various aspects of *King Lear* as it can or should be performed, I suggest that you use these terms as often and as casually as possible, thereby engendering students' understanding of and comfort with them. The terms include:

- *Blocking:* This word denotes the physical movements of actors on stage. Fight choreography falls under the umbrella of stage blocking, as do elements of actors' body language, routes and speeds of their movements around the stage, directions regarding entrances and exits, poses to be struck, and any other aspects of characters' physical performances. Blocking decisions generally are made by directors in preparatory rehearsals, although experienced or insightful actors often have a hand in their own characters' physicality, as well.

- *Delivery:* This term describes how lines of dialogue are to be said or delivered to an audience. Especially in Shakespeare, it is often debatable how given lines of text are best delivered. For example, Gloucester's "As flies to wanton boys are we to th' gods; / They kill us for their sport," legitimately can be spoken matter-of-factly, bitterly, furiously, incredulously, sadly, or in any combination of these ways (4.1.41–42). Debates between actors and directors concerning deliveries of ambiguous lines such as this one can get heated, but can also prove beneficial for delving into subtext, such as characters' motivation and background, that ultimately enhances the eventual performance.

- *Upstage, Downstage, Left, and Right:* To theatrical laymen, terms such as upstage, downstage-left, and even center stage can be confusing; most of this disorientation arises from people's uncertainty as to *whose* left is stage left located anyhow, the actors' or the audience's? The simplest answer is that these locations on stage are always considered from an actor's point of view. To move stage left, as an actor, is to move to *your* left, to move upstage is to move away from your audience, and to frown at someone located offstage right is to glare into the wings to your right. Figure 2 demonstrates all of these directions.

- *Set:* A theatrical set is the stage's physical and aesthetic layout, including what furniture or decoration is present, what backgrounds have been painted or adorned, and even what colors and shadings are included. Shakespeare's set directions are even scantier than his stage directions; it is clear that *King Lear* requires a hovel and a heath, for example, but directors otherwise are free to stage the drama as they wish. Thus, like almost all of the Bard's plays, this one has been performed in nearly every physical and aesthetic space, from traditional Elizabethan reproductions to wholly minimalist sets, and from adaptations of the play to settings

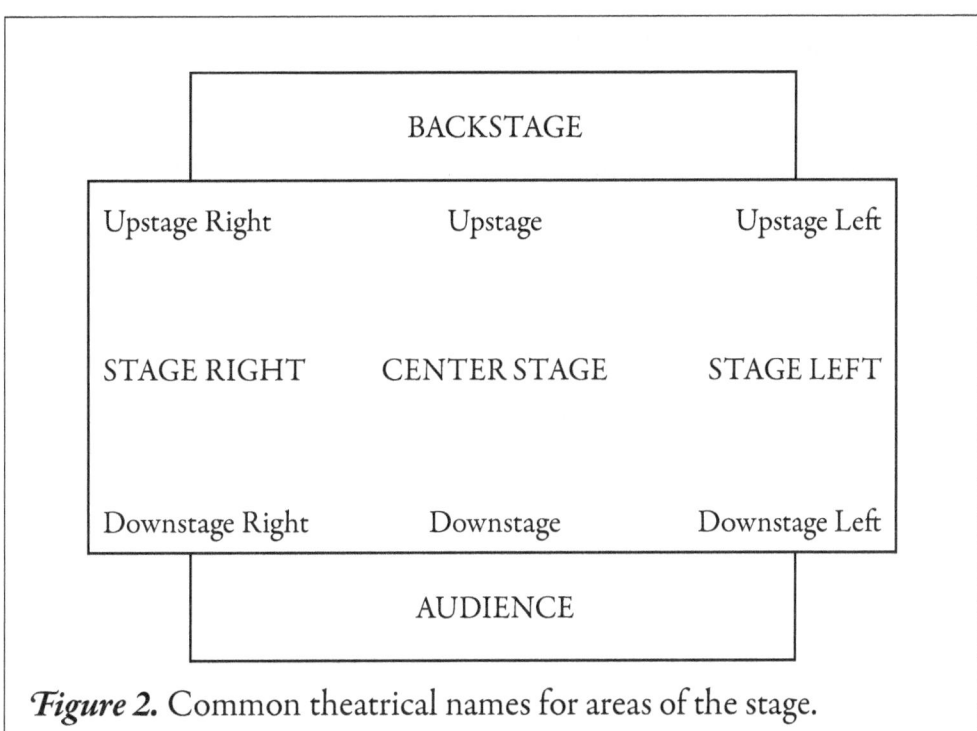

Figure 2. Common theatrical names for areas of the stage.

quite distinct from the British Isles to black-box theaters entirely devoid of recognizable aspects.

- *Prompt Book:* A prompt book is a copy of the text that has been marked up by its owner (usually a play's director, although actors will themselves have prompt books concerning their own roles in a production), noting details of blocking and delivery of lines, set decorations, and every bit of information needed to make a performance come off smoothly. Visually, a prompt book resembles a highly annotated script.

Understanding Characters: Questions for Discussion or Written Reflection

All thespians engaged in staging a play need to envision their ultimately performed product long before the curtain goes up. Actors especially benefit from thorough, textually based understandings of their characters in order to enact convincing portrayals of these "persons" who, until brought to life on the stage, are truly nothing but ink on pages. There surely is no better way to arrive at such deep understandings of characters than to analyze and discuss their attributes with fellow dramatists: characters' backgrounds, emotional dispositions, motivations for acting and speaking as they do at any given point during the play, the tones of their voices, and their relationships with other characters. To play a role realistically is often to climb inside of a character's skin, and there really is no way to do so without arriving at some understanding of who that character truly is and why.

To this extent, I here include several prompts and questions that should help students to analyze some important characters in *King Lear*, particularly ones who are not quite the "stars of the show." The following questions will not help students to block any scene, nor will they detail the deliveries of particular lines of dialogue, but if considered thoughtfully, they will help inquisitive actors to arrive at fundamental understandings (or at least their own opinions) of who these characters truly are and why, as well as how their roles should or can be performed as a result.

Character analysis regarding specific supporting characters might include the following:

- *The Fool:* Like Falstaff from Part I of *Henry IV* and Mercutio from *Romeo and Juliet*, Lear's Fool is a comedic scene stealer. His bits of wisdom masquerade as rhymed showmanship, allowing the Fool to voice to his master the audience's opinion of the goings-on, much like a traditional Greek chorus. He in all cases avoids true chastisement because of his evasive wit, and playgoers and readers generally lump him in with *King Lear*'s "good guys," despite the fact that the Fool effectively abandons Lear, Kent, and the rest following the central storm's passage from the stage. What, in your estimation, is the Fool's motivation for leaving at that point? Does it lessen his reputation as a laudable character, or does it simply illuminate personal qualities that were better hidden earlier in the play?

- *Oswald:* An extremely static character throughout the play, Oswald demonstrates no clear emotional growth between the text's covers. Thus, he comes off as simpler to apprehend than more dynamic characters in *King Lear*, and usually alienates sympathetic audience members with his mistreatment of Lear, Kent, and the others. Nevertheless, Oswald is, if viewed from one perspective, perhaps the most honest character in the entire play. He does not lie, disguise his identity, or in any way transgress the orders of his superiors. In your opinion, what is Oswald's motivation for acting as he does? On a related note, do you esteem Oswald as an intelligent person, regardless of his ethics?

- *Albany:* The Duke of Albany, identified early in the play solely as Goneril's husband, is perhaps a difficult character about whom to set an opinion. His defining characteristic throughout the drama's first half seems to be weakness, political and otherwise, yet he joins the rebellious Edgar's side in the end, ultimately sequestering rule of England from the royal family. What is your impression of Albany? What kind of a man is he truly? What does he apparently believe?

- *Cornwall:* A common belief holds that you can tell a lot about people by considering their dogs; certain types of individuals go with particular kinds of canines. True or not, this apprehension can likewise be applied to the three princesses, and by extension to their husbands. In other words, perhaps you can tell a lot about people by examining their spouses. Regan's spouse, the Duke of Cornwall, is portrayed almost entirely as a heartless villain. Moreover, while Goneril seems to control her own husband, Albany, Cornwall apparently exhibits control—or at least guidance—over his wife. What do you imagine a typical audience's reaction is to Cornwall? Beyond his obvious acts of cruelty (e.g., to Gloucester), what does his spoken dialogue indicate about his personal character, and what do you think has made him this way?

Questions such as the few above can also be asked regarding *King Lear*'s other characters. However, answers to such questions tend to be either tremendously complex, tied in large part to specific points of the plot in cases of focal, main characters such as Lear himself, or reductive and unsatisfying, based largely on conjecture in cases of characters so minor that we have very little dialogue upon which to make any inferences about them, such as the examples of Gloucester's Old Man. Nevertheless, it is *always* valuable to consider characters' essential personalities and the audience reactions that they engender.

You may wish that students consider these questions in informal, independent writing assignments or in discussion; perhaps a combination of both approaches would be ideal, whereby written reflection is used to fuel discourse among classmates. Regardless of how you choose to administer them, questions such as the above provide students with opportunities to react to roles in interpretive, considerate ways, fueling and augmenting the eventual decisions that they make regarding these characters' blocking, delivery, and emotions at particular moments of the script.

In a general sense, when it comes down to understanding individual scenes and interpreting dramatic moments, the following questions will prove more valuable in helping students to envision and articulate how they should be played. Again, these questions may be considered by students individually, although communal dialogue will probably produce a clearer, more substantiated vision and a deeper understanding by all pupils in the class of how an eventual staging should or might come off. The particular questions to ask of students include:

- What is the character thinking at this moment of the play?
- What is the character feeling at this point?
- How are the other characters onstage responding to this character, and why?
- How might the character's body language reflect his or her emotions?

Performing King Lear

- Can the other characters' thoughts be represented by their body language?
- How much personal space does this or other characters want right now, and why?
- What physical actions might this character take to emphasize clearly the point of his or her lines?
- Could a lack of movement by this character communicate his or her emotions or thoughts even more clearly than would action? Why or why not?
- Tone conveys a person's attitude, so in what tone of voice should these lines be delivered?
- If standing deadly still, how might this character communicate his or her emotions or thoughts clearly just by altering his or her delivery of these lines?

As usual, there are rarely definite answers to any of these questions, at least within the dramatic boundaries fixed by Shakespeare's content. (In other words, delivering his final lines of dialogue, having carried the dead Cordelia onstage in his arms, Lear clearly is neither feeling nor acting upbeat; students who interpret or attempt to enact the final scene in this way had better have some pretty good logic to support themselves!) If students respond to the questions above as they read or prepare to stage *King Lear*, then they will arrive at deep and personal understandings of the play and its characters, plus a clearer picture of just how Shakespeare's action "looks." All of these processes will aid their understanding, mastery, and retention of the play.

Prompt Books and Performance

Once students understand and are able to discuss fluently these various aspects of characterization and stagecraft, you may want to require that they practice their productive skills in an assessable way. Creating a prompt book, even a truncated one that "directs" and stages only a scene or two from a play, is an extremely valuable exercise in close reading and deep thinking. Successful prompt booking requires students to get into the minds of characters, envision sets and actors' uses of props, and block every character on stage throughout the entirety of the performance. If students are able to pull all of these aspects of stagecraft together, explaining their choices persuasively, then they definitely will have developed not only their close reading skills, but also their interpretive-analytical faculties, both of which they will need for ultimate success on the AP Literature exam.

I recommend that you assign hybrid assignments to your gifted and talented students, requiring sections (be they acts, scenes, or even just extended speeches) of *King Lear* to be outlined and directed in the style of prompt books and accompanied by short essays explaining the intellectual processes that students undertook and choices that they ultimately made when creating their prompt books. When prompt booking the final scene of Act III, for example, it is one thing for students to state that Cornwall should move smoothly stage-left as he draws his sword just as Regan shifts downstage, both with impassive but menacing countenances as they surround Gloucester's chair, but it is something quite different and cognitively more challenging for students to do the same, plus articulate logically why they chose such blocking maneuvers and delivery notes over other possibilities, especially in light of how the rest of the scene transpires. You might ask each student, for example, to create a prompt book for an individually chosen 100-line section of the play, as well as produce an essay explaining the decisions of delivery and blocking that he or she made as a hypothetical director, plus a sketch of an envisioned set for the excerpt. Quite an in-depth assessment! Even those students who consistently excel in the reading and interpretation of literature will probably be stretched to produce and articulately defend such a multifaceted product.

As a device for enhancing students' close reading and interpretation of text, prompt books are a pedagogical end in themselves, but theatrically they always serve as a means toward a larger end: eventual performance in front of an audience. Of course it is practicable to assign prompt book work to your students without requiring their public expositions; conversely, however, requiring that students perform speeches, scenes, and acts from *King Lear* without having designed preparatory prompt books is potentially disastrous, akin to beginning an impromptu recipe in one's kitchen without prior awareness of the ingredients or time required. If you are going to have your students perform the play or parts of it, then I strongly suggest that you first insist on their production of prompt books.

Lesson Plan: Nahum Tate's Alternative Lear

After learning about prompt books and various stage terminology, students are ready to put what they have learned into action. This activity introduces students to what for 150 years was the only version of "Shakespeare's" *Lear* performed on stage, a heavily edited version with a happy ending! They will consider excerpts from the revision relative to the Bard's original, performing or simply reading them aloud for their peers, and ultimately engage in evaluation of the texts and their audiences. This lesson plan can be found on pages 116–119, followed by the script that it utilizes, by Nahum Tate, on pages 120–127.

Comparisons of Various Cinematic Versions

Every teacher knows that students love "movie day." In my experience, however, the same students cheering for an announcement of film viewing soon zone out (or even fall asleep) once the movies begin rolling, at least when those films are Shakespearean adaptations. The stereotypical cinematic version of Shakespeare, as parodied so well by Robin Williams in *Dead Poets Society*, is banal, conceited, and overdramatized, probably including lots of unnecessary hand gestures and some kind of funny accent, too. I shall not argue against this stereotype, which is grounded in far too many examples to ignore. The key to opening students' minds to Shakespeare on film, in my opinion, is not to bore students (and reinforce that stereotype) by showing them entire 2-hour-plus-long movies, especially those versions shot in black and white. There is nothing inherently bad or inadequate about older films, of course; Laurence Olivier is arguably still the best interpreter of Shakespeare. My experience, however, is that 21st-century teenagers have a natural and immediate aversion to such seemingly antiquated performances.

This stereotype will be overcome not by subjecting students to overexposure, attempting to force appreciation down their figurative throats, but by showing them judiciously selected excerpts of older Shakespearean adaptations juxtaposed with more recent versions or alternatives set in adaptive locales. If your class examines several versions of one scene from *King Lear*—the same dramatic moment staged in two or three distinct ways—then students undoubtedly will recognize the great variety of potential interpretations that Shakespeare allowed his future directors and actors. This step is the first toward an appreciation of the Bard's inherent "flexibility." The natural malleability of Shakespearean theater can be pointed out to pupils in no better way than by comparing, contrasting, and dissecting various professionals' visions.

Relative to various other Shakespearean plays (i.e., *Romeo and Juliet* and *Hamlet*) filmed adaptations of *King Lear* are comparatively few. However, while your local library, rental hub, or retail store may not have a number of the play's cinematic adaptations, a variety of them are definitely available via the Internet. Previewing whatever versions you acquire is certainly the most advisable way to find particular scenes that differ in the hands of various directors and actors, but among the most plausible suspects for such diversity are the opening scene, the interactions between Lear and the Fool in Acts I and II, the pivotal storm scene on the heath, and the final scene, including both Edgar and Edmund's battle and Lear's harrowing finale. Juxtaposing Akira Kurosawa's 1985 production *Ran*, which is a samurai adaptation of *King Lear*, with a more traditional film version, such as Peter Brook's excellent release from 1970, surely will engender productive discussion regarding how students' own visions of a given scene differ from either director's staging.

Asking students to focus on specific aspects of stagecraft, moreover, such as blocking and vocal delivery, or on strictly cinematic touches like camera angles, also sharpens their analytical acumen, providing them with more precise material for discussion and debate. At the end of this chapter (pages 128–129), I have included two worksheets that you may use to help students compare and contrast just such particular elements as they watch different versions of Shakespearean scenes.

Conclusion

This chapter's activities offer a variety of ways to engage your class in dramatic, thoughtful, and otherwise inspiring performance of Shakespeare's text. By contrast, the next chapter focuses on considered, deliberate, substantiated discussion of the play: its relevancies, its themes, and its characters.

Chapter Materials

Lesson Plan 4

Nahum Tate's Alternative Lear

Purpose/Objective

This activity compares and contrasts the revised text of *King Lear*, edited and published by Nahum Tate, to Shakespeare's original drama in order to allow students an opportunity to consider the relative values of their diction, syntax, thematic unity, dramatic flourishes, realism, and pacing.

Placement

The first part of this activity, concerning the play's first scene, can be completed as early as Act I; the second half, however, should not be completed until after students conclude their reading of the play. At the teacher's discretion, on the other hand, the entire lesson can be delivered wholly after the conclusion of Shakespeare's drama.

Materials Required

Beyond the text of Shakespeare's *King Lear*, copies of selections from Tate's *History of King Lear*, found on pp. 120–127 of this text, are necessary. The selections compiled in this book have been slightly revised from the 1681 first edition text, tangibly housed at the University of Pennsylvania and available in several edited versions online, as noted in the References section; this book's particular selections retain the line numbers of the original text.

Duration

This activity is divisible into multiple pieces, each of which should last anywhere from 20–40 minutes. These pieces can be conflated and completed in one full class period of approximately 90 minutes, or they can be separated and accomplished over several days; in this sense, the activity's duration is very flexible. Furthermore, at the teacher's discretion, the discussions following performance can be expanded into full-blown Socratic seminars (see pp. 132–138 of this book for further information).

Lesson Plan

1. *Anticipatory Set:* Ask the class to consider a story with which most of them are familiar, but that has some sort of violent or sad conclusion, such as a film (e.g., *Bambi* or *Titanic*) or fairy tale (e.g., "Hansel and Gretel" or "The Three Little Pigs"); have them each write a brief synopsis of that story in their notebooks, including all important aspects of its plot. Students may pair and share their synopses with each other, and perhaps with the class as a whole. Next, ask students to rewrite the conclusion of the story in order to eliminate its violent or solemn outcome. For example, "The Three Little Pigs" might be rewritten so that rather than falling into a pot of boiling liquid when his only entrance into the brick house is a chimney, the Big Bad Wolf might reconsider his malevolent ways and offer recompense to the three pigs by rebuilding their blown-down houses himself, perhaps afterward deciding to live with them as a convivial lodger. These alternate endings should likewise be shared among students and aloud with the class, then used as springboards into a discussion of why they are perhaps better, less effective, sillier, less realistic, and so on. Ultimately, you might reach a point of discussion considering whether archetypal happy endings are, for whatever reason, artistically lesser than sorrowful or otherwise "difficult" endings.

2. *Communication of Objective:* Inform students that the purpose of this activity is to consider, relative to Shakespeare's original, the version of the play that was the most popular and prevalently performed during the 17th and 18th centuries. Inform them moreover that in the 17th century, Shakespeare was not quite the literary giant that he is considered today, and that therefore to amend his works was in no way considered inappropriate; thus Nahum Tate, a 17th-century English dramatist, did just that, editing and publishing "new" versions of various Shakespearean plays, the most famous of which remains *The History of King Lear*. Tate's version was so popular among audiences and thespians that it actually replaced the Bard's original for 150 years, being *the* version of *King Lear* performed from 1681–1834. This revised version was in fact one of the most successful English stage plays of its time, having been enacted by innumerable celebrity dramatists until it was finally ousted, in favor of Shakespeare's original, in the mid-19th century. Finally, tell students that you are going to examine the revised play's beginning and end, exploring it relative to Shakespeare's in several ways: (1) on its linguistic level, comparing Tate's diction and syntax to the Bard's; (2) on its dramatic level, considering how effective as a piece of staged drama (i.e., including dialogue that is intended to be spoken effectively) Tate's play compares to Shakespeare's;

and (3) on its thematic level, identifying how Tate's revision of *King Lear* impacts its overall meaning.

3. *Preparation:* Divide the students into four groups: one to perform the first scene of Shakespeare's *King Lear*, another to perform Nahum Tate's first scene, a third to perform the final scene of Shakespeare's version, and a final group to perform Tate's conclusion. Allow these groups to split up and work together, looking over their particular pieces of text and preparing to enact them before their classmates. This portion of the lesson can be accomplished in as few as 10 minutes, encouraging students to read and perform their scripts essentially impromptu, or it can be expanded into thorough prompt-booking (see pp. 110–111 of this text for further instructions and an explanation).

4. *Comparison of First Scenes:* Allow the first group of students to perform for their peers scene i from Shakespeare's Act I of *King Lear*. Next, allow the second group to perform Tate's first scene. As a class, follow these performances with a discussion of the two scenes' similarities and differences, focusing on these three areas of consideration:

   1) Linguistic Level
      - What portions of Shakespeare's dialogue did Tate choose to replace?
      - What characteristics—overarching or particular—does Tate's new dialogue have?
      - In terms of their syntax, diction, and poetical qualities, how do Tate's insertions compare to Shakespeare's original writing?

   2) Dramatic Level
      - What differences are there between Shakespeare's and Tate's first scenes in terms of their dramatic effectiveness (i.e., how your classroom audience responded to them)?
      - Do any of the characters in the two scenes "change" between the two versions (e.g., what do Tate's alterations do to the characterizations of Cordelia or Lear)?
      - Which of the two versions is, all things considered, most realistic and thus most believable in performance? Why?

   3) Thematic Level
      - Do the changes, omissions, and insertions described above change the atmosphere or foreshadowing of the first scene?
      - If students already recognize some of the play's major events, themes, or moments, then ask whether the alterations made by Tate in this first scene in any way impinge upon the thematic directions toward which Shakespeare's play travels after scene i.

5. *Anticipating Further Changes:* Ask students to imagine and describe in their notebooks what changes, based on their experience with the two opening scenes, they believe Tate may have made to the play's denouement. Have students pair and share their predictions with one another, and perhaps with the class as a whole.
6. *Comparison of Resolutions:* Following the same procedure for performance and discussion outlined above, allow the third and fourth groups of students to perform the different endings of *King Lear*, then consider their differences, similarities, and merits relative to one another. Again, the conversational portion of this activity can certainly be expanded into a graded Socratic seminar discussion (e.g., pp. 132–138) or even a classroom debate (e.g., pp. 138–144).

Closure

Perhaps the most telling fact concerning Nahum Tate's *The History of King Lear* is that it was the only version of *King Lear* performed for 150 years, literally replacing Shakespeare's drama on the stage. Ask students to consider what this fact demonstrates about audiences of the past (and perhaps of the present, as we now laud Shakespeare's version and largely slight Tate's), and thus about human nature. A comparison might be drawn between these alternative versions of the play and contemporary cinema; why is it, you might ask, that satirical, farcical, or otherwise lighthearted movies often top lists of Hollywood's most profitable films upon release, performing well with box office audiences, but such "happy ending" movies generally are passed over by scholarly groups tasked with choosing a year's most artistic or otherwise "best" movies? Must a story be solemn to be moving? To be truthful? Students can answer these sorts of questions in oral conversation or in their notebooks. Regardless, the popularity of Tate's fairy tale twist on *King Lear* is fodder for some great discussion regarding "classic" literature, its identifiable qualities, and its audience in general.

from Act One

[*Flourish. Enter* LEAR, CORNWALL, ALBANY, BURGUNDY, EDGAR, GONERIL, REGAN, CORDELIA. EDGAR *speaking to* CORDELIA, *at Entrance.*]

EDGAR
Cordelia, royal Fair, turn yet once more,
And ere successful Burgundy receive
The treasure of thy beauties from the King,
Ere happy Burgundy forever fold thee, 60
Cast back one pitying look on wretched Edgar.

CORDELIA
Alas what would the wretched Edgar with
The more unfortunate Cordelia,
Who in obedience to a father's will
Flies from her Edgar's arms to Burgundy's?

LEAR
Attend my Lords of Albany and Cornwall
With princely Burgundy.

ALBANY
We do, my Liege.

LEAR
Give me the map—know, Lords, we have divided
In three our kingdom, having now resolved 70
To disengage from our long toil of state,
Conferring all upon your younger years;
You, Burgundy, Cornwall and Albany
Long in our court have made your amorous sojourn
And now are to be answered—tell me, my daughters,
Which of you loves us most, that we may place
Our largest bounty with the largest merit.
Goneril, our eldest-born, speak first.

GONERIL
Sir, I do love you more than words can utter,
Beyond what can be valued, rich or rare. 80
Nor liberty, nor sight, health, fame, or beauty
Are half so dear, my life for you were vile,
As much as child can love the best of fathers.

LEAR
Of all these bounds, ev'n from this line to this
With shady forests and wide-skirted meads,
We make thee Lady, to thine and Albany's issue
Be this perpetual. What says our second daughter?

REGAN
My sister, sir, in part expressed my love,
For such as hers, is mine, though more extended.
Sense has no other joy that I can relish; 90
I have my all in my dear Liege's love!

LEAR
Therefore to thee and thine hereditary
Remain this ample third of our fair kingdom.

CORDELIA
Now comes my trial, how am I distressed. [*Aside*]
That must with cold speech tempt the chol'rich King
Rather to leave me dowerless, than condemn me
To loathed embraces!

LEAR
Speak now our last, not least in our dear love,
So ends my task of State—Cordelia speak,
What canst thou say to win a richer third 100
Than what thy sisters gained?

CORDELIA
Now must my love in words fall short of theirs
As much as it exceeds in truth—Nothing, my Lord.

LEAR
Nothing can come of nothing; speak again.

CORDELIA
Unhappy am I that I can't dissemble,
Sir, as I ought. I love your Majesty,
No more nor less.

LEAR
Take heed, Cordelia.
Thy fortunes are at stake; think better on't
And mend thy speech a little. 110

CORDELIA
O my Liege,
You gave me being, bred me, dearly love me,
And I return my duty as I ought,
Obey you, love you, and most honor you!
Why have my sisters husbands, if they love you all?
Happ'ly when I shall wed, the Lord whose hand
Shall take my plight will carry half my love,
For I shall never marry, like my sisters,
To love my father all.

LEAR
And goes thy heart with this?
'Tis said that I am chol'rich, judge me Gods.
Is there not cause? Now minion I perceive
The truth of what has been suggested to us,
Thy fondness for the rebel son of Gloucester,
False to his father, as thou art to my hopes.
And oh, take heed, rash girl, lest we comply
With thy fond wishes, which thou wilt too late
Repent, for know our nature cannot brook
A child so young and so ungentle.

CORDELIA
So young, my Lord, and true.

LEAR
Thy truth then be thy dow'r,
For by the sacred sun and solemn night
I here disclaim all my paternal care,
And from this minute hold thee as a stranger
Both to my blood and favor.

KENT
This is frenzy.
Consider, good my Liege —

LEAR
Peace Kent.
Come not between a dragon and his rage.
I loved her most, and in her tender trust
Designed to have bestowed my age at ease!
So be my grave my peace as here I give
My heart from her, and with it all my wealth.
My Lords of Cornwall and of Albany,
I do invest you jointly with full right
In this fair third, Cordelia's forfeit dow'r.
Mark me, my Lords, observe our last resolve,
Our self attended with an hundred knights
Will make aboard with you in monthly course,
The name alone of King remain with me;
Yours be the execution and revenues.
This is our final will, and to confirm it,
This coronet part between you.

KENT
Royal Lear,
Whom I have ever honored as my King,
Loved as my father, as my master followed,
And as my patron thought on in my pray'rs—

LEAR
Away—the bow is bent, make from the shaft.

KENT
No, let it fall and drench within my heart.
Be Kent unmannerly when Lear is mad.
Thy youngest daughter—

LEAR
On thy life, no more.

KENT
What wilt thou do, old man?

LEAR
Out of my sight!

KENT
See better first.

LEAR
Now by the Gods—

KENT
Now by the Gods, rash King, thou swear'st in vain.

LEAR
Ha, traitor—

KENT
Do, kill thy physician, Lear,
Strike through my throat, yet with my latest breath
I'll thunder in thine ear my just complaint,
And tell thee to thy face that thou dost ill.

LEAR
Hear me rash man, on thy allegiance hear me:
Since thou hast striv'n to make us break our vow
And pressed between our sentence and our pow'r,
Which nor our nature nor our place can bear,
We banish thee for ever from our sight
And kingdom; if when three days are expir'd
Thy hated trunk be found in our dominions,
That moment is thy death. Away.

KENT
Why, fare thee well, King, since thou art resolved
I take thee at thy word and will not stay
To see thy fall; the gods protect the maid
That truly thinks, and has most justly said.
Thus to new climates my old truth I bear.
Friendship lives hence, and banishment is here.

[Exit]

LEAR
Now Burgundy, you see her price is fal'n,
Yet if the fondness of your passion still
Affects her as she stands, dow'rless, and lost
In our esteem, she's yours, take her or leave her. 190

BURGUNDY
Pardon me, Royal Lear, I but demand
The dow'r your self propos'd, and here I take
Cordelia by the hand, Dutchess of Burgundy.

LEAR
Then leave her, sir, for by a father's rage
I tell you all her wealth. Away.

BURGUNDY
Then sir, be pleased to charge the breach
Of our alliance on your own will,
Not my inconstancy.
                    [*Exit.* EDGAR *and* CORDELIA *remain.*]

EDGAR
Has Heaven then weighed the merit of my love,
Or is't the raving of my sickly thought? 200
Could Burgundy forgo so rich a prize
And leave her to despairing Edgar's arms?
Have I thy hand Cordelia, do I clasp it,
The hand that was this minute to have joined
My hated rivals? Do I kneel before thee
And offer at thy feet my panting heart?
Smile, Princess, and convince me, for as yet
I doubt, and dare not trust the dazzling joy.

CORDELIA
Some comfort yet that 'twas no vicious blot
That has deprived me of a father's grace, 210
But merely want of that that makes me rich
In wanting it, a smooth professing tongue:
O sisters, I am loathe to call your fault
As it deserves, but use our father well,
And wronged Cordelia never shall repine.

EDGAR
O heav'nly maid that art thy self thy dow'r,
Richer in virtue than the stars in light,
If Edgar's humble fortunes may be graced
With thy acceptance, at thy feet he lays 'em.
Ha, my Cordelia! Dost thou turn away? 220
What have I done t'offend Thee?

CORDELIA
Talk't of Love.

EDGAR
Then I've offended oft, Cordelia too
Has oft permitted me so to offend.

CORDELIA
When, Edgar, I permitted your addresses,
I was the darling daughter of a King,
Nor can I now forget my royal birth,
And live dependent on my lover's fortune.
I cannot to so low a fate submit,
And therefore study to forget your passion, 230
And trouble me upon this theme no more.

EDGAR
Thus majesty takes most state in distress!
How are we tossed on fortune's fickle flood!
The wave that with surprising kindness brought
The dear wreck to my arms, has snatched it back,
And left me mourning on the barren shore.

CORDELIA [*Aside*]
This baseness of th' ignoble Burgundy
Draws just suspicion on the race of men,
His love was int'rest, so may Edgar's be
And he but with more complement dissemble; 240
If so, I shall oblige him by denying,
But if his love be fixed, such constant flame
As warms our breasts, if such I find his passion,
My heart as grateful to his truth shall be,
And cold Cordelia prove as kind as he.
                                        [*Exit*]

from ACT FIVE

[*Flourish. Enter before the tents,* ALBANY, GONERIL, REGAN, *Guards and Attendants.* GONERIL *speaking apart to the Captain of the Guards, entering.*]

GONERIL
Here's gold for thee. Thou knowst our late command
Upon your pris'ners lives. About it straight, and at
Our ev'ning banquet let it raise our mirth
To hear that they are dead.

CAPTAIN
I shall not fail your orders.
[*Exit*]
[ALBANY, GONERIL, REGAN *take their seats*]

ALBANY
Now, Gloucester, trust to thy single virtue, for thy sold'rs,
All levied in my name, have in my name
Took their discharge; now let our trumpets speak, 170
And read out this.
[HERALD *reads*]

If any man of quality, within the lists of the army, will maintain upon Edmund, suppos'd Earl of Gloucester, that he is manifold traitor, let him appear by the third sound of the Trumpet; He is bold in his defense.—Again, Again.
[*Trumpet answers from within*]
[*Enter* EDGAR, *armed*]

ALBANY
Lord Edgar!

BASTARD
Ha! My brother!
This is the only combatant that I could fear,
For in my breast guilt duels on his side,
But conscience, what have I to do with thee? 180
Awe thou thy dull legitimate slaves, but I
Was born a Libertine, and so I keep me.

EDGAR
My noble Prince, a word—e'er we engage
Into your Highness's hands I give this paper,
It will the truth of my impeachment prove
Whatever be my fortune in the fight.

ALBANY
We shall peruse it.

EDGAR
Now, Edmund, draw thy sword,
That if my speech has wrong'd a noble heart,
Thy arm may do thee justice; here i'th' presence 190
Of this high Prince, these Queens, and this crown'd list,
I brand thee with the spotted name of traitor,
False to thy gods, thy father and thy brother,
And what is more, thy friend; false to this Prince.
If then thou shar'st a spark of Gloucester's virtue,
Acquit thyself, or if thou shar'st his courage,
Meet this defiance bravely.

BASTARD
And dares Edgar,
The beaten routed Edgar, brave his conqueror?
From all thy troops and thee, I forced the field, 200
Thou hast lost the gen'ral stake, and art thou now
Come with thy petty single stock to play
This after-game?

EDGAR
Half-blooded man,
Thy father's sin first, then his punishment:
The dark and vicious place where he begot thee
Cost him his eyes. From thy licentious mother
Thou draw'st thy villainy, but for thy part
Of Gloucester's blood, I hold thee worth my sword.

BASTARD
Thou bear'st thee on thy mother's piety, 210
Which I despise; thy mother being chaste,
Thou art assured thou art but Gloucester's son,
But mine, disdaining constancy, leaves me
To hope that I am sprung from nobler blood,
And possibly a King might be my Sire.
But be my birth's uncertain chance as 'twill,
Who 'twas that had the hit to father me
I know not; 'tis enough that I am I.
Of this one thing I'm certain—that I have
A daring soul, and so have at thy heart 220
Sound trumpet.
[*Fight.* BASTARD *falls*]

GONERIL and REGAN
Save him, save him.

GONERIL
This was practice, Gloucester.
Thou won'st the field, and wast not bound to fight
A vanquished enemy, thou art not conquered,
But cozened and betrayed.

Performing King Lear

ALBANY
Shut your mouth, lady,
Or with this paper I shall stop it—hold, sir,
Thou worse than any name, read thy own evil.
No tearing, lady, I perceive you know it. 230

GONERIL
Say if I do, who shall arraign me for't?
The laws are mine, not thine.

ALBANY
Most monstrous! Ha, thou know'st it too.

BASTARD
Ask me not what I know.
I have not breath to answer idle questions.

ALBANY
I have resolved; your right, brave sir, has conquered,
 [*To* EDGAR]
Along with me, I must consult your father.
 [*Exit* ALBANY *and* EDGAR]

REGAN
Help every hand to save a noble life;
My half o'th' kingdom for a man of skill
To stop this precious stream. 240

BASTARD
Away, ye empericks,
Torment me not with your vain offices.
The sword has pierced too far; legitimacy
At last has got it.

REGAN
The pride of nature dies.

GONERIL
Away, the minutes are too precious.
Disturb us not with thy impertinent sorrow.

REGAN
Art thou my rival then professed?

GONERIL
Why, was our love a secret? Could there be
Beauty like mine, and gallantry like his 250
And not a mutual love? Just nature then
Had erred; behold that copy of perfection,
That youth whose story will have no foul page
But where it says he stooped to Regan's arms,
Which yet was but compliance, not affection,
A charity to begging, ruined beauty!

REGAN
Who begged when Goneril writ that? Expose it.
 [*Throws her a letter*]
And let it be your army's mirth, as 'twas
This charming youth's and mine, when in the bow'r
He breathed the warmest ecstasies of love, 260
Then panting on my breast, cried matchless Regan
That Goneril and thou should e'er be kin!

GONERIL
Die, Circe, for thy charms are at an end,
Expire before my face, and let me see
How well that boasted beauty will become
Congealing blood and death's convulsive pangs.
Die and be hushed, for at my tent last night
Thou drank'st thy bane, amidst thy rev'ling bowls.
Ha! Dost thou smile? Is then thy death thy sport,
Or has the trusty potion made thee mad? 270

REGAN
Thou com'st as short of me in thy revenge
As in my Gloucester's love; my jealousy
Inspired me to prevent thy feeble malice
And poison thee at thy own banquet.

GONERIL
Ha!

BASTARD
No more, my Queens, of this untimely strife.
You both deserved my love and both possessed it.
Come, soldiers, bear me in, and let
Your royal presence grace my last minutes.
Now, Edgar, thy proud conquest I forgive; 280
Who would not choose, like me, to yield his breath
T'have rival Queens contend for him in death?
 [*Exit*]

 SCENE, *A Prison.*
 [LEAR *asleep, with his head on* CORDELIA's *lap*]

CORDELIA
What toils, thou wretched King, hast thou endured
To make thee draw, in chains, a sleep so sound?
Thy better angel charm thy ravished mind
With fancied freedom. Peace is used to lodge
On cottage straw; thou hast the beggar's bed,
Therefore shou'dst have the beggar's careless thought.

And now, my Edgar, I remember thee.
What fate has seiz'd thee in this general wreck 290
I know not, but I know thou must be wretched
Because Cordelia holds thee dear.
O Gods! A sudden gloom o'erwhelms me, and the image
Of death o'er-spreads the place.—ha! Who are these?

[*Enter* CAPTAIN *and* OFFICERS *with cords*]

CAPTAIN
Now, sirs, dispatch, already you are paid
In part; the best of your reward's to come.

LEAR
Charge, charge upon their flank, their last wing halts;
Push, push the battle, and the day's our own.
Their ranks are broke, down, down with Albany.
Who holds my hands?—O thou deceiving sleep, 300
I was this very minute on the chase,
And now a prisoner here—What mean the slaves?
You will not murder me?

CORDELIA
Help Earth and Heaven!
For your souls' sakes, dear sirs, and for the Gods.

OFFICER
No tears, good Lady, no pleading against gold and preferment.
Come, sirs, make ready your cords.

CORDELIA
You, sir, I'll seize,
You have a humane form, and if no pray'rs
Can touch your soul to spare a poor King's life, 310
If there be any thing that you hold dear,
By that I beg you to dispatch me first.

CAPTAIN
Comply with her request. Dispatch her first.

LEAR
Off, Hell-hounds, by the Gods I charge you spare her;
'Tis my Cordelia, my true pious daughter:
No pity?—Nay, then take an old Man's vengeance.

[*Snatches a partisan, and strikes down two of them. The rest quit* CORDELIA, *and turn upon him. Enter* EDGAR *and* ALBANY.]

EDGAR
Death! Hell! Ye vultures, hold your impious hands,
Or take a speedier death than you would give.

CAPTAIN
By whose command?

EDGAR
Behold the Duke your Lord. 320

ALBANY
Guards, seize those instruments of cruelty.

CORDELIA
My Edgar, Oh!

EDGAR
My dear Cordelia, lucky was the minute
Of our approach, the Gods have weighed our suff'rings;
W' are past the fire, and now must shine to ages.

GENTLEMAN
Look here, my Lord, see where the generous King
Has slain two of 'em.

LEAR
Did I not, fellow?
I've seen the day, with my good biting falchion,
I could have made 'em skip; I am old now, 330
And these vile crosses spoil me—out of breath!
Fie—Oh, quite out of breath and spent.

ALBANY
Bring in old Kent, and, Edgar, guide you hither
Your father, whom you said was near,
[*Exit* EDGAR]
He may be an ear-witness at the least
Of our proceedings.
[KENT *brought in here*]

LEAR
Who are you?
My eyes are none o' th' best, I'll tell you straight;
Oh Albany! Well, sir, we are your captives,
And you are come to see death pass upon us. 340
Why this delay?—or is't your highness's pleasure
To give us first the torture? Say ye so?
Why here's old Kent and I, as tough a pair
As e'er bore tyrant's stroke—but my Cordelia,
My poor Cordelia here, O pity!—

Performing King Lear

ALBANY
Take off their chains—Thou injured majesty,
The Wheel of Fortune now has made her circle,
And blessings yet stand 'twixt thy grave and thee.

LEAR
Com'st thou, inhumane Lord, to sooth us back
To a fool's paradise of hope, to make 350
Our doom more wretched? Go to, we are too well
Acquainted with misfortune to be gull'd
With lying hope. No, we will hope no more.

ALBANY
I have a tale t' unfold so full of wonder
As cannot meet an easy faith,
But by that royal injur'd head 'tis true.

KENT
What would your Highness?

ALBANY
Know the noble Edgar
Impeached Lord Edmund since the fight, of treason,
And dared him for the proof to single combat, 360
In which the Gods confirmed his charge by conquest;
I left ev'n now the traitor wounded mortally.

LEAR
And whither tends this story?

ALBANY
Ere they fought,
Lord Edgar gave into my hands this paper,
A blacker scroll of treason, and of lust
Than can be found in the records of hell.
There, sacred sir, behold the character
Of Goneril the worst of daughters, but
More vicious wife. 370

CORDELIA
Could there be yet addition to their guilt?
What will not they that wrong a father do?

ALBANY
Since then my injuries, Lear, fall in with thine:
I have resolved the same redress for both.

KENT
What says my Lord?

CORDELIA
Speak, for me thought I heard
The charming voice of a descending God.

ALBANY
The Troops by Edmund rais'd, I have disbanded;
Those that remain are under my command.
What comfort may be brought to cheer your age 380
And heal your savage wrongs, shall be applied,
For to your Majesty we do resign
Your kingdom, save what part yourself conferred
On us in marriage.

KENT
Hear you that, my Liege?

CORDELIA
Then there are Gods, and virtue is their care.

LEAR
Is 't possible?
Let the spheres stop their course, the sun make halt,
The winds be hushed, the seas and fountains rest;
All nature pause, and listen to the change. 390
Where is my Kent, my Caius?

KENT
Here, my Liege.

LEAR
Why, I have news that will recall thy youth;
Ha! Didst thou hear 't, or did th' inspiring Gods
Whisper to me alone? Old Lear shall be
A King again.

KENT
The Prince, that like a God has pow'r, has said it.

LEAR
Cordelia then shall be a Queen, mark that:
Cordelia shall be Queen. Winds catch the sound
And bear it on your rosy wings to heav'n. 400
Cordelia is a Queen.
      [*Re-enter* EDGAR *with* GLOUCESTER]

ALBANY
Look, Sir, where pious Edgar comes
Leading his eye-less father. O my Liege!
His wondrous story will deserve your leisure,
What he has done and suffered for your sake,
What for the fair Cordelia's.

GLOUCESTER
Where is my liege? Conduct me to his knees to hail
His second birth of empire; my dear Edgar
Has, with himself, revealed the King's blest restoration.

LEAR
My poor, dark Gloucester. 410

GLOUCESTER
Oh let me kiss that once more scepter'd hand!

LEAR
Hold—thou mistak'st the Majesty; kneel here.
Cordelia has our pow'r, Cordelia's Queen.
Speak—is not that the noble suff'ring Edgar?

GLOUCESTER
My pious son, more dear than my lost eyes.

LEAR
I wronged him too, but here's the fair amends.

EDGAR
Your leave, my Liege, for an unwelcome message.
Edmund (but that's a trifle) is expired;
What more will touch you, your imperious daughters,
Goneril and haughty Regan, both are dead, 420
Each by the other poisoned at a banquet;
This, dying, they confessed.

CORDELIA
O fatal period of ill-governed life!

LEAR
Ingrateful as they were, my heart feels yet
A pang of nature for their wretched fall—But Edgar, I defer thy joys too long.
Thou serv'dst distressed Cordelia; take her crown'd,
Th' imperial grace fresh blooming on her brow.
Nay, Gloucester, thou hast here a father's right,
Thy helping hand t' heap blessings on their head. 430

KENT
Old Kent throws in his hearty wishes too.

EDGAR
The Gods and you to largely recompense
What I have done, the gift strikes merit dumb.

CORDELIA
Nor do I blush to own my self o'er-paid
For all my suff'rings past.

GLOUCESTER
Now, gentle Gods, give Gloucester his discharge.

LEAR
No, Gloucester, thou hast business yet for life;
Thou, Kent and I, retired to some cool cell,
Will gently pass our short reserves of time
In calm reflections on our fortunes past, 440
Cheered with relation of the prosperous reign
Of this celestial pair; thus our remains
Shall in an even course of thought be past,
Enjoy the present hour, nor fear the last.

EDGAR
Our drooping country now erects her head,
Peace spreads her balmy wings, and plenty blooms.
Divine Cordelia, all the Gods can witness
How much thy love to empire I prefer!
Thy bright example shall convince the world
(Whatever storms of fortune are decreed) 450
That truth and virtue shall at last succeed.

[*Exit. Finish.*]

EPILOGUE
[*Spoken by* CORDELIA]

Inconstancy, the reigning sin o' th' age,
Will scarce endure true lovers on the stage;
You hardly ev'n in plays with such dispense,
And poets kill 'em in their own defense.
Yet one bold proof I was resolved to give,
That I could three hours constancy outlive.
You fear, perhaps, whilst on the stage w' are made
Such saints, we shall indeed take up the trade;
Sometimes we threaten—but our virtue may
For truth I fear with your pit-valor weigh. 10
For (not to flatter either) I much doubt
When we are off the stage, and you are out,
We are not quite so coy, nor you so stout.
We talk of nunn'ries—but to be sincere
Whoever lives to see us cloistered there,
May hope to meet our critiques at Tangier.
For shame give over this inglorious trade
Of worrying poets, and go maul th' Alcade.
Well—since y' are all for blust'ring in the pit,
This play's reviver humbly does admit 20
Your abs'lute pow'r to damn his part of it;
But still so many master-touches shine
Of that vast hand that first laid this design,
That in great **Shakespeare**'s *right, he's bold to say,*
If you like nothing you have seen today
The play your judgment damns, not you the play.

Name: _____ Date: _____

King Lear on Film—Compare and Contrast

Film #1 Director: Year Released:	Film #2 Director: Year Released:
Costuming and Props	
Sets (i.e., Locations of Scenes)	
Camera Work (On Whom Does the Camera Focus, and From What Angles?)	

Name: _____ Date: _____

Physical Actions (i.e., Blocking)	
Actors' Deliveries of Lines	

Chapter 6

Talking About *King Lear*

As I noted previously in *Advanced Placement Classroom: Romeo and Juliet*, the National Board for Professional Teaching Standards requires of aspiring National Board Certified Teachers of English Language Arts only one self-reflection concerning students' development as both readers and writers, but twice as many portfolio entries regarding teachers' guidance of students' verbal interactions: one leading a class discussion and another helping small groups of children collaborate orally. Similarly, the National Council of Teachers of English incorporates dialoguing about literature in its 12 core standards, and the College Board does likewise in its communicating guidelines for AP Literature and Composition teachers. I therefore conclude here, as I did before, that some of the biggest authorities in English education today consider the collective, collaborative discussion of literature, involving real-time interactions among students and teachers, at least as important as—if not *more* critical than—the solitary processes of reading and writing about that literature. Two heads are better than one, but those two heads are even more insightful, effective, and productive if they accompany sets of vocal cords.

Anyone who has ever been involved in a truly engaging, illuminating college seminar discussion probably agrees. Listening actively and openly to other students' perspectives and playing them off one another helps students to mold their opinions regarding everything from themes to characters, and from motivations to symbolism. Such discussions, in my opinion, are the true core of any effective study of literature. After all, who among us English teachers doesn't enjoy a really profound conversation or a good debate?

This chapter presents several ways to assign and assess students' dialogue, including a variety of topics to spark good conversation. It focuses on two different types of classroom interactions: cooperative seminar-style discussions and competitive debates. For each type I provide suggested procedures to follow, questions to consider, and rubrics by which to assess students' interactions.

Socratic Seminar

In terms of classroom instruction, the phrase "Socratic seminar" and the Greek word *paideia* are often used synonymously. Some scholars and teachers choose to distinguish between the two practices, but they are truthfully very similar, both in their historical underpinnings and recent popularization at the hands of Mortimer Adler, Director of Chicago's Institute for Philosophical Research, plus in their diminishment of a teacher's instructional role from the lecturing "sage on the stage" to being either a fellow participant with students or a simple observer and evaluator of their dialogue. When these teachers ask questions, according to both models, the point is not just to find the "right" answer, especially because such an ideal response very well may not exist for such a deep, thematic, theoretical question as, "What does *King Lear* essentially say about the potentially transient nature of familial love?" The true point of any seminar dialogue is to interact, to bounce ideas off one another, to search collaboratively for meaning—even if that meaning is individualized and different for various persons in the discussion—and to develop communicative and interpretive-analytical skills. To paraphrase a cliché, it's not the destination that matters so much in a good seminar as the journey to it.

Among common difficulties facing teachers wishing to implement seminar discussions in their classes are some very pragmatic, important classroom issues: How do I ensure that my students will participate? How do I prevent them from settling for the simplest, quickest answer? What do I do about the shy kids who won't speak up? How do I assign grades?

A clearly established and communicated mechanism for assessing students' dialogue is necessary, and its use is optimized if shared with participants beforehand. Table 4 includes a sheet of grading criteria; it is the one that I distribute to my own students, AP and otherwise, prior to seminars.

Modeling also is an important component in prepping for successful seminar discussions. When I first distribute to my students this sheet of grading criteria, I describe to them what good and bad seminar discussions "look like," elaborating upon the points bulleted at the top of the page. I then give them some silent time to peruse the entire sheet, after which I ask them to use the criteria to assess three sample answers to a question that I provide: one mediocre (1 point), one

TABLE 4
Rubric and Guidelines for Socratic Seminar

Here are some general rules of thumb:
- The less the teacher has to talk, the better.
- A GOOD seminar looks like 20 people having a fun discussion on a literary topic, as if trying to solve one of the book's "puzzles" together.
- A BAD seminar resembles the Teacher-as-Dentist idea . . . asking questions should not be like pulling teeth!

	Here's How Each Answer Will Be Graded	
Potential Score	Where Your Response Comes From	What Your Response Might Contain
√++ (3 pts.)	You reply to other people's responses to the original question, either supporting an argument in agreement or refuting one in polite disagreement.	Your response ties together . . . - aspects of the discussion to this point, - passages from the text itself, and/or - relevant connections to extraneous studies or observations.
√+ (2 pts.)	You reply to other people's responses to the original question, either supporting an argument in agreement or refuting one in polite disagreement.	Your response is supported either by . . . - a passage or two from the text itself, or - relevant connections to outside studies or observations.
√ (1 pt.)	Your response is either your individual answer to the initially asked question or a response to another person's answer to the question.	Your response *may* also be supported either by . . . - textual passages or - relevant connections to outside resources.
√- (minus 1 pt.)	Your response is solely your individual answer to the initially asked question.	Regardless of the content of your response, it is a repetition of something already said in the discussion.
√-- (minus 2 pts.)	It is hard to tell, actually . . .	Your response contains nothing of value; you are talking just to hear yourself.

outstanding (3 points), and one silly or immaterial (minus 2 points). And, yes, I tell them when they inevitably ask, I really do take points away from their scores if they make random and irrelevant comments. All told, it takes between 5 and 10 minutes even to begin our first seminar discussion, but such modeling of my expectations ensures that all students begin on the right foot; as the classmates begin to talk, I usually inform the entire class of how I grade the first three or four comments made, explicitly tying students' points in "real time" to the printed grading criteria.

My process of evaluating students themselves is usually very simple. After asking students to rearrange their desks and chairs into a circle, I sit among them with a roster of their names, tallying checks as the discussion proceeds, interjecting my own thoughts and steering the dialogue when appropriate or necessary. Figure 3 is a sample checklist from one of my AP class's seminar discussions.

I never predetermine the total point value of any seminar discussion, but rather base its quantifiable endpoint on the length of time that the discussion consumed and how insightful high-scoring students' comments were. The discussion exhibited by this checklist lasted approximately 70 minutes, and based on the quality of students' responses, I determined that it should be worth 8 total points. Making such determinations on the spot may be difficult at first, but the more seminars you lead, the more skillful you will become at gauging their relative levels of success.

The checklist in Figure 3 also reveals some additional issues requiring consideration. As it evidences, during the discussion recorded, 11 of the 28 students involved did not contribute at all, and only 6 participants earned their full score of 8 points. It is simply the nature of the scholastic beast that there inevitably are going to be students who do not speak up, for any variety of reasons—shyness, lack of preparation or understanding, personal issues, etc.—during a particular discussion. I inform my own students prior to their first seminar in my classes that I recognize and accept this fact. "If you know right now that you are simply the type of student that will be more liable to sit and listen during this discussion than to speak up regularly," I tell them, "then I advise you to take notes on the flow of the conversation as it is occurring." Elaborating further, I explain to my students that I will allow them to take their notes home that night and write out what they would have said had they participated more in the discussion; the next day, I grade their written responses using the same criteria that I use to grade commentary during the seminar itself. A large percentage of my students take advantage of this policy following every graded discussion, especially because I also allow those participants who contributed somewhat, but not enough to garner their full share of points, to supplement their totals with additional points earned for written responses. On the downside, this policy obviously leads to additional homework for nonparticipatory students following any seminar, but it also eliminates the

Kris	Erik
Melissa - √, √+	Kelsey #3 - √, √+
Justin	Charlie - √+, √++, √, √, √
Kelsey #1 - √+, √+	Garrett
Juliet	Brittany
Corinne - √+, √++, √, √+, √+	Lily
Johannes	Ashlee - √++, √, √+, √++
Pete - √, √, √+	Kyle - √, √+, √++
Kelsey #2 - √++, √	Ada - √+, √+, √, √, √+, √+
Virginia - √+, √++, √+, √+	Amanda
Darian	Hannah - √, √+, √++, √
Val	Graham - √, √, √+
Cathryn - √	Lech - √+, √++, √
Andrew - √+, √+, √+, √+	Jack - √+, √

Figure 3. Sample assessment checklist from an AP class's Socratic seminar discussion.

inequity that would otherwise result among extroverted and introverted pupils' grades.

On the other hand, it is perhaps inevitable in classes composed primarily of gifted and talented students that certain of them will lead conversations and contribute inordinately more than other peers will. Such verbal inequity is likewise foreseeable, and I myself only see a problem with it when such outspoken persons dominate a particular conversation so much that other students are prevented from speaking their mind, and thus garnering their reasonable share of points. Attempting to prevent this unfairness, I inform my own students—again, before we hold our very first seminar discussion—that I shall actually begin to deduct points from students exhibiting this overly dominant behavior. In many classes, I have actually taken to using soccer referees' yellow and red cards to signal to students their statuses in this regard; flashing them a yellow card communicates that they are probably nearing their full score of points, but a red card indicates to them that they are speaking too often and that if they do not let peers get more words in edgewise, then I shall soon begin taking points away. This system provides students with a simple and clear method by which to gauge their own participation.

In seminar discussions of any literary work, there are generally two different types of questions considered: those considering particular and locatable parts of the text, focusing on such elements as symbolism, diction, and style, and those questions concerning thematically deeper "big picture" issues. The practical aspects of initiating and assessing seminar discussions really do not vary for either type, but the contents of these two types of discussions absolutely do. Tightly focused, textually centered discussions utilize numerous supportive quotations from the text, relying largely on close readings of particular points of the play in order to reach conclusions; on the other hand, more philosophical and/or thematic discussions refer less frequently to particular moments of dialogue and instead consider the narrative as a whole, examining larger issues that Shakespeare imparts over the course of five acts. Here are a number of questions of each type, to all of which, again, there are no particular "right" answers.

Textually Based Questions

- At the beginning of the play, Edmund's language changes depending upon exactly whom he is addressing. Compare his diction and syntax in several places throughout the first two acts. What do the differences imply about Edmund as a character?

- Character foils are opposites of one another, usually in several specific and important ways; this opposition accentuates the individual characteristics that each foil possesses. Apart from the obvious character foils in *King Lear*, such as Edmund and Edgar, some critics interpret Cordelia and Edmund as foils for one another. In what ways can you see a characteristic contrast between their personalities and apparent beliefs? Do you find that Edmund is perhaps a clearer foil with Lear himself?

- Scholars differentiate between the Shakespearean archetypes of the clown and the fool. Distinguished simply, the clown in any given Shakespearean

play is the butt of jokes, constantly laughed at by other characters, while the fool is the witty instigator of jokes, often an onstage representative of an audience's response to the play's events. Ignoring the obvious happenstance of his name, do you think that Lear's Fool is a clearer representative of the archetypal clown or fool?

- For innumerable audiences, Goneril and Regan are effectively seen as two sides of the same evil coin, their chief characteristics being fairly shared, if not identical. Considering the way in which *King Lear* unfolds, however, what differences can you discern between the two wicked elder sisters? Is one more evil than the other? Weaker or stronger? More insidious or honest?

- Lear is traditionally interpreted as a powerful depiction of the onset of madness. His descent into hallucination and apparent dementia are both frightening and realistic. Examining the play as a progression, consider Lear's mental and emotional journey, attempting to track his relative levels of sanity and/or insanity throughout the scenes and events of the drama. At what point does he reach a mental nadir, and what drives him to this point? By the end of the play, has he recovered at all?

Philosophical and Thematic Questions

- To what degree does *King Lear* portray a world without hope? Various critics over the centuries have cast this play as proto-nihilistic, a depressive representation of the hopelessness of the human condition. Do you agree or disagree with this assessment? If there is hope in the world of *Lear*, then where is it found? If there is not, then why?

- In terms of being relatable to people in the living, breathing world, which character in *King Lear* is the truest? On the other hand, which is the most unrealistic? Why, and what do these characters' realness or incredibility imply—about them, about you as an interpretive reader, and about our human world?

- One theory as to why *Lear*'s setting in time is unfixed, if not rather abstract, is that time and place actually matter little to the events portrayed by the play; where this drama really takes place, such theorists purport, is on the landscape of human emotion, where all of the play's characters represent virtues (e.g., loyalty, pride, greed, wisdom) intent on battling each other for dominion of the human soul. When explained in this way, perhaps the idea sounds a bit far-fetched, but it does merit an interesting inquiry: In this scenario, which virtues and vices might the various characters of *King Lear* represent?

❧ This play has been interpreted, among other things, as a treatise on culpability and innocence. Some analysts conclude that Lear deserves his fate, while others disagree. Some see Edmund's striving for power throughout the play as legitimately fair, while others demonize his tactics. Consider the play's various characters; which ones effectively get what they deserve in this play, and what do your conclusions imply about the world that Shakespeare creates in *King Lear*?

Lesson Plan: Landscapes With Several Falls

Once your students have some experience with Socratic seminars and with discussing the play in general, you could be ready to implement the lesson plan on pages 146–149. This lesson uses both visual art and poetry as springboards to a discussion of some of *King Lear*'s important thematic aspects.

Debate

Socratic seminar discussions are cooperative, but debates between groups of students pitted on opposite sides of a subjective issue are competitive. There are many ways to structure classroom debates, as well as a variety of questions to deliberate, yet I here propose two similar arrangements modified from procedures common among interscholastic debaters nationwide. Therefore, some of your pupils may be both familiar with these methods of interteam debate and perhaps proficient at them.

Simply stated, the questions to be debated during any competitive round should be answerable with either "yes" or "no" answers. Students' creativity is required and rewarded in such debates, not in their simple response to the question itself, but rather in the methods and textual support that they utilize to substantiate that answer. Each debate is conducted between two teams, one of which affirms the question (answers "yes") and the other of which denies it (answers "no"); per tradition, I here refer to these groups as the Affirmative and Negative teams, respectively. Moreover, each team is composed of two distinct participants, the first and the second speakers.

Each speaker—the 1st and 2nd Affirmative speakers, and the 1st and 2nd Negative speakers—are required to present either one or two speeches during the debate. If each speaker delivers two speeches, then they are distinguished as Constructive speeches, the purpose of which is to build a case, and Rebuttal speeches, the purpose of which is to defend one's own case from opposing argumentation (i.e., to rebut the other team's reasoning). A team's initial Constructive speeches

TABLE 5
Debate Round Utilizing Each Speaker Twice

Order of Speeches, Two Per Debater

Name of Speech	Time	Purpose of Speech	Preparation
1st Affirmative Constructive	5 min.	To present the affirmative team's initial case affirming (answering "yes" to) the question.	This speech should be prepared before the debate and include a variety of quotations from the text.
1st Negative Constructive	5 min.	To present the negative team's initial statement denying (answering "no" to) the question.	This speech should be prepared before the debate and include a variety of quotations from the text.
2nd Affirmative Constructive	5 min.	To build further the affirmative team's affirmation of the question, plus to respond to aspects of the negative team's first constructive speech.	Portions of this speech may be prepared before the debate, but parts of it will be impromptu responses to the opposing team's arguments.
2nd Negative Constructive	5 min.	To build further the negative team's denial of the question, plus to respond to aspects of the affirmative team's constructive arguments.	Portions of this speech may be prepared before the debate, but parts of it will be impromptu responses to the opposing team's arguments.
1st Affirmative Rebuttal	2 min.	To rebut any arguments against the affirmative team's case made by the negative team.	This speech will be prepared impromptu.
1st Negative Rebuttal	2 min.	To rebut any arguments against the negative team's case made by the affirmative team.	This speech will be prepared impromptu.
2nd Affirmative Rebuttal	2 min.	To reinforce the affirmative team's case affirming the question, plus to contribute any final remarks upon the negative team's opposing case.	This speech will be prepared impromptu.
2nd Negative Rebuttal	2 min.	To reinforce the negative team's case denying the question, plus to contribute any final remarks upon the affirmative team's opposing case.	This speech will be prepared impromptu.

should be prepared prior to the debate round (i.e., as homework prior to the classroom debate) and include abundant textual support for the case being made, all taken from the play itself. Rebuttal speeches, and to some extent 2nd Constructive speeches, are prepared impromptu, based largely on the direction in which the teams' argumentation proceeds. Table 5 is an outline of the times that should be allowed for each speech, as well as each speaker's individual responsibilities.

The details of each speech are, of course, occasioned by the particular issue/question that is being debated. You may choose to assign questions—and thus match pairs of teams—in advance of the debate, thereby allowing students to prepare for homework, or you may wish to reveal such match-ups immediately prior

TABLE 6
Debate Round Utilizing Each Speaker Only Once

Order of Speeches, One Per Debater

Name of Speech	Time	Purpose of Speech	Preparation
1st Affirmative	6 min.	To present the affirmative team's initial case affirming (answering "yes" to) the question.	This speech should be prepared before the debate and include a variety of quotations from the text.
1st Negative	6 min.	To present the negative team's initial statement denying (answering "no" to) the question.	This speech should be prepared before the debate and include a variety of quotations from the text.
2nd Affirmative	6 min.	To rebut the negative team's case denying the question, plus to reinforce the affirmative team's case affirming the question.	This speech should be prepared impromptu.
2nd Negative	6 min.	To rebut the affirmative team's case affirming the question, plus to reinforce the negative team's case denying the question.	This speech should be prepared impromptu.

to a round, thus allowing both teams a truncated amount of time to mine the play for supportive evidence, compose a cogent argument and speech, and anticipate their opponents' dissimilar argument. I caution you that while the latter procedure certainly adds to the excitement of any debate round, it is really only feasible with teams of students who know the play very well and can therefore navigate its intricacies in search of textual details quickly.

The second arrangement for a debate round allows each debater to speak only once, albeit for a slightly extended length of time. Because the outcome of this second type of debate hinges so clearly on the delivery of the 2nd Affirmative and Negative speeches, it is critical—perhaps unlike the requirements of the first organization, which allows every speaker two times at bat, so to speak—that the second speakers for each team be very quick-thinking, loquaciously persuasive speakers. Table 6 is an outline of this second format for debates.

Regardless of which arrangement you choose to utilize in your classroom, note that each team engaged in any round should be allowed 4–5 minutes of preparatory time to use as it sees fit. During this time, the teammates should be allowed to search the play for evidence, prepare argumentation, outline their upcoming speeches, discuss strategy, and whatnot, and while the opposing team and the judges of any round will have little to do but sit there during this preparatory time (well, the opposing team would actually be wise to prepare themselves simultaneously, too), your allowance of it will prove invaluable in raising the ultimate quality of the debate itself. After all, even a moment or two to gather one's thoughts can greatly aid logic and communicative clearness.

Perhaps the most enjoyable role to be played during any debate round is that of the judge. Because each round requires only four total speechmakers, I advise you to allow the remainder of your class to judge the participating teams' performances. Roman-style verdicts via thumbs placed up or down may be simple to orchestrate, but focusing your student judges' attention on less holistic details of a round surely will enhance their judicial skill and the legitimacy of the outcome, plus provide valuable feedback to the debaters themselves and to you. Table 7 includes a ballot for you to use in judging these rounds; if distributed to every observing student in your class prior to each debate, then a sum total or average of the many judges' points might be used to determine the winning side.

All portions of this ballot should be completed by the judges, and you may wish to photocopy the lot of them to pass on to the participants of each debate. All of us, of course, love getting feedback from our peers! Any teacher of the gifted, too, will admit that students' intellectual competitiveness can sometimes devolve into unsportsmanlike or otherwise immature behavior. You may or may not wish to include sportsmanship as a component of the decision-making process in your class's debate rounds, but I here provide a separate ballot (see Figure 4) considering just this element. If you do include it alongside the other three criteria for judgment, then the total points possible during any round, of course, will rise from 15 to 20.

Finally, I here include a number of questions to be debated. Because four students are involved in any debate round, these five questions account for the involvement of every member of a class of 20 students.

Questions for Debate

- Is Edmund's betrayal of his family justified? Make sure to support your argument with examples from the text.
- Is Lear as much to blame for the events of the play as his daughters? Justify your argument with textual support and feasible logic.
- Is Cordelia truly pure of heart, or does she exhibit ulterior motives just as her sisters do? Support your point of view with sound logic and clear evidence from the text.
- Is Lear himself a heroic figure? Make sure to support your argument with a clear and well-wrought definition of heroism.

TABLE 7
Interteam Debate Ballot

King Lear

Date _____ Judge _____

Topic _____

Affirmative Team _____

Negative Team _____

Before allotting to students any points or ranks, or determining the winning team, fill out the following table. Assess the four debaters separately in each category. Do not assign more points in any category than the maximum possible. Then, rank each debater in order of performance (1 for the most successful, 2 for the next highest performer, etc.).

1st Affirmative	2nd Affirmative		1st Negative	2nd Negative
Points:	Points:	Delivery (Pace, Clarity, Tone, Sportsmanship) **5 Pts. Maximum**	Points:	Points:
Reasons Why:	Reasons Why:		Reasons Why:	Reasons Why:
Points:	Points:	Persuasiveness (Organization, Argumentation) **5 Pts. Maximum**	Points:	Points:
Reasons Why:	Reasons Why:		Reasons Why:	Reasons Why:
Points:	Points:	Textual Support (Quotations, Logical Analysis) **5 Pts. Maximum**	Points:	Points:
Reasons Why:	Reasons Why:		Reasons Why:	Reasons Why:

1st Aff. _____   1st Neg. _____

Total Points _____   Rank _____   Total Points _____   Rank _____

2nd Aff. _____   2nd Neg. _____

Total Points _____   Rank _____   Total Points _____   Rank _____

Total Score, Affirmative Team _____   Total Score, Negative Team _____

In my opinion, the better debating was done by the _____, for these reasons:
(Affirmative or Negative)

Signature of Judge _____

Interteam Debate Sportsmanship Ballot
King Lear

Date _____   Judge _____
Topic _____
Affirmative Team _____
Negative Team _____

Please score the four debaters in terms of their portrayal of ethical, sportsmanlike behavior. Consider their delivered speeches, as well as their body language, tones of voice, and general attitudes during the debate.

Sportsmanship Rating	*1st Affirmative Debater*	*1st Negative Debater*	*2nd Affirmative Debater*	*2nd Negative Debater*
5: Outgoing, friendly, civil, and fair throughout the debate				
4: Civil and fair throughout the debate				
3: Civil and fair throughout most of the debate, but bordering on unfriendliness in places				
2: Somewhat civil during part of the debate, but rather unfriendly or combative at certain times				
1: Unfriendly or combative throughout most of the debate, bordering on offensive disrespect				

Figure 4. Optional ballot for student sportsmanship.

- Does the setting of *King Lear*, in terms of both time and place, actually matter to its events and themes? Justify your answer with sound logic and substantive argumentation.

Lesson Plan: Critical Interpretation Flashcards

This lesson introduces students to a variety of scholars and critics of *King Lear* from years, and in some cases centuries, past. Rather than assign large and relatively unwieldy selections of Shakespearean criticism, you can implement this lesson in several different ways, sampling small excerpts from the play's profoundest interpreters. The complete lesson plan and its accompanying flashcards are included on pages 150–156.

Conclusion

I have presented the techniques and activities outlined in this chapter to enhance your students' deep understanding of *King Lear* by getting them talking about it. In the next chapter, I propose various methods by which you can help them to write about it, from traditional analytical essays to original, potentially nonlinguistic creative-interpretive projects. I also include in Chapter 7 a variety of original assignment sheets, instruments, and grading rubrics.

Chapter Materials

Lesson 5

Landscapes With Several Falls

Purpose/Objective

This activity connects the events of *King Lear* to an iconic European painting and two poems that comment on that painting in order to accomplish two learning goals: (1) to reinforce students' understandings of the major themes, motifs, and characters found in *King Lear*, and (2) to discover and verbally articulate intertextuality between Shakespeare's play and other works of art.

Placement

This activity should be conducted when students have read through the first three acts of the play.

Materials Required

Copies of Pieter Bruegel the Elder's painting *Landscape With the Fall of Icarus* (1558), William Carlos Williams's poem "Landscape With the Fall of Icarus" (1962/2000), and W. H. Auden's poem "Musée de Beaux Arts" (1938/1962); all three works are easily accessible online, in which case Internet access is also required. Please note that sources for each of these items are listed in the References and Internet Resources sections of this book, found on pp. 215–222. Moreover, a computer projector or document camera projector is necessary to display the painting during discussion with the class.

Duration

This activity should take one class period of approximately 60 minutes, including examination and interpretation of the painting and two poems in question, followed by application of those common themes to *King Lear*. The teacher's option is to subdivide this lesson into 2 days' of activities, saving the reflection upon King Lear for a second class period and expanding the discussion into a full-blown Socratic seminar (see pp. 132–138 of this book for further information).

Lesson Plan

1. *Anticipatory Set:* At the beginning of the class period, introduce the day's activity with the proverb "A picture is worth a thousand words." Discuss with students what the saying means, perhaps inquiring whether they agree or disagree with it. Present to your class a painting or photograph *not* related explicitly to Shakespeare, but that is emotionally or connotatively rich; my recommendations are Andrew Wyeth's painting *Christina's World* or Dorothea Lange's Great Depression photograph "Mother of Seven Children," as it is commonly called, either of which might be interpreted as portraying loneliness, frustration, desperation, perseverance, resolve, hope, or any other host of emotions. As you present your chosen image, ask students to interpret what it expresses, first with each other, and then to the rest of the class. It is important, even as you kick off this 2-day activity, that you emphasize to your students the fact that there is no interpretive "right" answer, no more in this anticipatory set than in the subsequent investigations of other works of art. After you have discussed the "thousand words" (give or take) that your anticipatory image portrays, if your students are unaware of the word "intertextuality" and its meaning, then explain that thematic or other similarities between works of art, as between a painting and a poem, can be identified as intertextuality, a word composed of the root "text" and the prefix "inter-," meaning "between."

2. *Communication of Objective*: Inform students that the purpose of this activity is to discover and present examples of intertextuality between *King Lear* and three other works of art: one painting and two poems. The class will examine a particularly famous painting that, while not explicitly related to *Lear*, nevertheless represents themes, emotions, and characteristics of the play, followed by two poetic commentaries upon that painting.

3. *Visual Art:* Display for your students Pieter Bruegel's *Landscape With the Fall of Icarus*, without identifying the painting by its title. As this painting includes a great number of minutiae, the larger and more clearly you can display it, the better. Ask students what they see in this painting; a discussion of details should follow, and you may direct the conversation by asking leading questions such as, "What do you think the artist is attempting to portray here?" or, "In what kind of a mood do most of these people seem to be?" If after several minutes no student has noticed or pointed out the human legs sticking out of the ocean in the painting's lower righthand corner, then point them out yourself, inquiring as to whose they might be and what they potentially signify. At this point, share with students this painting's title, discussing with them the legend of Icarus's waxen wings. Next, shift from Icarus and refocus the conversation upon the other peo-

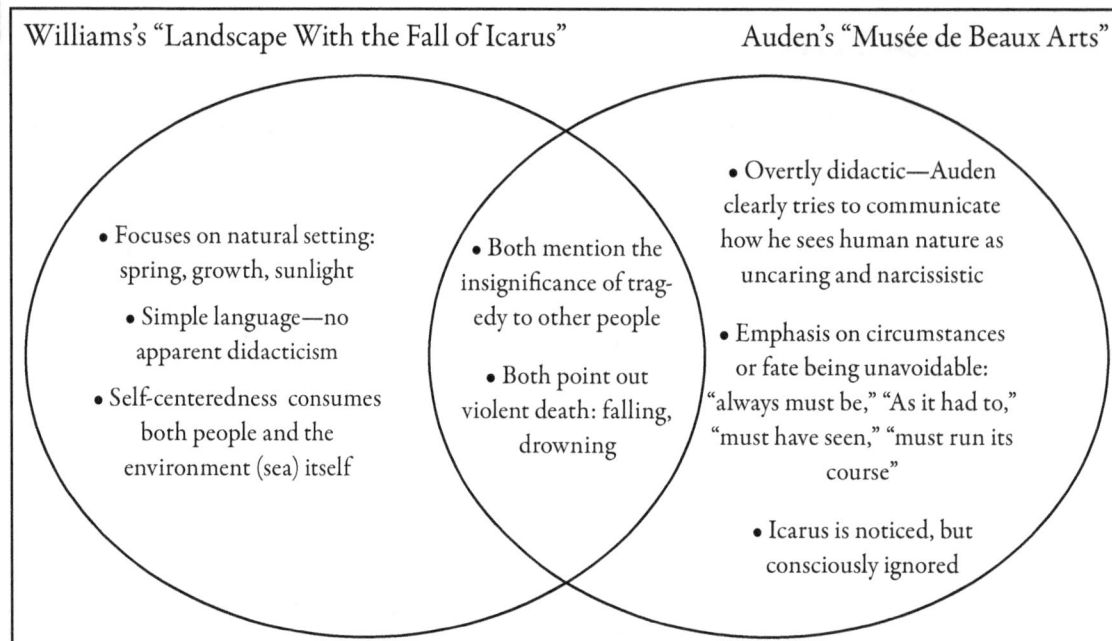

Figure 5. Venn diagram outlining intertextuality between William Carlos Williams's "Landscape With the Fall of Icarus" and W. H. Auden's "Musée de Beaux Arts."

ple, all of whom seem to be paying little attention to the boy's splash. Once again ask what the artist might be trying to communicate, attempting to lead students into a discussion of the painting's themes or connotations.

4. *Poetical Art:* Leaving Bruegel's painting visible, share with students William Carlos Williams's "Landscape With the Fall of Icarus," reading it together. Lead them in a similar discussion of this apparently simple descriptive poem, attempting to dig further into thematic import or communicative point by asking what aspects of the painting Williams highlights and what his motivation might be. Follow this discussion by sharing W. H. Auden's "Musée de Beaux Arts," reading it together. Once again, discuss what aspects of Bruegel's painting Auden found important and attempt to determine why; by this point, students should be discovering a thematic unity among all three works of art—the ignorance of the comfortable many when faced with the obvious suffering and peril of the helpless few—and the discussion should turn in this way.

5. *Similarities and Differences:* Ask students in their notebooks to draw and complete a simple Venn diagram concerning the two poets' different reactions to Bruegel's painting. Above is a sample Venn diagram, completed for the two works.

6. You may ask that students share with each other their Venn diagrams, which outline concisely the intertextual details of these poems. Again, it

is important during this final stage of the activity to emphasize to your class the fact that no single "right" answer exists regarding any of the chosen works of art, and thus that no interpretation is any less valid than others. Nevertheless, discuss with the class that what both poems share is perhaps Bruegel's pictorial message; in Auden's (1938/1962) words, all three of these artists qualify as "Old Masters [who] well . . . understood [suffering's] human position," how its personal significance to the sufferer is relative insignificance to the multitude, and thus perhaps all three are here commenting that human nature is to ignore the plight of the downtrodden and infirm when we ourselves are not suffering (ll. 2–3). A discussion as to whether students agree or disagree with this didactic conclusion based on their own lives or experiences could of course follow.

7. *What It Has to Do With Lear:* Having concluded Act III of *King Lear*, students should be able to find and verbalize many parallels between this interpretation and circumstances throughout the play: Goneril and Regan's uncaring dismissal of their father, Edmund's betrayal of his family, Lear's realization on the heath that he has heretofore ignored the plight of the homeless and impoverished, even the Fool's apparent abandonment of Lear at the end of the act. You may wish to guide inquiry further by asking whether this point seems to be Shakespeare's message: that human nature is to ignore imperiled others. Such a discussion would achieve two ends: First, it would approach the topic of author's purpose, attempting to decipher what Shakespeare's thematic intention seems to be, at least at this point of the play; and second, it would broach the related issue of hope, effectively asking students to predict how they foresee the play ending, either happily or—per Bruegel—painfully. The cognitive skills inherent in both of these topics are taxonomically high, so the discussion of these points is quite worth having.

Closure

Following this conversation, you may wish to have students write responses to what they discussed, how they felt during the discussion, whether they agreed or disagreed with the conclusions, and perhaps even whether today's topic in any way hit close to home for them. These written responses might then be shared verbally in pairs or with the entire class; regardless, engaging students in reflective writing concludes the lesson by personalizing its outcome for each student.

Lesson Plan 6

Critical Interpretation Flashcards

Purpose/Objective

The purpose of this activity is twofold: to consider various scholarly critics' interpretations of the play's themes, events, and characters; and to develop students' abilities to discuss the play, both as reflective conversationalists and in a leadership role.

Placement

This lesson can be delivered in two ways. On one hand, the accompanying Critical Interpretation Cards (pp. 153–155) can be assigned to students as they progress through the play, at various points of the text appropriate to the particular quotations. In this way, students' interpretive presentations and discussions can occur on a near-daily basis throughout your reading of the play. On the other hand, the various cards' quotations can be appointed to students after the play's conclusion, allowing the class to engage in the accompanying discussions all at once.

Materials Required

You will require copies of the Critical Interpretation Cards found on pp. 153–155 of this book. Additionally, each student should be given a copy of the Grading Checklist for Student Presentations and Discussions, found on p. 156, which is the mechanism by which they can be assessed individually.

Duration

This lesson consists of a series of analytical conversations, each of which should last anywhere between 5 and 10 minutes. The teacher's option is to separate these discussions or to conduct them at once, back-to-back, in which case the activity's duration will coincide with the total number of students in class.

Lesson Plan

1. *Anticipatory Set:* Present to your class a well-known proverb that in some way relates to *King Lear*, such as "the grass is always greener on the other

side" or "when the cat's away, the mice will play." Without pointing out to your students the exact levels of analysis in which you engage, discuss the proverb and model for them the discursive process in which they will engage during this activity: comprehension (in which you explain what the proverb means in a general sense), reflection (in which you relate the proverb to *King Lear* specifically, demonstrating how it might apply), evaluation (in which you either agree with the proverb's point of view relative to *King Lear* or disagree and claim its ultimate irrelevance), and conversation (in which you lead students in a short discussion of whether or not they think the particular proverb is insightful of *King Lear*).

2. *Communication of Objective:* Inform students that the lesson requires them to consider individually a number of scholarly quotations regarding King Lear. If students are unaware of what literary criticism entails, then explain to them what scholarship written by critics is, resembles, and/or accomplishes. Distribute to them copies of the Grading Checklist for Student Presentations and Discussions, found on p. 156. Referring to your conversation about the proverb, demonstrate how all four portions of the discussion are identifiable on the checklist. Finally, explain that students will engage in the same process as they analyze and lead their classmates in discussions of particular quotes, written by literary critics, concerning the play. You may wish to distribute to students their quotations by separating and affixing their respective cards to the bottom of their checklists.

3. *Preparation:* Students should not engage in presentations and discussions immediately after receiving their cards. The eventual products will prove far better, especially in terms of textual substantiation, if students are allowed at least one evening to prepare for them. Thus, you should instruct students to plan for presentations occurring on a later day. Moreover, you have the ability at this point of the lesson to add particular criteria to your grading calculus; if, for example, you want students to support their positions at the evaluative level with several quoted lines of dialogue from the play, then you should inform them of the requirement here; if you want students to make visuals to accompany their oral presentations, then this point of the activity is an appropriate place to communicate it. Obviously, there is much flexibility in this regard to include in students' assignments various skills, templates, or products on which you may have been working or want to reinforce.

4. *Series of Discussions:* Students' delivery of their quotations and analytical presentations should run rather smoothly, truth be told. If they know ahead of time that they are to be evaluated using the accompanying Grading Checklist, then they should organize themselves according to it.

The portion of this activity in which you may need to help somehow is the final one: students leading each other in discussion. You may, of course, insert your opinions and aid as you see fit, but otherwise, regardless of whether you sprinkle these quotation analyses throughout your reading of the play or lump them at its end, students' engagement in the process should be reliably straightforward.

Closure

Having considered various literary critics' perspectives on *King Lear*, students may enjoy composing their own concise, insightful quotes regarding the play. Instruct students, therefore, to compose in their notebooks short sentences or paragraphs that comment upon the play in some way. I have found success in my own classes with what is describable simply as "the fortune cookie method": if your pupils were to describe or explore some aspect of *King Lear*—its characters, its themes, its situations—in a message packaged inside of a stereotypical fortune cookie, then what would it say? Having composed their concise commentaries, students should pair and share them with one another, and perhaps with the entire class.

Critical Interpretation Cards for Discussion of *King Lear*

"It is part of Shakespeare's genius not to have Edmund and Lear address even a single word to each other in the entire play, because they are apocalyptic antitheses: the king is all feeling, and Edmund is bare of all affect."
—Harold Bloom (1998)

"... the theme of *King Lear* may be stated in psychological as well as in biological terms. So put, it is the destructive, the ultimately suicidal character of unregulated passion, its power to carry human nature back to chaos."
—Harold C. Goddard (1951)

"If the fool would persist in his folly, he would become wise."
—William Blake (1790/1979a)

"Lear is essentially impossible to be represented on a stage."
—Charles Lamb (1818)

"[The great Shakespearean Tragedies] are not primarily treatments of characters with a so-called 'fatal flaw,' whose downfall is brought about by the decree of just if inscrutable powers ... the fundamental flaw is not in them but in the world they inhabit: in the political state, the social order it upholds, and likewise, by projection, in the cosmic state of shifting arbitrary phenomena called 'Fortune.'"
—J. W. Lever (1987)

"In the storm scene Lear is at his most powerful and, despite moral considerations, at his noblest; the image of man hopelessly confronting a hostile universe and withstanding it only by his inherent powers of rage, endurance, and perpetual questioning, is perhaps the most purely 'tragic' in Shakespeare."
—Barbara Everett (1960)

"The experience of *Lear* depends on the paradox that people are at the same time connected and separate, a paradox to which both sympathy and anger are responses.... Anger and sympathy are both signs of human vulnerability and relationship."
—Marianne Novy (1984)

"Are we to assume that Edmund is simply evil and therefore so is his philosophy? I want to argue that we need not ... bear in mind a crucial fact: Edmund's skepticism is made to serve an *existing* system of values; although he falls prey to, he does not introduce his society to its obsession with power, property and inheritance; it is already the material and ideological basis of that society."
—Jonathan Dollimore (1984)

"The contrast between Goneril and Regan, on the one hand, and Cordelia, on the other, owes something to the traditional tendency in Western literature to split the image of woman into devil and angel, Eve and Mary."
—Marianne Novy (1984)

"If a way to the better there be, it exacts a full look at the worst."
—Thomas Hardy (1901)

"Edmund has no passions whatsoever; he has never loved anyone, and he never will. In that respect, he is Shakespeare's most original character."
—Harold Bloom (1998)

"Lear is not a study in redemption but in outrageousness and in being outraged . . . he is Shakespeare's perfection in the poetics of outrage . . . [thus appealing] primordially to the universal outrage of all those acutely conscious of their own mortality."
—Harold Bloom (1998)

"We love the things we love for what they are."
—Robert Frost, "Hyla Brook" (1916/1969)

"Experimentally, we can approach Lear not as a linear narrative, but as a cluster of relationships. First we try to rid ourselves of the notion that because the play is called *King Lear* it is primarily the story of one individual."
—Peter Brook (1968)

"Western culture is genetically incapable of producing an audience not conditioned to identify itself with the youngest of three sisters and to recognize transparent vessels of wickedness in elder sisters pleasing to their parent."
—Stephen Booth (1983/1987)

"Love is no healer in *The Tragedy of King Lear*; indeed, it starts all the trouble, and is a tragedy in itself."
—Harold Bloom (1998)

"A play in which the wicked prosper, and the good miscarry, may doubtless be good, because it is a just representation of the events of human life . . ."
—Samuel Johnson (1765/2008)

"*King Lear* seems to me Shakespeare's greatest achievement, but it seems to me *not* his best play. And I find that I tend to consider it from two rather different points of view. When I regard it strictly as a drama, it appears to me, though in certain parts overwhelming, decidedly inferior . . ."
—A. C. Bradley (1904)

"In *King Lear*, the father who imagined that he 'gave his daughters all' extracts from his daughter at the end of the play the same price he demanded in the opening scene—that she love her father all. . . . Cordelia returns to her father, and the final scene stages the most sterile of altar tableaux: a dead father with his three dead daughters, the wheel having come full circle back to the opening scene of the play."
—Lynda E. Boose (1982/2008)

"Producers have found it virtually impossible to cope with the plot of *King Lear*. When realistically treated, Lear and Gloster [sic] were too ridiculous to appear tragic heroes. If the exposition were treated as a fairy tale or legend, the cruelty of Shakespeare's world, too, became unreal."
—Jan Kott (1964/2008)

". . . Machiavelli's knowledge of the world is present; not just in his attitudes of realism and cynicism, but in his experience of the condition to which these attitudes are appropriate—in which the inner and outer worlds have become totally disconnected, and man's life is all public, among strangers, seen only from outside."
—Stanley Cavell (2002)

"The central focus is on the horror of a society divided between extremes of rich and poor, greed and starvation, the powerful and the powerless, robes and rags, and the impossibility of real justice and security in such a world. Lear himself, like the faithful Gloucester, discovers this only when his own world is turned upside down, when he himself is destitute and mad, and at last sees authority with the eyes of the dispossessed."
—Margot Heinemann (1992/2008)

"*King Lear* is a play about the disintegration of the world."
—Jan Kott (1964/2008)

"Despite Lear's recurrent attempts to find a just Thunderer in the storm [in Act III] its violence ultimately epitomizes not the just masculine authority on which Lear would base his own but the dark female power that everywhere threatens to undermine that authority."
—Janet Adelman (1992)

Grading Checklist for Student Presentations and Discussions Using Critical Interpretation Cards

☐ *Comprehension Level*: Presenter understands and communicates the essential meaning of the selected passage.
    Key Verbs: read → understand → convey

☐ *Reflection Level*: Presenter accurately relates the selected passage to the events, characters, themes, and/or overarching drama of *King Lear*.
    Key Verbs: reflect → connect → explain

☐ *Evaluation Level*: Presenter states agreement or disagreement with the passage, supporting his or her point of view with logically sound evidence and/or explanation.
    Key Verbs: consider → judge → support

☐ *Conversation Level*: Presenter effectively leads classmates in a discussion of the passage and its legitimacy relative to the play as a whole.
    Key Verbs: ask → interact → guide

Chapter 7

Writing About *King Lear*

Just as I opened a similar chapter in *Advanced Placement Classroom: Romeo and Juliet*, I here reiterate that writing is the bread and butter of academic scholarship, the chief method by which scholars gain, record, and communicate knowledge. Extraneous to students' studies of literature and composition in traditional English classes, no matter what academic disciplines students gravitate toward in college, they will be evaluated in large part based on their abilities to write well. As such, it is simply a professional responsibility to train our students how to write effectively in a variety of styles and formats.

That point being made, however, it would be imprudent of me not to acknowledge the large burden the grading of students' essays is on English teachers. Especially in this age of increased class sizes and standardized assessment, it is simply hard to find time to assess pupils' written products adequately, in manners that offer both timely and productive feedback. Nevertheless, it remains a simple fact that if a student cannot compose organized, substantiated essays, then he or she will not perform well on the AP English Literature and Composition examination . . . period.

To that end, this chapter presents a variety of writing assignments and assessment instruments, from which I hope that you will cull as suits your educational needs. I here identify, discuss, and provide materials for five dissimilar genres of writing activities, two of which I have modeled on the types of writing that students are asked to produce on the Scholastic Aptitude Test and the AP English Literature and Composition examination. The SAT requires children to write argumentatively and persuasively on a debatable topic; essays of this type are timed to 25 minutes each. The AP English Literature exam, by contrast, asks students to analyze literary works, either excerpted or in their entireties, that they probably have never before encountered, dissecting their styles, structures, effects, and literary devices within a span of 40 minutes; essays found on the SAT are argumentative in nature, but these AP essays are expository.

Additionally, most essays at the undergraduate level, at least in English courses, replicate this latter analytical function, although they are usually much longer and more complex exegeses of larger works of literature; I thus identify college-length literary analyses as formulating their own genre of composition. Research-based and informed writing, on the other hand, usually presents students' findings on a particular topic of individual interest, rather than engages in and offers scholarly criticism of anything; oftentimes, a pupil's presentations of his or her research findings need not even take the form of composed text, as many professors in a variety of academic disciplines eschew academic traditionalism in favor of potentially more engaging in-class oral presentations. Finally, an assignment requiring students to interpret, reframe, and reproduce in original ways a thematic aspect (or several) of a literary work is entirely creative in nature, harnessing advanced learners' abilities to meld real-world, often modern issues with fictional literature. I consider all five of these distinct methodologies and compositional styles in this chapter.

25-Minute Argumentative SAT-Style Essays

The writing portion of the SAT, introduced immediately after the turn of the millennium, asks test-takers to consider an issue that is highly debatable, although perhaps not controversially so. Essay questions usually ask students how they feel about such an issue, which often is presented in its prompt as a dichotomy (e.g., do you agree with this statement or not?), and the test allows 25 minutes in which each student must compose one well-organized, strongly supported answer. The College Board itself makes available many sample SAT questions and related grading rubrics, plus anchor papers that teachers and parents can use to gauge their proficient assessment of written answers.

It is a debatable issue whether standardized test preparation in and of itself is a contractually, or even legitimately, expected part of any professional educator's job. There is value, of course, in training students for success on the SAT, which holds much sway over the collegiate choices that will be available to them after high school, but "teaching to the test" as a pedagogical methodology suffers a poor reputation among teachers and evaluators who consider aptitude tests extraneous to the disciplined curricula of high school. I teach English literature, a teacher may muse, not test-taking. Nevertheless, the type of focused, argumentative, substantiated, think-on-your-feet writing that students are asked to produce for the SAT requires valuable skills, especially in traditional English classes in which teachers perhaps engage their students more commonly, if not exclusively, in analytical writing reminiscent of literary criticism and scholarship.

The argumentative essay is a different beast altogether than the literary exegesis and the common book report. Credible, effective argumentation, especially with a time limit as demanding as the SAT's, requires students to think and organize themselves quickly, logically, and proficiently, culling support from suitable sources that may or may not involve literature, but that certainly uphold their taken position on a given essay topic. To write an effective SAT-style essay in 25 minutes is difficult, and the personal time management that is so necessary for success on this task is itself a useful skill to be learned or improved through repeated practice.

For all of these reasons, I offer a variety of questions designed to engage students' persuasive and argumentative faculties. If you wish to mimic the demanding conditions of the actual SAT in your classroom, then limit your class's composition time to 25 minutes. It is also useful, prior to administering any writing assignment, to model for your students sample questions and responses, such as anchor papers, interpreting together what does and does not make a successful argumentative essay in general.

Sample Questions

- In *The Canterbury Tales*, Chaucer's (1387/1987) Miller comically opines that "youthe and elde is often at debaat," an observation with which generations of parents and children would surely agree (l. 3230). Many people would perhaps amend the aphorism to read, "youthe and elde [are always] at debaat." Considering *King Lear*, other studies, and your own observations, do you agree that younger and older generations are fated to fight? Organize and compose an essay in which you consider this issue. Support your argument with examples academic or otherwise.

- Shakespeare culled inspiration for *King Lear* from several accounts of a historical Lear, King of Britain, whose reign was purportedly premedieval. In the Bard's version of Lear's story, setting is rather inconsequential; mention is made, and to some degree important, of various locales such as Dover and France, but there seems to be nothing in particular tying *King Lear* to any specific time or place. In your opinion, is the setting of this play important, or could the story take place elsewhere and at another time, proving just as effective? Organize and compose an essay in which you consider this issue. Support your argument with examples academic or otherwise.

- Cordelia and Edmund, both the youngest children of their respective fathers, are antithetical foils. When one is honest, the other connives;

when one betrays, the other is loyal. Probably due to this extremism, some commentators have found either or both of these characters rather unrealistic, examples of severe characterization rather than portrayals of "potentially real people." Do you agree with this opinion? Are Cordelia and Edmund realistically credible persons? Organize and compose an essay in which you consider this issue. Support your argument with examples academic or otherwise.

- The Earl of Gloucester is a problematic character to interpret. He comes off to the audience in one way at the play's beginning, then dynamically shifts in terms of his characterization and reception as the drama progresses. Opinions of scholars, readers, and theatergoers alike are somewhat divided when it comes to Gloucester, for while he probably winds up a pitiable elder, well, as the saying goes, you never get a second chance to make a first impression. In your estimation, is he a villainous character, worthy of the audience's abhorrence, a sympathetic character, or something else? Organize and compose an essay in which you consider this issue. Support your argument with examples academic or otherwise.

- Edgar, and by extension Shakespeare, concludes *King Lear* by stating, "we that are young / Shall never see so much nor live so long" (5.3.394–395). This statement's implication, that tragedy of the magnitude of *King Lear* becomes less feasible as the world and its societies age, is of course debatable. Do you agree with it? Organize and compose an essay in which you consider this issue. Support your argument with examples academic or otherwise.

- At the core of it all, who or what do you feel is to blame for the massive tragedy of this book? Is it a person, a phenomenon, or something else that causes this play's terrible destruction and sorrow? Organize and compose an essay in which you consider this issue. Support your argument with examples academic or otherwise.

Grading Rubric

What students can gain from any writing process is not optimized, of course, without a teacher's prompt provision to them of useful feedback. Table 8 is an original grading rubric designed to mirror the expectations of the College Board on the writing portion of the SAT. As with any essay actually prepared for the SAT, your students' products are here gauged on a 6-point scale.

You may want to institute a peer-assessment process among your students, whereby they evaluate each others' argumentative essays using this instrument. Please note, however, that such peer assessment is by and large invalid if students

TABLE 8
Grading Rubric for 25-Minute SAT-Style Essays

	Grade of 6	Grade of 5	Grade of 4
Overall Impression	An exceptional composition, indicating obvious and even mastery	A successful composition, indicating reasonably even mastery	A capable composition, indicating sufficient mastery
Essayist's Point of View	Sharply discerning point of view	Able and perceptive point of view	Lucid point of view
Support for Position/ Argument	Obviously suitable examples, reasons, and evidence are used	Suitable examples, reasons, and evidence are used	Sufficient examples, reasons, and evidence are used
Organization and Focus	Excellent organization and focus	Solid organization and focus	Coherent organization and acceptable focus
Progression of Ideas	Skillful progression of ideas	Articulate progression of ideas	Reasonable progression of ideas
Usage of Vocabulary	An apparently practiced and exact use of varied vocabulary	Appropriately varied vocabulary	Acceptable but inconsistent use of varied vocabulary
Sentence Structure	A significant and expressive range of sentence structures	A range of sentence structures	A limited range of sentence structures
Grammar, Usage, and Mechanics	Free of all major and minor errors	Nearly free of errors	A number of errors exist
	Grade of 3	Grade of 2	Grade of 1
Overall Impression	An inadequate composition, indicating emergent mastery	A highly inadequate composition, indicating slight mastery	An essentially deficient composition, indicating little or no mastery
Essayist's Point of View	Apparent point of view	Unclear point of view	No viable point of view
Support for Position/ Argument	Insufficient examples, reasons, and evidence are used	Poorly chosen examples, reasons, and evidence are used	Few or no examples, reasons, and evidence are used
Organization and Focus	Limited organization and focus	Poor organization and focus	Disorganized and unfocused
Progression of Ideas	Some faults are present in the progression of ideas	Highly faulty progression of ideas	Disorderly or unintelligible progression of ideas
Usage of Vocabulary	Pedestrian and somewhat incorrect use of vocabulary	Inadequate and often incorrect use of vocabulary	Elementary errors in vocabulary
Sentence Structure	No range of sentence structures	Widespread difficulties in sentence structure	Extreme errors in sentence structure
Grammar, Usage, and Mechanics	Frequent errors exist	Major errors confuse the essayist's point in places	Widespread, serious errors greatly interfere with the essayist's point

are not trained beforehand on how the rubric "works" and what various graded essays "look like"; thus, anticipatory consideration of scored anchor papers with your class is very valuable in ensuring that all of your pupils are on the same evaluative page, so to speak. Additionally, I encourage you to implement peer assessment on an identity-blind basis, whereby students' essays are photocopied and distributed for assessment, minus their authors' names.

40-Minute Analytical AP-Style Essays

The AP English Literature and Composition examination requires that students compose three different essays after answering a battery of multiple-choice questions. Distinct from the argumentative compositions found on the SAT, all three of these essays are analytical, interpreting creative literary works' effects, purposes, themes, and the like. To write this kind of essay, a student must be an exegete, able to mine texts—one excerpt of poetry, another of prose, and a work of choice—for symbolism, aspects of syntax and other style, elements of formal structure, key passages, and whatnot. A solid background in literary devices and compositional techniques is essential preparation and critical ammunition for writing such an essay.

These essays must be just as organized as the position papers required by the SAT, and they should also be supported by precise textual details, gleaned by careful and intricate reading of literary selections. Keep in mind, too, that these AP-style essays should be generally longer and better executed, as students are allowed nearly twice as long to write each of them as they are to compose for the SAT: 40 minutes as opposed to 25, respectively. Once again, the College Board consistently releases to the public AP essay prompts and examples of students' responses to them, taken fully from the Literature and Composition exam; modeling for your class several College Board-scored anchor papers is excellent preparation for students' engagement with essays of this type.

Teachers are safe to assume that the literary pieces presented to students on the AP Literature and Composition examination will be unfamiliar ones; it is technically possible, but improbable, that the College Board asks test-takers to analyze such common works as Blake's "The Tyger" or Frost's "Birches." Therefore, students who take the exam should prepare by honing their analytical, compositional, *and* time management skills, as all three are requisite during a 2-hour block of time in which test-takers write three different essays on anything from a poet's syntactical patterns to the satirical elements of a prose piece, or from the didacticism evident in a provided excerpt to the importance of an urban setting in a novel read independently and long ago. Although different than the composition of a good argumentative essay, the process in which students engage here is no less dif-

ficult, and constant practice and constructive feedback from teachers are critical to students' improvement and eventual success.

To help you to prepare your students, I have included five sample AP-style essay prompts in this chapter's materials section (see pp. 182–186), each excerpted from a particular act of *King Lear*. Students who compose all five essays will practice analyzing a variety of literary devices, techniques, and purposes, all of which are legitimate and reasonable topics and foci for which to prepare as they work toward the actual AP Literature and Composition examination.

Grading Rubric

As with all essays, students' improved performance in writing timed analyses is heightened by prompt, focused feedback. The grading rubric in Table 9, which I have designed to mirror the College Board's expectations for success on the AP Literature and Composition exam, can help your expedient delivery of such feedback. It is a mechanism for assessing students' products on a 9-point scale, as per the AP exam's instrument, and considers a wide range of compositional factors.

Once again, peer assessment among students is a potentially helpful endeavor in their preparation for the AP Literature exam. Please recall, though, that the legitimacy and importance of peer assessment as a method for improvement is lessened if your class is not trained beforehand on proper use of the rubric and comparative analysis of evaluated anchor papers, which is valuable in ensuring that all students understand not only the rubric's criteria, but also how to differentiate among dissimilar written responses. As with SAT-style position papers, I encourage you here to implement peer assessment on an identity-blind basis, omitting students' names from any responses that are shared among members of your class.

Extended "College-Length" Analytical Essays

The phrase "English paper" probably conjures in the minds of most high-achieving high school and college students slight variations on one thing: a lengthy exposition of the themes, didactic morals, technical structure, cultural importance, ambiguous interpretability, or covert symbolism of any given work of literature, probably measured between 6–10 pages and including numerous quotations, citations, and references or works cited at its back. Yes, such products are common in English courses, especially at undergraduate and graduate levels of literary study, where they constitute the majority of students' written products.

The College Board assumes that teachers of AP courses replicate college-level instruction, going so far as to approve or deny teachers' unique course syllabi in order to monitor consistent rigor, so we as language arts professionals would be

TABLE 9
Grading Rubric for AP-Style 40-Minute Essays

Score of 9	Score of 8	Score of 7
• Rhetorical and stylistic devices analyzed correctly with precision *or* • Persuasive argument is cogent, convincing, and well supported	• Rhetorical and stylistic devices analyzed well *or* • Persuasive argument is cogent and convincing, but only somewhat supported	• Rhetorical and stylistic devices analyzed competently *or* • Persuasive argument is cogent, but a lack of development or support is somewhat unconvincing
• Frequent, succinct, and appropriate references to the text, either directly or indirectly	• Some appropriate references to the text, either directly or indirectly	• A few appropriate references to the text, either directly or indirectly
• Point of view is clearly articulated and reinforced extremely well	• Point of view is clearly articulated and reinforced appropriately	• Point of view is clearly articulated, but reinforced only somewhat
• Extremely well written... any existent errors are inconsequential	• Well written... very few and only minor errors are made	• Some errors exist, but they do not interfere with the writer's clear expression of ideas

Score of 6	Score of 5	Score of 4
• Rhetorical and stylistic devices analyzed somewhat haphazardly *or* • Underdeveloped and undersupported persuasive argument is only slightly convincing	• Relevant rhetorical and stylistic devices are analyzed very little *or* • Persuasive argument is underdeveloped and undersupported, and thus unconvincing	• Only secondary rhetorical and stylistic devices are analyzed *or* • Persuasive argument is superficial, perhaps missing the point of the question/prompt
• A few references to the text, directly or indirectly, are only somewhat relevant	• The writer refers to the text, directly or indirectly, very little, and only somewhat relevantly	• Almost no relevant references to the text are made, either directly or indirectly
• Point of view is vaguely articulated and reinforced only somewhat	• Point of view is vaguely articulated and reinforced hardly at all	• Point of view is developed incoherently and only somewhat clear
• Errors exist, very few of which are serious enough to interfere with the writer's clear expression	• Errors in diction, syntax, or grammar interfere with the writer's clear expression of ideas	• Immature errors exist, demonstrating the writer's lack of control over diction and syntax

Score of 3	Score of 2	Score of 1
• Secondary rhetorical and stylistic devices are incorrectly analyzed *or* • Persuasive argument is seriously flawed, as well as mostly off the topic of the question/prompt	• Any attempted analysis of rhetorical or stylistic devices is extremely simplistic *or* • Persuasive argument is seriously flawed, irrelevant, and unorganized	• No attempt is made to analyze rhetorical or stylistic devices *or* • Irrelevant persuasive argument is excessively flawed and extremely unorganized
• No direct references to the text are made, and indirect references are mostly irrelevant	• No relevant references to the text are made, either directly or indirectly	• No references to the text are made at all, either directly or indirectly
• The writer's point of view is unclear and disjointed	• The writer's point of view is expressed quite unclearly	• The writer's point of view is incomprehensible
• Very immature errors exist, demonstrating the writer's lack of control over standard English syntax and grammar	• Overly simplistic errors demonstrate the writer's lack of control over basic English diction, syntax, and grammar	• Overwhelming errors indicate the writer's extreme lack of control over basic English diction, syntax, and grammar

Scores of 0 are given for blank papers, simple paraphrases of prompts, or essays not on assigned topics.

remiss to ignore long "collegiate" exegeses completely in favor of shorter, timed, in-class prompts aimed solely at higher scores on the AP test. Although it is true that students' performances on the exam ultimately determine their potential reception of undergraduate credit, it is no less critical that once they actually matriculate to college they are familiar with the procedure and experience of writing eight-page papers, not just five-paragraph handwritten essays.

A large potential hazard of which many high school teachers are aware, though, exists with regard to these lengthy essays: high-achieving, academically driven students are sometimes prone to plagiaristic urges when left to their own compositional devices, especially with the senior year's stakes of potential college admissions added to normal scholastic pressures. Additionally, the proliferation of Internet sites, including many that charge fees for previously written essays, has enhanced students' abilities and opportunities to plagiarize work; one simple web search, plus an electronic copy and paste or two, can save young writers hours of late-night stress. Especially for ambitious high schoolers eyeing the future, the temptation to "write" in this way is probably natural. I personally have found that the best way to prevent plagiarism is to be proactive, requiring analytical papers from my AP classes, the assignments for which are formatted in ways that discourage dishonesty.

First, rather than ask open-ended interpretive questions of students or request their submission of a vaguely defined paper on a topic of their choice (e.g., "write a paper analyzing *King Lear*'s symbolism"), I distribute to them a closed list of potential essay theses. I allow each student to choose whichever thesis he or she wishes to defend, requiring him or her to include it—word for word—in the submitted essay, probably within its introductory paragraph. This mandate absolutely lessens students' potential to discover a useable essay elsewhere, for the likelihood of other people having not only written, but also published a legitimate essay on that precise topic is remote. Secondly, I reward students with extra credit points for using in their essays a multitude of higher-level vocabulary words that we have previously learned in class. In this way, essays come to me dotted with contextualized words that serve dual purposes: students' use of the vocabulary reinforces their definitions, plus acts as an indicator of students' honest composition of a given essay. After all, random people publishing essays on the Internet do not know to highlight my classes' specific vocabulary words, and thus are unlikely to include them with frequency in their papers.

Here is a list of potential theses concerning *King Lear*. I encourage you to assign them to your class wholly as a "menu of choices," from which students can select. Moreover, I recommend that you suggest essays' lengths not in terms of their numbers of total pages, but in terms of their aggregate word counts; writers can adjust the amount of text on computerized pages by altering font and margin sizes, but this is impossible if students need to produce a set number of words.

Consider the fact that an average page typed in a standard size and style of font, bounded by one-inch margins, contains approximately 250–300 words; using this formula you can estimate the required page length of your students' essays.

Sample Essay Theses

- Contrary to Lear's own assertion that "nothing will come of nothing," Shakespeare implies in his play that nothingness is actually the source of most everything truly valuable in the world (1.1.99).

- Although vision, both outward and inward, represents security in the world of *King Lear*, Shakespeare's text suggests that blindness is more common among human beings, who are therefore collectively doomed.

- In the seemingly backward reality of *King Lear*, Shakespeare implies that foolishness and nonsense, contrary to their respective denotations, are not folly in truth, but actually wisdom and insight.

- With 29 and 13 occurrences throughout *King Lear*, respectively, "make" and "made" are among the most common words in the play; their frequency is potentially misleading, however, as Shakespeare in the drama suggests that humans' ability to create is illusory, ultimately undermined by people's natural tendencies to destroy.

- In *King Lear*, Shakespeare portrays Nature as a deific force that is not indifferent to human life, but rather malevolent and ultimately destructive.

- Contrary to common human belief, Shakespeare suggests in *King Lear* his view that individual identity is not tied to personal worth, but that a person's refusal and resultant lack of autonomous identity are intrinsically valuable.

- In *King Lear*, words, regardless of their content, are inherently untrue to various degrees; one's realization of truth, Shakespeare claims in the text, ultimately arises not through verbiage, but through the experience of pain.

- Shakespeare implies in *King Lear* that age and hope are inversely related, for the passage of time parallels the growth of hopelessness for many of the drama's main characters.

Grading Rubric

I evaluate my students' lengthy analytical essays using the included instrument (see p. 168), which focuses on specific criteria, like any rubric does, yet is flexible enough to allow some degree of the holistic assessment common among many undergraduate English professors. In other words, I highlight particular skills and requirements in this rubric, but I also allow room to judge essays on my overall impression of them. Because I reward my AP students with extra credit for their contextualized usage of vocabulary words in their essays, I always determine an initial score for each essay using this rubric, then add to that score for each vocabulary word.

Submissions and Returns

I believe that the more ways in which I can turn summative assessment into formative assessment, helping my students to learn even as they are being assessed, the better. If even a test is a learning opportunity, then the short time that I have to work with pupils is closer to maximized. To this end, in my own AP classes I vary in particular ways two mundane procedures that are necessary to the assignment and evaluation of long essays: my collection of students' papers and my subsequent redistribution of them to their authors.

On essay due dates, many teachers anticlimactically cap the compositional process simply by collecting papers, then moving without transition or praise to other activities, perhaps to the next unit, leaving the essays themselves forgotten or ignored by the class until they eventually are returned with grades and feedback. I personally feel that children who work so hard to produce these essays should be provided a sense of closure or culmination greater than that allowed by a simple passing of papers to the front of the classroom; all teachers want students to feel proud of their work and to share it with their classmates. Extrinsic motivation for praise is a powerful human motivator, of course.

For this reason, I allow my own AP students not only to read each others' work as a form of peer editing, but also to modify their own as they garner ideas for improvement from their classmates' products. Many teachers utilize peer editing as an evaluative, rather than a creative, tool, whereby students find and correct mistakes in their classmates' essays. Learners' incentive for performing well or concentrating as they do so is low; after all, especially after a presumably late night spent writing their own papers, to nitpick grammatical and stylistic errors from friends' essays is hardly engaging, especially when there is no immediate personal benefit to a student editor.

Figure 6 contains instructions to students on how otherwise to engage in "peer editing" as they improve and submit their own essays. My use of the technique outlined by these instructions has been positive and productive, raising students' motivation to read each other's works and allowing them one last opportunity to amend their own before it is evaluated. I invite you to distribute this sheet of directions to your own students or to reproduce it on the front board the next time that they submit college-length essays.

Name: _____ Date: _____

Scoring Rubric for Extended Analytical Essays

– A + (90–100 points)	– B + (80–90 points)	– C + (70–80 points)	– D + (60–70 points)	– F + (below 60 points)
Essays earning grades of "A" are outstanding in their clear and consistent mastery of analytical skills, demonstrating their writers' exceptional control of effective writing techniques, sustaining extremely insightful and in-depth analysis of complex ideas, and developing and supporting their main points with logically compelling scrutiny and highly persuasive examples. Such essays are clear, interesting, and correct, including strong and highly effective introductory and conclusive paragraphs, as well as appropriate transitions both within paragraphs and across the entire piece. They are sharply focused and well organized, demonstrating coherent unity and a smooth analytical progression, as well as referring frequently and carefully to the text, both directly and indirectly. These essays display excellent use of language, highlighted by effective sentence variety and precisely apt vocabulary; they demonstrate their authors' superior facility with sentence structure, grammar, usage, and mechanics, including few, if any, errors.	Essays earning grades of "B" are effective in their clear and reasonably consistent mastery of analytical skills, demonstrating their writers' considerable control of effective writing techniques, sustaining generally insightful analysis of complex ideas, and developing and supporting their main points with logically sound scrutiny and well-chosen, appropriate examples. Such essays are clear, interesting, and mostly correct, including skillful and effective introductory and conclusive paragraphs, as well as transitions that are generally appropriate and relatively widespread throughout the piece. They are clearly focused and well organized, demonstrating good overall coherence and an apparent analytical progression, as well as referring frequently to the text, both directly and indirectly. These essays display fluent use of language, highlighted by generally effective sentence variety and appropriate vocabulary; they demonstrate their authors' good control of sentence structure, grammar, usage, and mechanics, including occasional, though not overly numerous, errors.	Essays earning grades of "C" are competent in their fairly clear and developing mastery of analytical skills, demonstrating their writers' adequate control of effective writing techniques, sustaining relevant analysis of important ideas, and supporting their main points with acceptable inquiry and sufficient examples. Such essays are reasonably clear and mostly correct, including satisfactory introductory and conclusive paragraphs, as well as occasional usages of appropriate transitions. They are passably focused and organized, demonstrating reasonable coherence and a sufficient analytical progression, as well as referring commonly to the text, either directly or indirectly. These essays display adequate use of language to convey meaning, including some sentence variety and generally appropriate vocabulary; they demonstrate their authors' satisfactory control of sentence structure, grammar, usage, and mechanics, including frequent errors, very few of which are simplistic in nature.	Essays earning grades of "D" are inadequate, revealing limited mastery of analytical skills, demonstrating their writers' inconsistent control of effective writing techniques, sustaining weak analysis of important ideas, and addressing relatively unsupported main points with brittle inquiry and insufficient examples. Such essays are superficial, though mostly correct, and include cursory introductory and conclusive paragraphs, as well as few, if any, appropriate transitions. They are disjointedly focused and organized, demonstrating the writer's overall inability to compose coherently and logically, as well as referring vaguely and indirectly to the text. These essays display weak use of language to convey meaning, including little sentence variety and commonly awkward vocabulary; they demonstrate their authors' unsatisfactory control of sentence structure, grammar, usage, and mechanics, including widespread errors, some of which are simplistic in nature.	Essays earning grades of "F" are seriously flawed or limited, revealing very little mastery of analytical skills, demonstrating their writers' lack of control of effective writing techniques, sustaining seriously flawed analysis of important ideas, and addressing main points without support or examples. Such essays are simple and in many ways incorrect, including little or no introductory and conclusive paragraphs, as well as very few appropriate transitions. They are disorganized and/or unfocused, demonstrating the writer's fundamental inability to compose coherently and logically, as well as exhibiting an almost total neglect of reference to the text. These essays display deficient use of language to convey meaning, including almost no sentence variety and highly awkward vocabulary in many places; they demonstrate their authors' inadequate control of sentence structure, grammar, usage, and mechanics, including pervasive errors, many of which are simplistic in nature.

Total Points (out of 100): _____

> **Procedural Directions for Essay Submissions**
>
> 1. Carefully checking that all of your pages are in the correct order, please staple your essay, then place and leave it on top of your desk.
> 2. Please stand up, move about the classroom, and choose an essay to read; do so carefully, thoroughly, and silently. When you are finished reading that essay, please return it to the author's desk and choose another to read similarly.
> 3. I am going to collect the essays "permanently" in 30 minutes. You have that amount of time not only to read as many peers' essays as possible, but to edit your own in any way that you wish. If you want to add or amend anything to/in your essay, then please do so in pen. I shall read and grade any such additions or amendments as if they were included, typed, as original portions of your essay. Keep in mind, please, that while you may add anything to your essay at all, from quotations to extra sentences of explanation, from extra transitions to formatting minutiae, I am going to grade all such insertions exactly as I would any other portion of your typed analysis (i.e., watch your grammar, punctuation, spelling, etc.).
> 4. Make sure (e.g., through the usage of arrows) that I can tell easily where each insertion is supposed to go in your text. If you do not wish to make any changes to your essay, of course, then you need not. You have 30 minutes.
>
> *Figure 6.* Instructions for peer editing procedures during essay submission process.

On the other hand, it is human nature in any class, when receiving one's evaluated essay back from a teacher, to look immediately at the score received, then probably to file the essay away, reading few if any of the teacher's comments scattered throughout it. If a writer is happy with the grade received, then why bother reading the comments? On the other hand, if a writer is disappointed or upset by the grade, then he or she may be too disgusted to peruse the reasons for that perceived "failure" to achieve. Either way, the efforts of teachers who spend so much time and take so much care in commenting upon students' essays largely are wasted.

These statements are generalizations, but as one of those stereotypical English teachers who edits and comments upon students' papers extensively—it often takes me about an hour to assess fully one undergraduate-length essay submitted in my AP classes—I want to ensure as best as I am able that students actually peruse the notes and markings that I make; I do not like "wasting" my own time any more than students like to waste theirs. I therefore utilize two procedures

> **Do You Want 2 Points Added Immediately
> to the Total Score of Your Essay?**
>
> 1. Find two grammatical errors that you commit very commonly in your essay (you must commit each error a minimum of three times to qualify as "very common").
> 2. Complete, type or handwrite, and submit to me the following four sentences by tomorrow:
>
>   One of my most common errors is [name or precise explanation of error], which can be found [first location of error, including a complete description of it], as well as [second location of error, including a complete description of it] and [third location of error, including a complete description of it].
>
>   I plan to avoid making this error on my next essay by [explanation of tactic].
>
>   Another of my most common errors is [name or explanation of error], which can be found [first location of error, including a complete description of it], as well as [second location of error, including a complete description of it] and [third location of error, including a complete description of it].
>
>   I plan to avoid making this error on my next essay by [explanation of tactic].
>
>   *(There is no need to underline all of your insertions when you type these sentences; it is simply done so here for editorial purposes.)*
>
> 3. No more steps, actually. I shall add 2 points to the total grade for your essay.
>
> **Figure 7.** Instructions for garnering additional points on essays through retroactive editing.

to encourage my students to read my feedback on their essays, the first of which is that I do not give them their actual grades—numerical or otherwise—when I redistribute their marked-up papers. Rather than staple my rubric and final grade to each pupil's essay, I hold them back for a day; students' immediate and natural impulse to look at the numerical grade is thus preempted, and they instead look through the annotated pages of the essay, searching for clues as to how it was evaluated. The next day, I distribute to them their rubrics, once they have had time to consider and digest my commentary upon their work.

Moreover, because I spend so much of the time that it takes to assess papers in the correction of students' grammatical errors, I reward them for following in my editorial footsteps. As Figure 7 indicates, if students are able to identify and correct several errors that they made repeatedly in a given essay, then I augment

their scores after the fact. I invite you to make use of the procedure outlined by Figure 7 in your own classes.

Research Projects and Essays

Learners' engagement in and presentation of original research is another important experience that prepares them for undergraduate work, in English or otherwise. In all disciplines, many college professors nationwide expect matriculating freshmen to be familiar with the process for undertaking and completing research on an assigned topic, as well as to be proficient at fusing and presenting their findings clearly. In our field, Shakespeare's life and times offer to students a large and engaging field to research, containing mysterious episodes about which few records were kept, as well as periods of clarity about which we know much. After all, countless scholars have made careers out of researching the Bard!

If you wish to require your students to compose traditional research essays, then the rubric that I offer for the assessment of college-level analyses (see p. 168) can be used here as well. Keep in mind, however, that research essays are far more documentary than they are interpretive, so the rubric's emphasis on persuasion and analysis should be discounted as irrelevant in regard to research papers.

On the other hand, in my own classes I prefer more engaging, creative in-class presentations of students' research findings. Providing learners with opportunities to express themselves in a variety of ways is good professional practice, I believe, as it encourages children to develop full academic faculties; in other words, for a student who is used to writing essays, composing a visual and oral presentation instead may be a spur to developing abilities that are perhaps too seldom accessed in school.

I therefore offer below a number of plausible research topics designed with such presentations, oral or otherwise, in mind. Each one can be altered slightly in order to suit more traditional essay products.

Sample Research Projects

- Scholars have had difficulty determining exactly when Shakespeare wrote *King Lear*. Certainly it dates from between 1603, when Samuel Harsnett's *A Declaration of Egregious Popish Impostures* was published, and December 26, 1606, when it was first performed at the court of King James I. Research scholars' previous attempts to date Shakespeare's composition of the play, paying particular attention to his sources, professional activities, and family life.

- Shakespeare took inspiration for *King Lear* from many sources, including Raphael Holinshed's *Chronicles of England, Scotland, and Ireland* (2nd ed.), Edmund Spenser's *The Faerie Queene*, and John Higgins's *A Mirror for Magistrates*. Research these sources, pinpointing what aspects of Shakespeare's drama are traceable to them, and share your findings in a well-documented presentation.

- *King Lear*, with its bloodshed, betrayal, and tragedy, perhaps seems an unlikely story to be set to music, but on the other hand, maybe it's perfect for this kind of adaptation! In 1978, German composer Aribert Reimann set the story as an opera, nearly 150 years after Frenchman Hector Berlioz turned it into a symphonic work. Gather these musical interpretations of the play, then compare and contrast their portrayals of some of the plot's critical moments, such as the famous storm scene of Act III. Compare your findings to a cinematic adaptation of the play, such as Japanese director Akira Kurosawa's *Ran*, from 1985, or Russian director Grigori Kozintsev's version from 1971. How are their interpretations of these moments similar to or different than one another? Which of these adaptations do you feel is truest to the spirit of Shakespeare's *King Lear*? Do the adaptations from different parts of the world impress upon you their geographic uniqueness in any way? Do you conclude that the story is best presented as a musical piece, a drama *sans* music, or a mixture of both? Present your findings and conclusions in a well-developed multimedia presentation.

- To some degree, textual analysis of all of Shakespeare's plays is difficult because different versions of each script exist. Just as modern movies are often released to the public in original, special edition, and/or expanded versions, the Bard's works are extant in several different Quarto (Q1 and Q2) and Folio (F) texts. When it comes to *King Lear*, the differences among these versions are sometimes profound. Locate excerpts from or the entireties of these different versions, then compare and contrast their texts. Highlighting a particular scene or two, what are some major and minor differences that you find among them? What effect might these distinctions have upon characterization, theme, pacing, and other dramatic elements?

- Within the span of a century, the story of Lear, historical King of Britain, was presented popularly on the English stage no fewer than three times: the first version was the anonymous *The True Chronicle History of King Leir* [sic] *and his three daughters*, the second was Shakespeare's *King Lear*, and the third was Nahum Tate's *History of King Lear*. Compare and contrast the scripts of these three different versions of the same story, paying particular attention to diction and syntax. How is the evolution of

the English language explicated by a comparison of these three different drama's versions of one or two selected scenes? Present your findings in a well-documented manner.

- The geographic setting of *King Lear* is clear; the drama takes place in England, extending southeastward to Dover, on the edge of the English Channel. The temporal setting, on the other hand, is ambiguous. We learn from various sources that there once was a Lear (or Leir) who was a British king, but exactly when and over what constituency he reigned is apocryphal. There also was supposedly an Edgar who was at one point king; he is noted, we are told, for ridding Britain of wolves. It is debatable how much of this information is historically accurate and temporally locatable, for while some sources suggest that King Lear reigned near the Middle Ages, others propose that he was quasi-Druidic, to which end Laurence Olivier's 1983 on-screen version of *King Lear* incorporates Stonehenge! Investigate the historical Lear (or Leir), learning as much as you are able about the drama's eponymous ruler, then present your findings to the class. To expand your project, research the historical Edgar, as well.

- Prior to 1576, professional theaters were outlawed in Puritan-controlled London; by extension, they were rare, if extant at all, throughout all of England at that time. In that year, however, James Burbage, a former carpenter and professional actor himself, obtained permission to construct in the northern London suburb of Shoreditch the first permanent playhouse, a structure devoted wholly to the staging of plays. Appropriately, it was simply called the Theatre. Following its construction, Puritan and otherwise governmental opposition to playhouses lessened, and Burbage's Theatre was soon followed by many similar edifices, constructed to satisfy the public's rising demand for staged entertainment. Research the events leading up to and surrounding the construction of the Theatre, including preconstruction civic attitudes and statutes, Burbage's stated motivations for his playhouse's erection, and its immediate impact on London's artistic scene; likewise, research the rise of theatergoing as a socially and/or morally acceptable pastime in pre-Elizabethan England. Share your findings with the rest of your class in a well-organized presentation.

Grading Rubric

Table 10 is an original grading rubric that you can use to assess students' research presentations. To adapt the rubric's point values to a 100-point grading scale, simply multiply students' scores by 6.25. Please note that the final assessment criterion outlined by this rubric considers predetermined parameters such as time

TABLE 10
Grading Rubric for Student's Research Presentations

	4	3	2	1
Content	The project's content is totally legitimate and highly detailed, exhibiting a strong research base.	The project's content is legitimate and detailed, though not exceedingly deep, exhibiting a solid research base.	The project's content is mostly legitimate, but less detailed overall, exhibiting solid research in only some areas.	The project's content is largely illegitimate and lacks detail and depth, exhibiting major deficiencies in the research base.
Organization	The project's organization is outstandingly logical, and the flow between ideas or sections is superbly smooth, demonstrating much forethought and preparation.	The project's organization is logical, with fluid transitions between most ideas or sections, demonstrating good preparation.	The project's organization is logical to some extent, but the flow between ideas or sections would benefit from stronger transitioning; overall, solid, but not exceptional, preparation is evidenced.	The project's organization is largely illogical, and the flow between ideas or sections is awkward and/or jumpy in many places, demonstrating haphazard preparation.
Engagement of Audience/ Theatricality	The presentation to the audience is cleverly creative, highly original, and thoroughly engaging, exhibiting strong theatricality.	The presentation to the audience is creative, somewhat original, and engaging at many points, exhibiting present, but limited, theatricality.	The presentation to the audience is solid, but lacks creativity and originality at most points; the audience is engaged sporadically, but the presentation overall lacks theatricality.	The presentation to the audience is largely mundane or routine, greatly lacking originality; the audience's response is generally indifferent to the presentation's banality.
Adherence to Project Parameters	The presentation fits perfectly all of the assignment's parameters, such as time limit and/or included elements. *or* The presentation exceeds the assignment's parameters through the use of additional resources or elements.	The presentation fits most of the assignment's parameters, such as time limit and/or included elements.	The presentation fits only a limited amount of the assignment's parameters, such as time limit and/or included elements.	The presentation fits none of the assignment's parameters, such as time limit and/or included elements.

Total Score (out of 16 possible): _____

limits, which are certainly flexible according to your instructional purposes and the abilities and talents of your pupils.

Individualized Creative-Interpretive Projects

Another of my own educational beliefs is that the most truly valuable, enduring learning that students accomplish in schools occurs not in some kind of academic vacuum, but rather in a synthesis of scholastic theory and real-world relevance. Humans in general are more apt to remember events, details, and facts that hold personal meaning, that relate in some way to the occurrences and details of their own lives. Our favorite poems or novels are just that, our *favorites*, because they hold personal significances for us; these works' ascension to that title is not arbitrary, nor should students' engagement of classic works and themes of literature be. As teachers, if we want our lessons and our students' learning to last, to impact their lives beyond the finite boundaries of classroom walls and school calendars, then we must help our pupils to personalize their learning.

Too commonly in high school English classes nationwide, students are asked to recognize, absorb, and interpret the intentions, styles, and products of canonical authors and poets in a somewhat vacuous context, without being given the opportunity to reflect upon or reframe those authors' and poets' visions and themes as they relate to students' own lives. I attempt to prod my students toward greater contextual and personal awareness by asking such simplistic, albeit difficult to answer, questions as "So what?" "Why should you care?" and "Why is this stuff relevant to your life?" Students who are able to answer these questions, no matter what work of literature is being considered, can find, digest, and personalize a work's humanness, the true and lasting reasons why the posterity of canonical artists is timelessly relevant.

Yes, we can utilize *King Lear* as a tool to teach classes of young people about primogeniture, iambic pentameter, figurative language, and dramatic stagecraft, but unless some theme, idea, conflict, or character in the play connects powerfully with an individual student somehow, then few if any of those academic details are liable to stay with that child beyond his or her classroom experience. How many nonteachers do you imagine can recall what work of literature they wrote about on their own senior AP exam? Isn't the point of reading literature at all—or studying anything, for that matter—to help you understand more clearly yourself, your life, and your world? In my case, those understandings are why I chose to major in English rather than mathematics. Literature truly can be life-changing, and your assignment that students create individualized creative-interpretive projects aims to augment students' learning in just those ways.

I have required such original products from my AP students for years, and the great diversity of submissions that I have received from them testifies to their profound, entertaining, and too often untapped creative talents. One former student composed, using a marimba and toms, a suite portraying *Hamlet*'s implication that knowledge and intelligence are a burdensome curse; another wrote, sang, and recorded a song concerning the abandonment of Frankenstein's monster, expressing how that betrayal mirrored her own experience as the daughter of divorcees. One year, someone related King Lear's obstinate hubris to modern athletics, designing and filming a mock sports report concerning the misguided blindness of arrogance and greed; others have painted and drawn thematic visualizations, skinned and tanned leather and molded wood for a *Hamlet* dream catcher, designed and compiled photographic essays, and composed original narrative poems, short stories, or one-act plays. I've received shadow boxes, works of stained glass, mobiles and marionettes, stop-motion LEGO movies, computerized short films, and interpretive dances! And, of all of the assignments that I require of my AP students, these creative-interpretive projects are by far the most enjoyable to grade; I look forward to their creative expressions every year.

The following assignment sheet (see p. 177) is one that you may distribute to your own students if you choose to engage them in this intellectually stimulating, profoundly rewarding endeavor. It is important that students understand the difference between creatively interpreting (i.e., reframing) aspects of *King Lear*, and simply regurgitating the plot or its characters in an alternative, albeit extremely similar, setting or situation; the former is the goal of this project, for personalized learning occurs when students are freed from the constraints of Shakespeare's original to focus instead on the truly human, universal heart of the story.

In order to encourage students' honest consideration of themes, emotions, and other elements of both their own artwork (self-reflection) and Shakespeare's original (critical interpretation), I require them to submit short explanations of their artistic products, their interpretive and creative goals in producing them, and the relative success that they feel they have achieved in this undertaking. This explanatory portion of the creative project ensures that students submit original works that truly are relevant to the literature being studied, plus verbalize the intertextual ties between that literature and themselves.

Rather than a traditional rubric highlighting gradients of success on various criteria, I assess students' creative-interpretive projects using the "numerical checklist" on p. 178, which allows for a large diversity of products. The grading criteria defined by this checklist are flexible enough that no matter what a student produces and submits, you can assess it using this instrument. Moreover, the checklist's relatively holistic focus contrasts with the fastidious nature of most hierarchical rubrics; considering students' products that are themselves works of art, I personally see this wide-angle view as optimal.

Creative-Interpretive Project
King Lear

In higher level English classes nationwide, students are too often asked to reflect upon, interpret, and digest the artistic intentions of famous authors without being given the opportunity to reflect upon, interpret, and digest the importance of those authors' visions and themes as they relate to students' own lives. If you cannot relate a theme or philosophical concept to your world, then why bother to study it? Such an idea, an idea without personal utility, becomes inherently useless. In brief, the point of reading literature at all—or any idea, for that matter—is to help you understand better yourself, your own life, and your own world. I hope that this assignment provides you with an opportunity to do just that!

Requirements

- You are going to submit and reflect upon a creative interpretation—wholly of your own design—of one of *King Lear*'s major themes.

- This interpretation can take any artistic shape that you wish: a self-made movie, a narrative poem, a one-act play, a song (sung and/or played), a series of related photographs, a painting, an interpretive dance, a short story, a symbolic marionette or collage, a mock news broadcast, a sculpture, some amalgamation of many of the above, etc.

- Your artistic piece does not need to mirror the story of *King Lear* in any way, nor does it have to represent any of the literature's characters, settings, situations, or other elements. What it ***must*** do is represent in some tangible way one of the work's major ***themes*** (i.e., philosophical ideas such as the futility of fighting mortality, the emotional difficulty of divided loyalties, the timeless clashes of generations, the self-destructive nature of humans).

- Your creation is to be accompanied by a 400–600-word analysis, a self-reflection, of both your creative work of art and the play that influenced its creation, explaining just what theme(s) are portrayed in your own work, plus how and why they are important to you not just as a reader of literature, but also as a living, breathing, emotional human being.

Name: _____ Date: _____

Grading "Checklist" for Creative-Interpretive Project
King Lear

Conceptual Validity
- The interpretive concept underlying the work of art is well-thought-out, as explicated either by the work of art itself or by the accompanying analytical paper _____/10
- It is clear, either upon viewing the work of art itself or after reading the accompanying paper, that at least one major theme of *King Lear* is present and central to the concept of the newly created work of art _____/10
- The artist's conceptualization of both this major theme and its representation in the new work of art is *not* contrary to Shakespeare's original conceptualization of the same theme, but parallel to it _____/10

Accompanying Reflective Analysis
- The analytical paper that accompanies the work of art is between 400–600 words, and there are no major grammatical errors in it _____/10
- The analytical paper reflects clearly and validly upon both the original work of literature and its inspirational effect upon the new work of art, explicating such important factors as their thematic bond, their philosophical views, and/or their sameness of mood _____/10
- It is clear from the paper that the artist/student has thought about the original work of literature, its themes, and his or her own art not only thoroughly, but also well _____/10

Overall Impression
- After viewing the work of art, I as the assessor feel that the artist/student has worked hard on this project, both intellectually and artistically _____/20
- After viewing the work of art, I as the assessor am impressed both with the student's capacity for analyzing and reflecting upon philosophical, thematic literature and with his or her ability to correlate that literature with the "real world" of his or her life _____/20

Total Score (Out of 100): _____

Conclusion

The contents of this chapter offer a variety of ways in which students, at the end of their study of *King Lear*, can demonstrate their mastery, ownership, and synthesis of many disparate threads woven into the drama's unified whole. Any of the five writing styles highlighted in this chapter might legitimately serve to engender an end-of-unit assessment, but I recommend that you assign and overlap several of them at once, helping your students to consider and interpret the play in a variety of compositional ways.

Finally, although I suggest that you conclude your *King Lear* unit with a writing product, this book's five pedagogical chapters need not be followed in order. I have always felt that the most effective teachers, and thus the most memorable classes, interweave various activities simultaneously, disparate threads all attached to one central hub: On one day pragmatic AP exam practice, on another a Socratic seminar discussion of theme and form, and on a third an interpretive performance activity requiring close reading, all the while moving forward toward the end goal of essay composition and creative-interpretive reframing. In this way, while you certainly might use the contents of this book as a step-by-step guide to successful instruction of *King Lear*, I rather encourage you to mix and match its offerings to suit your own style and goals. After all, the most personal and energetic teaching, like the most personal and energetic learning, is creative and individual. No matter what approach you take in moving students through the world of *King Lear* on their road toward the AP exam, I certainly hope that this guidebook serves you well.

Chapter Materials

Name: _____ Date: _____

AP-Style Essay Prompt
King Lear, Act I

Read carefully the two speeches found below, both spoken in Act I of *King Lear*. Then compose a well-organized essay in which you compare and contrast the two speakers' apparent points of view regarding human beings' ability to determine their own characters, actions, and fates. Consider such elements as diction, imagery, tone, and figurative language. **Time limit– 40 minutes.**

Spoken by Gloucester
Act I, scene ii

Line 5
10
15

These late eclipses in the sun and moon portend no good to us. Though the wisdom of nature can reason it thus and thus, yet nature finds itself scourged by the sequent effects. Love cools, friendship falls off, brothers divide; in cities, mutinies; in countries, discord; in palaces, treason; and the bond cracked 'twixt son and father. This villain of mine comes under the prediction: there's son against father. The King falls from bias of nature: there's father against child. We have seen the best of our time. Machinations, hollowness, treachery, and all ruinous disorders follow us disquietly to our graves.—Find out this villain, Edmund. It shall lose thee nothing. Do it carefully.—And the noble and true-hearted Kent banished! His offense, honesty! 'Tis strange.

Spoken by Edmund
Act I, scene ii

Line 5
10
15

This is the excellent foppery of the world, that when we are sick in fortune (often the surfeits of our own behavior) we make guilty of our disasters the sun, the moon, and stars, as if we were villains on necessity; fools by heavenly compulsion; knaves, thieves, and treachers by spherical predominance; drunkards, liars, and adulterers by an enforced obedience of planetary influence; and all that we are evil in, by a divine thrusting on. An admirable evasion of whoremaster man, to lay his goatish disposition on the charge of a star! My father compounded with my mother under the Dragon's tail, and my nativity was under Ursa Major, so that it follows I am rough and lecherous. Fut, I should have been that I am, had the maidenliest star in the firmament twinkled on my bastardizing.

Name: _____ Date: _____

AP-Style Essay Prompt
King Lear, Act II

Read carefully the following excerpt from Act II of *King Lear*. Then compose a well-organized essay in which you analyze Shakespeare's methods of characterization in this brief scene. Consider elements such as tone, diction, meter, and punctuation. **Time limit–40 minutes.**

Cornwall This is some fellow
Who, having been praised for bluntness, doth affect
A saucy roughness and constrains the garb
Quite from his nature. He cannot flatter, he.
5 An honest mind and plain, he must speak truth!
An they will take it, so; if not, he's plain.
These kind of knaves I know, which in this plainness
Harbor more craft and more corrupter ends
Than twenty silly-ducking observants
10 That stretch their duties nicely.

Kent
Sir, in good faith, in sincere verity,
Under th' allowance of your great aspect,
Whose influence, like the wreath of radiant fire
On flick'ring Phoebus' front—

Cornwall What mean'st by this?

Kent
15 To go out of my dialect, which you discommend so much. I know,
sir, I am no flatterer. He that beguiled you in a plain accent was a
plain knave, which for my part I will not be, though I should win your
displeasure to entreat me to 't.

Cornwall [*to Oswald*] What was th' offense you gave him?

Oswald
20 I never gave him any.
It pleased the king his master very late
To strike at me, upon his misconstruction;
When he, compact, and flattering his displeasure,
Tripped me behind; being down, insulted, railed,
25 And put upon him such a deal of man
That worthied him, got praises of the King
For him attempting who was self-subdued;
And in the fleshment of this dread exploit,
Drew on me here again.

Kent
30 None of these rogues and cowards
But Ajax is their fool.

Cornwall Fetch forth the stocks.—
You stubborn ancient knave, you reverent braggart,
We'll teach you.

Name: _____   Date: _____

AP-Style Essay Prompt
King Lear, Act III

Read carefully the two soliloquies found below, both spoken in Act III of *King Lear*. Then compose a well-organized essay in which you compare and contrast the two speakers' emotions and thoughts. Consider such elements as diction, syntax, tone, and figurative language. **Time limit–40 minutes.**

Spoken by Lear
Act III, scene iv

>   Prithee, go in thyself. Seek thine own ease.
>   This tempest will not give me leave to ponder
>   On things would hurt me more. But I'll go in.—
>   In, boy; go first.—You houseless poverty—
> 5   Nay, get thee in. I'll pray, and then I'll sleep.
>   [*Fool exits.*]
>   Poor naked wretches, wheresoe'er you are,
>   That bide the pelting of this pitiless storm,
>   How shall your houseless heads and unfed sides,
>   Your looped and windowed raggedness defend you
> 10 From seasons such as these? O, I have ta'en
>   Too little care of this. Take physic, pomp.
>   Expose thyself to feel what wretches feel,
>   That thou may'st shake the superflux to them
>   And show the heavens more just.

Spoken by Edgar
Act III, scene vii

>   When we our betters see bearing our woes,
>   We scarcely think our miseries our foes.
>   Who alone suffers suffers most i' th' mind,
>   Leaving free things and happy shows behind.
> 5   But then the mind much sufferance doth o'erskip.
>   When grief hath mates and bearing fellowship.
>   How light and portable my pain seems now
>   When that which makes me bend makes the King
>   bow!
>   He childed as I fathered. Tom, away.
> 10 Mark the high noises, and thyself bewray
>   When false opinion, whose wrong thoughts defile
>   thee,
>   In thy just proof repeals and reconciles thee.
>   What will hap more tonight, safe 'scape the King!
>   Lurk, lurk.

AP-Style Essay Prompt
King Lear, Act IV

Read carefully the following excerpt from Act IV of King Lear. Then compose a well-organized essay in which you analyze Shakespeare's portrayal and usage of irony throughout the brief scene. Consider elements such as tone, diction, and characterization. **Time limit–40 minutes.**

Edgar
    Yet better thus, and known to be contemned,
    Than still contemned and flattered. To be worst,
    The lowest and most dejected thing of fortune,
    Stands still in esperance, lives not in fear.
5   The lamentable change is from the best;
    The worst returns to laughter. Welcome, then,
    Thou unsubstantial air that I embrace.
    The wretch that thou hast blown unto the worst
    Owes nothing to thy blasts. But who comes here?

[Enter Gloucester and an old man]

10   My father, poorly led? World, world, O world,
    But that thy strange mutations make us hate thee,
    Life would not yield to age.
Old Man
    O my good lord, I have been your tenant
    And your father's tenant these fourscore years.
Gloucester
15   Away, get thee away. Good friend, begone.
    Thy comforts can do me no good at all;
    Thee they may hurt.
Old Man
              You cannot see your way.
Gloucester
    I have no way and therefore want no eyes.
    I stumbled when I saw. Full oft 'tis seen
20   Our means secure us, and our mere defects
    Prove our commodities. O dear son Edgar,
    The food of thy abusèd father's wrath,
    Might I but live to see thee in my touch,
    I'd say I had eyes again.
Old Man
              How now? Who's there?
Edgar
25   *[aside]* O gods, who is 't can say "I am at the worst"?
    I am worse than e'er I was.
Old Man
              'Tis poor mad Tom.
Edgar
    [aside] And worse I may be yet. The worst is not
    So long as we can say "This is the worst."
Old Man
    Fellow, where goest?
Gloucester
              Is it a beggar-man?
Old Man
30   Madman and beggar too.
Gloucester
    He has some reason, else he could not beg.
    I' th' last night's storm, I such a fellow saw,
    Which made me think a man a worm. My son
    Came then into my mind, and yet my mind
35   Was then scarce friends with him. I have heard more since.
    As flies to wanton boys are we to th' gods;
    They kill us for their sport.

Name: _____ Date: _____

AP-Style Essay Prompt
King Lear, Act V

Read carefully the two excerpts found below, both spoken in Act V of *King Lear*. Then compose a well-organized essay in which you compare and contrast the atmospheres and tones of both excerpts. Consider such elements as diction, punctuation, syntax, and imagery. **Time limit– 40 minutes.**

Excerpt A

Edmund
    Some officers take them away. Good guard
    Until their greater pleasures first be known
    That are to censure them.
Cordelia [*to Lear*]
                      We are not the first
Line   Who with best meaning have incurred the worst.
5   For thee, oppressèd king, I am cast down.
    Myself could else outfrown false Fortune's frown.
    Shall we not see these daughters and these sisters?
Lear
    No, no, no, no. Come, let's away to prison.
    We two alone will sing like birds i' th' cage.
10   When thou dost ask me blessing, I'll kneel down
    And ask of thee forgiveness. So we'll live,
    And pray, and sing, and tell old tales, and laugh
    At gilded butterflies, and hear poor rogues
    Talk of court news, and we'll talk with them too –
15   Who loses and who wins; who's in, who's out –
    And take upon 's the mystery of things,
    As if we were God's spies. And we'll wear out,
    In a walled prison, packs and sects of great ones
    That ebb and flow by th' moon.
Edmund
                      Take them away.

Excerpt B

Lear
    Howl, howl, howl! O, you are men of stones!
    Had I your tongues and eyes, I'd use them so
    That heaven's vault should crack. She's gone
        forever.
Line   I know when one is dead and when one lives.
5   She's dead as earth.—Lend me a looking glass.
    If that her breath will mist or stain the stone,
    Why, then she lives.
Kent
                  Is this the promised end?
Edgar
    Or image of that horror?
Albany
                  Fall and cease.
Lear
    This feather stirs. She lives. If it be so,
10   It is a chance which does redeem all sorrows
    That ever I have felt.
Kent
                  O, my good master—
Lear
    Prithee, away.
Kent
                'Tis noble Kent, your friend.
Lear
    A plague upon you, murderers, traitors all!
    I might have saved her. Now she's gone forever—
15   Cordelia, Cordelia, stay a little. Ha!
    What is 't thou sayst?—Her voice was ever soft,
    Gentle, and low, an excellent thing in woman.
    I killed the slave that was a-hanging thee.
Gentleman
    'Tis true, my lords, he did.
Lear
                  Did I not, fellow?
20   I have seen the day, with my good biting falchion
    I would have made him skip. I am old now,
    And these same crosses spoil me.

Glossary

- *alliteration:* Alliteration is the name for repeated sounds—though not necessarily letters—at the beginnings of words in proximity, such as, "Chronological queens created many kaleidoscopes."

- *allusion:* In a work of literature, an allusion is a reference to characters, events, or elements from a separate literary work. William Blake's (1794/1979b) "The Tyger," for example, alludes to the myths of Icarus and Prometheus, respectively, in lines 7–8: "On what wings dare he aspire? / What the hand dare seize the fire?"

- *analogy:* An analogy is a comparison of things by way of their similarities. If *King Lear* were a story set in the stereotypical jungle, one might analogize, then Lear himself would be an aged lion.

- *anaphora:* When Charles Dickens began *A Tale of Two Cities* (1859/1981) with "It was the best of times, it was the worst of times, it was the age of wisdom, it was the age of foolishness, it was the epoch of belief, it was the epoch of incredulity . . . " he utilized anaphora, the emphatic repetition of particular words or phrases at the beginnings of successive clauses or phrasal structures (p. 1).

- *antagonist:* The antagonist of any story is the character, institution, or force that opposes the tale's protagonist. It is a common misconception that one should be able to identify in any work of literature a singular antagonist; the collective antagonists at the end of Dickens's *A Tale of Two Cities*, for example, are the rebelling Parisian Jacquerie. Moreover, in George Orwell's *1984*, Big Brother is an institutional antagonist, while the truest antagonist to be found in William Golding's *Lord of the Flies* is the intangible, half-imagined Beast.

aphorism: Truth be told, there is little difference between aphorisms and proverbs; thus, the explanatory definition of *proverb* also applies here. Perhaps the truest distinction to be made between the two is that aphorisms tend to be didactic, whereas proverbs are perhaps more observational or philosophical in nature.

apostrophe: An apostrophe is a calling out or reaching out: to a deific force, an absent person, a deceased individual, an inanimate object, or anything else that is essentially incapable of response and/or comprehension. Two famous examples from Shakespeare are Antony's speech to the suddenly murdered Caesar in *Julius Caesar* (1599/1971)—"O, pardon me, thou bleeding piece of earth / That I am meek and gentle with these butchers!" (3.1.254–255)—and, from *Macbeth* (1606/1971), Lady Macbeth's bewildered and frustrated "Out, damned spot! Out, I say!" (5.1.32).

archaism: An archaism is something archaic (old and outdated). Both criteria must be met, so while the English language, for example, is quite old, it is not yet outdated, and thus not archaic; on the other hand, the particular words "thee" and "wherefore" are both old and outdated, so they are classifiable as archaisms.

aside: There are two different types of dramatic commentary classifiable as asides. First, moments arise in a scripted performance when a character briefly ceases speaking to others on stage and instead speaks directly to the audience, apparently the only people who can hear these comments; this type of aside is common in television sitcoms. Second, asides can be brief speeches wherein an actor on stage speaks only to himself or herself, inaudible to any other characters, as if he or she is simply thinking out loud; muttering under one's breath is a common example of this type of aside.

assonance: Assonance is the repetition of vowel sounds, as in the sentence "About the town the bough could not be found," wherein the words "About," "town," "bough," and "found" all contain identical vowel sounds, regardless of their distinct spellings.

atmosphere: Students sometimes misconstrue a piece of writing's atmosphere for the author's tone, considering them synonymous, but there is a distinction. Whereas a writer's tone demonstrates his or her emotional or intellectual attitude, as communicated by diction and syntax, the atmosphere of a piece of literature is how that writing feels *to a reader*; the terms are effectively two sides of the same coin, therefore, and it is viable to conclude that an author's tone creates atmosphere.

cacophony: The word *cacophony* describes harsh, discordant, probably loud noises, and it only is rarely applicable to textual writing, especially polished work of art. Nevertheless, sometimes authors and poets do piece together, to make a particular point, words that are cacophonous if read aloud; Charles Dickens's (1859/1981) description of the storming of the Bastille, from *A Tale of Two Cities*, is a clear example of his attempt to replicate an aural cacophony: "Flashing weapons, blazing torches, smoking wagonloads of wet straw, hard work at neighbouring barricades in all directions, shrieks, volleys, execrations, bravery without stint, boom, smash and rattle, and the furious sounding of the living sea…" (p. 200).

caesura: Caesurae occur when natural pauses arise within lines of metrical verse. They are commonly noted by a double-slash "//" which is not to be confused with the single-slash "/" indicating line breaks. Terminologists debate whether a pause for punctuation technically qualifies as a caesura, but the majority opinion is that it does, as in Polonius's advice to Laertes in *Hamlet* (1600/1970): "This above all, // to thine own self be true, / And it must follow // as the night the day / Thou canst not then be false // to any man" (1.3.78–80).

characterization, direct and indirect: Characterization is the way in which an author illuminates a character's personality; it has less to do with someone's size or physical appearance than with his or her personality. Direct characterization occurs when the audience is explicitly told something about a character, such as, "Kassandra was really friendly and energetic." Indirect characterization requires that the audience infer characteristics from someone's actions, dialogue, or decisions, or from another's description; one can infer from this sentence, for example, the student's shy, scholarly personality: "Abby always arrived early to class, but rarely contributed even a word to the goings-on of the group, though the concentration of her eyes, sometimes compounded with a contented slight smile, consistently demonstrated her intellectual engagement."

chiasmus: A rhetorical device that is analogically described as a syntactical palindrome or as "mirror-image parallelism," chiasmus is the effect of juxtaposed clauses that include a relative reversal of word order and/or structure; it is closely related to and often confused with *antimetabole*, as demonstrated in the famous incantation from *Macbeth* (1606/1971), "Fair is foul, and foul is fair" (1.1.10).

climax: The climax of any narrative is the moment of highest suspense, excitement, and drama, the last moment when it might be possible for the characters to "turn back the clock," so to speak, and return to the ways that they were at the beginning of their story. At the climax of Homer's

The Odyssey, he finally arrives home in Ithaca, sheds his beggarly disguise, thereby revealing his true identity, and enacts violent and long-overdue vengeance upon the indignant, panicked suitors.

complication: A story's complication is the plot twist that actually makes the rest of the narrative interesting, exciting, or dramatic; it commonly is confused with the inciting incident, which is the moment of time when the complication arises. In *Romeo and Juliet*, the complication is the love at first sight felt by Romeo and Juliet at the Capulets' ball, for if the lovers never actually love one another, well, then there's no rest of the story.

conflict: Generally defined as a clash or struggle between opposing characters or forces, there are six major types of literary conflict: human vs. human (as Edmund vs. Edgar), human vs. nature (as in *Lord of the Flies*), human vs. self (exemplified clearly by both Hamlet and Lady Macbeth), human vs. the supernatural (portrayed strongly in *The Odyssey*), human vs. society (as in *1984*), and human vs. technology (as in Shelley's *Frankenstein*). As a rule, the greater the variety of conflicts in a story, the more engaging it will be.

consonance: Consonance is the repetition of consonant sounds in close proximity, as in the sentence, "The archetypal arachnid attacked the critical acrobat's katydid," where the hard "k" sound is repeated six times.

contraction: Shakespeare's iambic pentameter, like all lines of metrical verse, requires a set number of syllables per line. Oftentimes, the Bard needed to say something within a line of verse, but could not do so without contracting a word into fewer syllables. "Thou think'st 'tis much that this contentious storm / Invades us to the skin. So 'tis with thee" is an example, as the contraction of the polysyllabic "it is" and "thinkest" into one syllable each retains the necessary 10 syllables in both lines (3.4.8–9).

couplet, rhyming and unrhymed: A poetic couplet is a series of two successive lines. They need not rhyme, but when they do, they are classified as a rhyming couplet: "Tyger! Tyger! burning bright / In the forests of the night" (Blake, 1789/1979b, ll. 1–2). Otherwise, a couplet is simply unrhymed: "Shall I compare thee to a summer's day? / Thou art more lovely and more temperate" (Shakespeare, Sonnet 18, 1609/1997, ll. 1–2). For an even more particular type of rhyming couplet, please see *heroic couplet*.

deification: Deification is the treatment of something, usually an abstract noun, as some kind of higher power or force, independent of and probably more powerful or influential than humans. Concepts or objects deified in this way are indicated in text by their capitalization, as is Power in Percy Shelley's poem "Mont Blanc."

- *denouement:* The *denouement* of any story, also known as the resolution, is the end result, where the characters, conflicts, and situations stand on the last page, so to speak. The word itself is French, and means "the unwinding" or "unknotting"; thus, the *denouement* of *King Lear* is that all members of the royal family are dead, as are numerous other nobles, but Edgar and Albany have resolved to take up leadership of the land.

- *dialogue:* A true dialogue is a conversation between two persons, but the word also describes any conversation among three or more individuals. Any portion of a staged drama (that is neither a monologue nor a soliloquy) is a dialogue.

- *diction:* Diction is one's choice of words. I explain to my own students the differences among vocabulary, diction, and syntax as per this three-step process: one's vocabulary is his or her treasure chest of all the words that he or she knows; diction is the process of rummaging through that chest in order to choose words to use at any given moment; and syntax is the arrangement of them in a logical way, thereby creating linguistic meaning.

- *enjambment:* Enjambment is a poetic device whereby syllables, within lines of patterned verse, run over into subsequent lines, making the lines of regularized, syllabic verse "irregular." For example, Dr. Seuss's (1960) famous couplet "I do not like green eggs and ham. / I do not like them, Sam-I-Am" is written in iambic tetrameter (p. 16). Were he to utilize enjambment, however, then the lines might read instead, "I will not eat green eggs / And ham, I will not eat them, Sam I Am." Poets often use enjambment to highlight or emphasize certain words or phrases over others.

- *enunciation:* In metrical poetry, to enunciate is to read as a separate syllable one part of a word that normally would not be read. For example, the word "martyred" is normally spoken as a two-syllable word; to enunciate the final suffix, "martyrèd," is to make it a three-syllable word. Poets commonly enunciate syllables to retain metrical regularity, and they often indicate enunciated syllables through the use of an *accent grave* ("è").

- *epiphora:* Sometimes called "epistrophe," epiphora is the repetition of words or phrases at the ends of successive clauses or phrasal structures, such as in the observation, "As plants are reborn, as the seasons are reborn, so opportunity can be reborn."

- *euphony:* The opposite of cacophony, euphony is the grouping together of harmonic, pleasing sounds. Much poetry is naturally euphonic, engen-

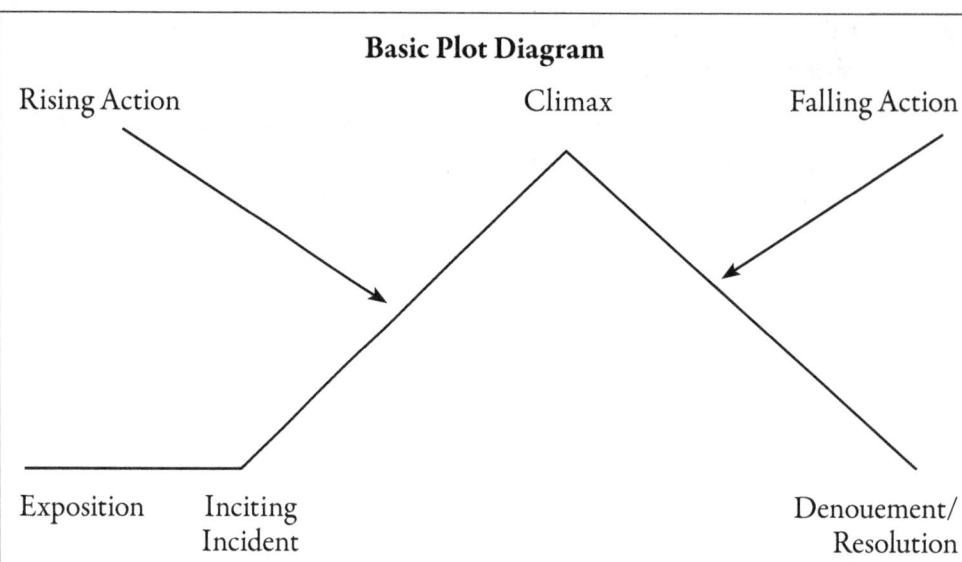

Figure 8. An illustration of any chronological narrative's plot; the progress of time is depicted horizontally, while the story's incorporation of suspense, excitement, and drama is represented vertically.

dered by such devices as alliteration and consonance, such as in these lines from Robert Frost's (1923/1969) "Nothing Gold Can Stay": "Nature's first green is gold, / Her hardest hue to hold. / Her early leaf's a flower; / But only so an hour. / Then leaf subsides to leaf" (ll. 1–5).

- *exposition:* In any chronological narrative, the exposition occurs prior to the introduction of the major complication via the inciting incident. It contains a near-complete lack of tension and excitement—its purpose, after all, is to explicate basic elements such as characters and setting—so any story's suspense rises only after its exposition's conclusion, hence the rising of the graph in Figure 8 toward the climax. The exposition of *King Lear* is quite short, consisting in the primary plot of fewer than 100 lines of text, and in the secondary and parallel plot solely of the play's first scene. Contrast this rapidity with the exposition of *Romeo and Juliet*, which lasts almost the entirety of the first act.

- *falling action:* A story's falling action occurs after the passage of its climax. For example, at the top of any rollercoaster's first hill, up which the cars go slowly and steadily, there is that last possible moment when the ride could be stopped mechanically, when the cars would cease their progress and nobody would have to speed downhill; after the passage of that last possible moment of stoppage, however, gravity takes over, and the cars must speed inevitably downward. If that last moment before gravity takes

over is the story's climax, then the speeding downhill is the falling action, during which it is literally impossible to stop the plot's action and return to the narrative's beginning unaltered.

- *figurative language:* Figurative language describes one thing in terms of something else, though not meant to be understood literally. It is the larger categorical umbrella under which metaphors, similes, analogies, allegories, symbols, and the like all fit. The statement that "It's raining cats and dogs" often is called a "figure of speech," a phrase derived from the description "figurative language."

- *foils:* Foils are, widely speaking, opposites in one or more characteristic ways; foils need not be total opposites, and they need not be characters, which are more particularly classified as "character foils." In *King Lear*, Edmund and Cordelia are both young, both nobly or royally born, and both antagonized early by their fathers, yet they qualify as foils because of their opposite temperaments and approaches to that antagonism: While Edmund insidiously plots his vengeful overthrow of Gloucester, Cordelia is the epitome of forgiveness and filial love.

- *foreshadowing:* Authors foreshadow future events when they hint or suggest at what may be to come. In *Romeo and Juliet* (1594/1992), as Juliet watches Romeo descend from her balcony in Act III, scene v, she prophetically remarks, "O God, I have an ill-divining soul! / Methinks I see thee, how thou art so low, / As one dead in the bottom of a tomb," a clear example of foreshadowing (ll. 54–56).

- *hemistich:* Among the questions most frequently asked of teachers by students new to reading Shakespeare is why the beginnings of certain dialogic lines are indented far beyond the leftmost margin, seeming in fact to begin in the middle of the page. The answer is that these indented half-lines function with the truncated lines above them to form complete units of metrical verse. In other words, in the first scene of *Macbeth* (1606/1971), when one witch asks, "Where the place?" and another responds (indented halfway into the page), "Upon the heath," these two sentences constitute one full line of trochaic tetrameter (1.1.6). A hemistich is a half-line of metrical verse, so it is accurate to say that when Shakespeare cut off one line of verse early and indented a second one below it, he was in most cases composing a full line of metrical dialogue using two hemistiches.

- *heroic couplet:* A traditional heroic couplet is formed by two lines of iambic pentameter, including masculine end rhyme. *King Lear*'s concluding sentence constitutes a heroic couplet.

- *hyperbole:* Hyperbole is extreme exaggeration, often used to emphasize the power or depth of emotions. Saying, "I'm so hungry that I could eat a horse!" is an example.

- *imagery:* Imagery is language that appeals to or enlivens one's senses, recreating sensations of sight, touch, taste, smell, and hearing. Consider this excerpt from *Lord of the Flies* as an example:

    > Toward noon, as the floods of light fell more nearly to the perpendicular, the stark colors of the morning were smoothed in pearl and opalescence; and the heat—as though the impending sun's height gave it momentum—became a blow that they ducked, running to the shade and lying there . . . " (Golding, 1954/2006, p. 58).

- *implied metaphor:* An implied metaphor is a symbolic comparison that the author does not state outright, but instead simply suggests by using words connotative of the comparison. In Coleridge's (1798/1973a) "Kubla Khan," for instance, phrases such as "oh! that deep romantic chasm" (l. 12), "woman wailing for her demon lover" (l. 16), "this earth in fast thick pants were breathing" (l. 18), and "a mighty fountain momently was forced" (l. 19) imply a sexual subtext quite distinct from Kubla's attempt to build a riverside home in Xanadu.

- *inciting incident:* The moment when a story's complication is introduced, an inciting incident follows the narrative's exposition and begins the rising action.

- *internal rhyme:* Internal rhyme occurs, apropos of its name, internally within individual lines of poetry. Consider this description of ice from line 61 of Coleridge's (1798/1973b) "The Rime of the Ancient Mariner": "It cracked and growled, and roared and howled." There is no need to look at any other lines for evidence of rhyme, since "growled" and "howled" here fit the bill within their own singular line.

- *irony:* Irony generally is defined as a difference between expectation and reality. If one walks into a restaurant, then he or she expects the presence of food, dishes, and utensils, so a restaurant devoid of these staples is an example of irony. There are also specific variants, including dramatic irony, occurring when an audience knows something that characters on stage do not, and verbal irony, whereby what a person says is different than what he or she actually means.

- *juxtaposition:* The placement of disparate objects, characters, or other elements in close proximity is called juxtaposition, the purpose of which is to highlight the differences between the two things set against one another, often identifiable as foils.

legend: A legend is a story that has some basis, however small, in historical fact, but that has grown over time. The famous story of George Washington cutting down his father's cherry tree is one such tale. The story of King Lear and his three daughters is another.

metaphor: A metaphor is a figurative comparison between two things or their qualities, made without the words "like" or "as." "Jacob is a riot!" is a simple metaphor describing a humorous student. As a metaphor does not explicate two things' *likeness*, implying by the omission of "like" or "as" their *sameness*; it is arguably more figurative than a simile.

meter: A thorough explication of poetic meter, including all of its potential variations and subtleties, requires much more space than this short entry allows, perhaps even than this entire book provides. Nevertheless, it is important not to neglect the fact that Shakespeare wrote the majority of his dialogue in metrical verse, predominantly in iambic pentameter. An iamb is a two-syllable pattern wherein the second syllable is more strongly or highly stressed than the first; its converse is the trochee. Examples of iambic words are "forget," "regard," "askew," and "around," all of which are naturally said with greater stress on the last syllable. The word "pentameter" is just a simple way to denote the fact that there are five iambs in one line of verse, as "penta-" comes from the Greek word for five. Thus, one line of iambic pentameter contains 10 syllables, the even-numbered of which are stressed; a clear example of iambic pentameter occurs in King Lear's famous response to Cordelia's honesty, "Nothing will come of nothing. Speak again" (1.1.99). It is perhaps important to note for students, moreover, that Shakespeare sometimes also composed in trochees (e.g., *Macbeth*'s three witches) and in metrical patterns other than pentameter (e.g., the fairies in *A Midsummer Night's Dream*).

metonymy: A figure of speech with which an author refers to something indirectly, metonymy references the name of something else with which it is associated; it differs from a regular symbol in its reliance on a name, not an object, as the associative link. Uncle Sam is a clear use of metonymy, for rather than being an actual person, Uncle Sam is simply a name with which the United States government is associated.

monologue: A monologue is a long speech by one person to an audience of any number of people. Any extended speech to another character qualifies. In Shakespeare, Antony's "Friends, Romans, countrymen, lend me your ears" speech from *Julius Caesar* (1599/1971) is a fine example of a monologue, as is every political speech ever made (3.2.73).

- *motif:* An object, idea, phenomenon, or circumstance that communicates figurative value or meaning in a work of literature is symbolic, but a symbol does not become a motif unless it appears repeatedly, accruing interpretability as it continues to arise in different situations. F. Scott Fitzgerald's continual emphasis on characters' (and even disembodied) eyes in *The Great Gatsby* is a fine example.

- *motivation:* Simply stated, one's motivation is the reason why he or she pursues a particular course of action; one's motivation for riding a bicycle rather than walking to a destination, for example, is probably speed.

- *paradox:* A paradox (often called a catch-22) is a close cousin of the oxymoron, yet they differ in that an oxymoron is strictly linguistic in nature, while a paradox is actually a situation, a combination of factors in life that are seemingly self-contradictory. A paradox to which many teenagers can relate concerns the quest for employment: One needs work experience to get a job, but one needs a job to gain work experience.

- *parallel plots:* Narrative plots that occur simultaneously in "real time" in a work of literature, though their circumstances are separate, are called parallel plots. For most of *A Tale of Two Cities*, for example, the narrative line occurring in England is separate from, but concurrent with, the events happening in France.

- *parallelism:* Parallelism is a word that describes the construction of a piece of writing in some kind of repetitive or otherwise logically structured way. Compare-and-contrast essays are generally written utilizing parallelism, for they tend to alternate extendedly and repetitively between two considered items.

- *personification:* When a writer attributes human characteristics to inhuman things, it is called *personification*. A very simple example is an "angry storm."

- *prose:* The opposite of verse, prose is most easily described as "normal" sentence-and-paragraph-style writing; it contains no clearly intentional metrical or otherwise syllabic structure, and its lines are not restrained by numbers of syllables. Novels and newspapers are written in prose, while poems are written in verse.

- *protagonist:* The protagonist of any narrative is the main character around whom the story revolves. I like to think of the protagonist as the central hub around which all of the spokes of a story's wheel rotate; remove that hub from the plot, and the story simply falls apart. By this calculus, Charles Dickens explicitly identifies Lucie Manette-Darnay, rather than any of his male characters who are granted considerably more dialogue, as the protagonist of *A Tale of Two Cities*; if Lucie were not present, then the story's concentration of characters, and thus its plot, would simply never cohere.

- *proverb:* A proverb is an old, common saying that makes a wise observation about life. "A bird in the hand is worth two in the bush" is an English proverb; ironically enough, many of Shakespeare's more quotable observations about life have actually reached proverb status, such as King Claudius's poignant observation in *Hamlet* (1600/1970), "When sorrows come, they come not single spies, / But in battalions" (4.5.78–79), which actually echoes another, much more common, proverb: "When it rains, it pours."

- *pun:* A pun is a play on like-sounding, but distinctly meaningful words (homonyms). Much of the sexual humor extant in *Romeo and Juliet* (1594/1992) arises from characters' punning, as does its introductory banter concerning coals, choler, and colliers (1.1).

- *refrain:* Anything that is repeated or returned to constantly can be called a refrain. If asked, many teenagers are likely to identify daily refrains of showering and brushing their teeth, weekly refrains of Saturday sleep-ins, monthly refrains of full and new moons, and annual refrains of holiday celebrations. A strong example of a literary refrain is F. Scott Fitzgerald's continued mention of Daisy Buchanan's green light in *The Great Gatsby*.

- *rhetorical question:* A rhetorical question is one to which the inquirer actually expects no response. "What's up?" is a standard rhetorical question, often asked in passing, as is the affixation of "you know?" at the ends of sentences.

- *rhyme, feminine and masculine:* Children learn about rhyme as they learn to talk and read. Few students, however, recognize the difference between the two major types of rhyme. Feminine rhyme occurs when multiple syllables at the ends of words are rhymed, such as "toaster" and "roaster," or "pigeon" and "religion." Masculine rhyme, by contrast, occurs when only the last syllable shared by words is rhymed, such as "principal" and "recital," or "Shakespeare" and "dear." The effect of feminine rhyme often is faster-paced and/or more comedic than masculine rhyme, which is simpler and ostensibly less contrived.

- *rhyme scheme:* A poem or dramatic excerpt's rhyme scheme is the pattern created by an author's use of end rhyme. The first rhyme used in any pattern is labeled rhyme A, the second rhyme used, regardless of the line on which it arises, is labeled rhyme B, and so on. Thus, poems written strictly in rhyming couplets utilize a rhyme scheme labeled AABBCC, while lines of alternating rhyme, such as the first three quatrains of any Shakespearean sonnet, are classifiable according to an ABAB scheme. Not all verse, of course, rhymes according to regularized schemes, such as blank verse, which by definition incorporates no rhyme scheme.

- *rising action:* The rising action of any plot occurs after the inciting incident's introduction of the main complication. This name, rising action, effectively describes the period of any story between its inciting incident and climax, wherein tension, drama, and action supposedly rise parallel to the progress of time. In *Macbeth*, every event that occurs following Macbeth's midnight murder of King Duncan qualifies as part of the rising action, leading the power-hungry, paranoid Scotsman ultimately and inevitably to his climactic confrontation with Macduff.

- *setting:* Details regarding where and when a story takes place contribute to that story's setting. *Romeo and Juliet* is set in Verona, Italy, circa 1590, while the setting of *The Great Gatsby* is New York City during the Roaring Twenties. Not all narratives require clearly distinguishable settings (e.g., *Waiting for Godot*), and it is certainly possible for a story to have more than one setting.

- *simile:* Like a metaphor, a simile is a figurative comparison between two things or their qualities, although a simile makes that comparison more explicit, incorporating the comparative words "like" or "as." For example, in describing students, I might say that "Lana is as sharp as a tack," while "Nate has a memory like a steel trap."

- *slant rhyme:* Slant rhyme, also known as approximate rhyme, occurs when authors attempt to rhyme words that, well, simply do not rhyme exactly. "What immortal hand or eye / Could frame thy fearful symmetry?" Blake (1789/1979b) asks in an infamous example of slant rhyme from "The Tyger" (ll. 3–4). Readers generally are supposed to overlook slant rhyme's inexactness, granting the poet or author artistic license for the sake of making his or her literary point.

- *soliloquy:* Commonly confused with monologue, a soliloquy is a long speech wherein a person speaks to no one but himself or herself, thinking privately but aloud. The two most famous soliloquies in all of Shakespeare occur in *Romeo and Juliet*'s balcony scene and *Hamlet* (1600/1970)—"To be or not to be—that is the question" (3.1.56). Edmund's "Thou, Nature, art my goddess" soliloquy is perhaps a close third (1.2.1).

- *sonnet, Shakespearean or English:* My experience is that high school students somehow pick up the misconception that Shakespeare "invented" the sonnet. Although he may have perfected it, depending on one's literary tastes, the poetic form itself arose long before the Bard ever took his first breath. Moreover, the form known as the Shakespearean or English sonnet, written in iambic pentameter and incorporating the rhyme scheme ABABCDCDEFEFGG, is far from the only style extant; technically, all that a poet requires in order to pen a sonnet is 14 lines, a rhyme scheme, and a regularized metrical pattern. Thus, there are potentially as many sonnet forms in the world as there are creative sonneteers. Nevertheless, Shakespeare's is by far the most recognizable and common type of sonnet in English.

stage directions: Stage directions in most Shakespearean plays are scant, which is one reason why directors and actors so love the creative license afforded them by the Bard; *King Lear*, relative to other Shakespearean plays, actually has quite a few stage directions. In all of his dramas they serve the same purposes that they do in other plays—to direct actors' movements and emotions, as well as to describe stage settings. The most famous stage direction in all of Shakespeare occurs in Act III, scene iii of *The Winter's Tale* (1611/1971), where Antigonus is directed to "*Exit, pursued by a bear.*"

suspense: Everything from fearful anxiety and apprehension to pleasant excitement, suspense is the quality felt by a reader or audience that is engaged in a narrative, unknowingly anticipating its outcome. We can imagine the suspense that *King Lear*'s first audiences felt as the unnamed soldier rushes to the castle on Edmund and Edgar's joint command to save Cordelia's life in Act V, scene iii.

synecdoche: Synecdoche is a figure of speech whereby something is identified only by mention of a smaller part of itself. "I soared into the air as the wheels left the runway" is an example of synecdoche used to describe an airplane's departure, for while the entire aircraft became airborne, only its wheels are mentioned.

syntax: The placement of words in a logical order to create communicative meaning, syntax follows diction as the next step in the linguistic process; once one has chosen the words "dog," "ran," "my," "door," "to," and "the," they need to be placed syntactically into a sensible order to communicate meaning.

theme: A literary theme is a philosophical idea, conjecture, or belief that is communicated through a work's dialogue, events, circumstances, or outcome. The difficulty of love (not just the abstract concept of love itself) is a clear theme in *Romeo and Juliet*.

- *tone:* The word *tone* usually is associated with speaking voice, but a person's tone can come across on paper just as easily as it can face-to-face. What someone's tone illuminates is his or her attitude toward a subject; on the printed page, that attitude is communicated via a writer's choice of words. One author's description of the "banal, anachronistically cute soiree" differs significantly from another's "enjoyably lighthearted picnic," though both writers may be describing the same event, toward which their attitudes obviously differ.

- *verse, blank and rhymed:* Verse is a synonym for metrical poetry (i.e., poetic lines that adhere strictly to patterns of meter). Because all verse, therefore, must by definition contain meter, the only issue is whether that verse rhymes (rhymed verse) or does not rhyme (blank verse). Percy Shelley's "Ozymandias" is an example of a near-sonnet written in blank verse, for while it contains 14 lines and is written in iambic pentameter, there is no regularized rhyme scheme to be found.

Appendix A

Notations on *King Lear*'s Literary Devices

	ACT I, SCENE 1 [Enter KENT, GLOUCESTER, and EDMUND]	The play's exposition, in which we are introduced to characters, setting, and background information (like these points concerning Edmund and Gloucester's relationship) begins immediately.
The reference to the Duke of Cornwall simply as "Cornwall" is an example of metonymy (in this case, referring to people as the places with which they are associated), as are later references to France, Burgundy, and Gloucester himself.	**KENT** I thought the king had more affected the Duke of Albany than Cornwall. **GLOUCESTER** It did always seem so to us, but now in the division of the kingdom, it appears not which of the dukes he values most, for equalities are so weighed that curiosity in neither can make choice of either's moiety. **KENT** Is not this your son, my lord? **GLOUCESTER** His breeding, sir, hath been at my charge. I have so often blushed to acknowledge him that now I am brazed to 't.	
Gloucester here puns upon Kent's usage of "conceive," playing with its double meaning.	**KENT** I cannot conceive you. **GLOUCESTER** Sir, this young fellow's mother could, whereupon she grew round-wombed, and had indeed, sir, a son for her cradle ere she had a husband for her bed. Do you smell a fault?	A background conflict (that Edmund is unloved) in the Edmund-Edgar-Gloucester parallel plot is here revealed.
In these comments to Kent, Gloucester here characterizes himself indirectly as insensitive, unloving, cruel, irresponsible, and perhaps foolish.	**KENT** I cannot wish the fault undone, the issue of it being so proper. **GLOUCESTER** But I have, sir, a son by order of law, some year elder than this, who yet is no dearer in my account. Though this knave came something saucily to the world before he was sent for, yet was his mother fair, there was good sport at his making, and the whoreson must be acknowledged.—Do you know this noble gentleman, Edmund? **EDMUND** No, my lord. **GLOUCESTER** My lord of Kent. Remember him here-after as my honorable friend. **EDMUND** My services to your lordship. **KENT** I must love you and sue to know you better. **EDMUND** Sir, I shall study deserving.	Gloucester's comparison of Edmund and Edgar establishes them immediately as foils.

| | **GLOUCESTER**
 He hath been out nine years, and away he shall again. *[Sennet.]*
 The king is coming.

 [Enter KING LEAR, CORNWALL, ALBANY, GONERIL, REGAN, CORDELIA, and Attendants]

 LEAR
 Attend the lords of France and Burgundy, Gloucester.
 GLOUCESTER
 I shall, my lord.

 [Exit GLOUCESTER and EDMUND] | At the entrance of the royal court, Shakespeare switches his dialogue from prose to verse, probably to indicate increased formality. |
| Lear's usage of the royal "we" here and elsewhere is essentially inverted synecdoche.

 "Our daughters' several dowers... strife" is an example of alliteration, creating euphony.

 This speech, as is much of the dialogue at the beginning of the play, is written in blank verse (i.e., solemnly formal).

 Goneril here delivers a monologue explaining her love, which she claims to be | **LEAR**
 Meantime we shall express our darker purpose.—
 Give me the map there.   *[He is handed a map.]*
       Know that we have divided
 In three our kingdom, and 'tis our fast intent
 To shake all cares and business from our age,
 Conferring them on younger strengths, while we
 Unburdened crawl toward death. Our son of Cornwall,
 And you, our no less loving son of Albany,
 We have this hour a constant will to publish
 Our daughters' several dowers, that future strife
 May be prevented now.
 The two great princes, France and Burgundy,
 Great rivals in our youngest daughter's love,
 Long in our court have made their amorous sojourn,
 And here are to be answer'd. Tell me, my daughters,—
 Since now we will divest us both of rule,
 Interest of territory, cares of state,—
 Which of you shall we say doth love us most,
 That we our largest bounty may extend
 Where nature doth with merit challenge. Goneril,
 Our eldest-born, speak first.
 GONERIL
 Sir, I love you more than word can wield the matter,
 Dearer than eyesight, space, and liberty,
 Beyond what can be valued, rich or rare, | Lear's mention of a "darker purpose" perhaps constitutes foreshadowing.

 The prevalence of caesurae in Lear's opening monologue communicates both the solemn tension of the circumstance and Lear's venerable age.

 Lear's decision to "divest [himself] of rule... territory [and] cares of state" serves as the complication of the drama's central plot. His request for his daughters' flattery in exchange for wealth and power is its inciting incident, signaling the end of the play's exposition. |

Appendix A: Notations on King Lear's Literary Devices   203

"more than word can wield" … a clear paradox.	No less than life, with grace, health, beauty, honor; As much as child e'er loved, or father found; A love that makes breath poor, and speech unable. Beyond all manner of so much I love you.	
Rhetorical questions are common occurrences in Shakespearean asides.	**CORDELIA** *[Aside]* What shall Cordelia speak? Love, and be silent. **LEAR** *[Pointing to the map]*	
Lear's description of Goneril's inheritance includes much euphonic consonance and assonance.	Of all these bounds, even from this line to this, With shadowy forests and with champains riched, With plenteous rivers and wide-skirted meads, We make thee lady. To thine and Albany's issue Be this perpetual.— What says our second daughter, Our dearest Regan, wife of Cornwall? Speak. **REGAN**	
	I am made of that self mettle as my sister And prize me at her worth. In my true heart I find she names my very deed of love; Only she comes too short, that I profess Myself an enemy to all other joys Which the most precious square of sense possesses, And find I am alone felicitate In your dear Highness' love.	Indirect, but clear, characterization arises from Goneril and Regan's unhesitating engagement in flattery, juxtaposed against Cordelia's anguished statements that she cannot do so, her love for Lear being "more ponderous than [her] tongue."
The break between Regan's monologue and Cordelia's aside is a clear use of hemistiches.	**CORDELIA** *[Aside]* Then poor Cordelia! And yet not so, since I am sure my love's More ponderous than my tongue. **LEAR**	
	To thee and thine hereditary ever Remain this ample third of our fair kingdom, No less in space, validity, and pleasure Than that conferr'd on Goneril.—Now, our joy,	In lovingly addressing his "joy," Cordelia, Lear here establishes her as a foil to her sisters, implying an underlying antagonism among the three.
Lear's description of vines' and milk's "striv[ing]" qualifies as personification.	Although our last and least, to whose young love The vines of France and milk of Burgundy Strive to be interested, what can you say to draw A third more opulent than your sisters'? Speak. **CORDELIA**	
In contrast to the preceding iambic verse, the startlingly terse succession of these lines	Nothing, my lord. **LEAR** Nothing?	The word "nothing" and the "infertility" of nothingness are here introduced; they act as thematic refrains throughout the play.

indicates a sudden shift in the scene's tone.	**CORDELIA** Nothing. **LEAR** Nothing will come of nothing. Speak again.	
Cordelia's "unhappy … heave … heart" qualifies as consonance.	**CORDELIA** Unhappy that I am, I cannot heave My heart into my mouth. I love your Majesty According to my bond, no more nor less. **LEAR** How, how, Cordelia? Mend your speech a little, Lest you may mar your fortunes.	The irony of Cordelia's statement is that her love "according [strictly and solely] to [her] bond" is the strongest and truest love in the play; her own words here thus qualify as both verbal and situational irony.
Cordelia's description of their relationship—"begot me, bred me, loved me … obey you, love you, and most honor you"—is largely an example of parallelism and particularly an example of epiphora.	**CORDELIA** Good my lord, You have begot me, bred me, loved me. I return those duties back as are right fit: Obey you, love you, and most honor you. Why have my sisters husbands if they say They love you all? Haply, when I shall wed, That lord whose hand must take my plight shall carry Half my love with him, half my care and duty. Sure I shall never marry like my sisters, To love my father all. **LEAR** But goes thy heart with this? **CORDELIA** Ay, my good lord. **LEAR** So young and so untender? **CORDELIA** So young, my lord, and true.	
"By all the operations of the orbs" is among the most assonant lines in the entire script, followed immediately by the alliterative "paternal care, / Propinquity, and property."	**LEAR** Let it be so. Thy truth, then, be thy dower, For by the sacred radiance of the sun, The mysteries of Hecate and the night, By all the operation of the orbs From whom we do exist and cease to be, Here I disclaim all my paternal care, Propinquity, and property of blood, And as a stranger to my heart and me Hold thee from this forever. The barbarous Scythian, Or he that makes his generation messes	Lear's allusions to the sun's "sacred radiance," to Hecate, and to "the orbs" that govern human life imply his religious paganism.

Appendix A: Notations on King Lear's Literary Devices

	To gorge his appetite, shall to my bosom Be as well neighbored, pitied, and relieved As thou my sometime daughter. **KENT** Good my liege— **LEAR**	Lear's disowning of Cordelia recalls Gloucester's dismissal of his own bonds with Edmund, establishing the two children as parallel characters.
"Come not between the dragon and his wrath"... a clear metaphor and a probably wise aphorism.	Peace, Kent. Come not between the dragon and his wrath. I loved her most, and thought to set my rest On her kind nursery. *[To CORDELIA.]* Hence, and avoid my sight!— So be my grave my peace, as here I give Her father's heart from her.—Call France. Who stirs?	
Lear angrily personifies pride as a conjugal partner.	Call Burgundy. *[Attendant exits.]* Cornwall and Albany, With my two daughters' dowers digest the third. Let pride, which she calls plainness, marry her. I do invest you jointly with my power,	
Shakespeare's shortening of "the addition" to the two-syllable "th' addition" is an example of contraction, while the final syllable in "Belovèd" is an example of enunciation; in both cases, his purpose is to maintain metrical regularity.	Preeminence, and all the large effects That troop with majesty. Ourself by monthly course, With reservation of an hundred knights By you to be sustained, shall our abode Make with you by due turn. Only we shall retain The name, and all th' addition to a king. The sway, revenue, execution of the rest, Belovèd sons, be yours, which to confirm, This coronet part between you.	The moment of Lear's abdication of power both establishes a paradox (that he wants to be called King, but not actually be a king) and dramatic irony, as the audience may suspect that his plan will surely fall through.
	[Giving the crown.] **KENT** Royal Lear, Whom I have ever honored as my king, Loved as my father, as my master followed, As my great patron thought on in my prayers— **LEAR**	
Lear threatens with figurative language.	The bow is bent and drawn. Make from the shaft. **KENT**	
Kent counters figuratively, effectively aiding the analogy.	Let it fall rather, though the fork invade The region of my heart. Be Kent unmannerly When Lear is mad. What wilt thou do, old man? Think'st thou that duty shall have dread to speak	

206   *King Lear*

Power bowing to flattery is another example of personification.	When power to flattery bows? To plainness honor's bound When majesty falls to folly. Reverse thy state, And in thy best consideration check This hideous rashness. Answer my life my judgment, Thy youngest daughter does not love thee least, Nor are those empty-hearted whose low sounds Reverb no hollowness.	
Kent here alludes to the proverb "Empty vessels have the loudest sounds."	**LEAR** Kent, on thy life, no more. **KENT**	
In a simile, Kent casts himself as a pawn.	My life I never held but as a pawn To wage against thine enemies, nor fear to lose it, Thy safety being motive. **LEAR** Out of my sight! **KENT** See better, Lear, and let me still remain The true blank of thine eye. **LEAR** Now, by Apollo— **KENT**	Shakespeare introduces a motif, that of misleading sight and reliance on others for true insight.
At this point, metrical verse dissolves into prose shouting, a dialogic device to convey terse, heated atmosphere.	Now, by Apollo, king, Thou swear'st thy gods in vain. **LEAR** O, vassal! Miscreant! *[Grabbing his sword.]* **ALBANY, CORNWALL** Dear sir, forbear. **KENT** Kill thy physician, and thy fee bestow Upon the foul disease. Revoke thy gift, Or whilst I can vent clamour from my throat, I'll tell thee thou dost evil. **LEAR** Hear me, recreant; on thine allegiance, hear me!	
"… to make us break" qualifies as internal rhyme.	That thou hast sought to make us break our vows— Which we durst never yet—and with strained pride To come betwixt our sentence and our power, Which nor our nature nor our place can bear,	Lear's banishment of Kent for his truthfulness both demonstrates the king's

Appendix A: Notations on King Lear's Literary Devices

	Our potency made good, take thy reward: / Five days we do allot thee for provision / To shield thee from disasters of the world, / And on the sixth to turn thy hated back / Upon our kingdom. If on the tenth day following / Thy banished trunk be found in our dominions, / The moment is thy death. Away! By Jupiter, / This shall not be revoked.	chosen ignorance of reality, the wrongness of which he shall later recognize on the heath, and commences the central plot's rising action.
"Fare thee well, king. Sith thus thou…" includes much euphonic consonance.	**KENT** / Fare thee well, king. Sith thus thou wilt appear, / Freedom lives hence, and banishment is here.	
	[To CORDELIA]	Kent's remarks, firstly to Cordelia and then to Goneril and Regan, juxtapose the former and latter as foils; he also explicitly allies himself here with Cordelia.
	The gods to their dear shelter take thee, maid, / That justly think'st and hast most rightly said.	
	[To GONERIL and REGAN]	
In two successive rhyming couplets, Kent's pairing of "approve" and "love" qualifies as approximate rhyme (i.e., slant rhyme); his rhyming of "adieu" and "new" creates masculine rhyme.	And your large speeches may your deeds approve, / That good effects may spring from words of love.— / Thus Kent, O princes, bids you all adieu. / He'll shape his old course in a country new.	
	[Exits] / *[Flourish. Enter GLOUCESTER, with FRANCE, BURGUNDY, and Attendants]*	
	GLOUCESTER / Here's France and Burgundy, my noble lord.	
Lear's initial address to Burgundy includes much consonance, particularly with a somewhat cacophonous repetition of "r."	**LEAR** / My lord of Burgundy, / We first address toward you, who with this king / Hath rivaled for our daughter. What in the least / Will you require in present dower with her, / Or cease your quest of love?	
	BURGUNDY / Most royal Majesty, / I crave no more than hath your Highness offered, / Nor will you tender less.	

King Lear

	LEAR	
	Right noble Burgundy,	
	When she was dear to us, we did hold her so,	
	But now her price is fallen. Sir, there she stands.	
	If aught within that little seeming substance,	Per Lear's earlier prediction
	Or all of it, with our displeasure pieced	("Nothing will come of
	And nothing more, may fitly like your Grace,	nothing"), his own offer
	She's there, and she is yours.	of "nothing" to Burgundy
	BURGUNDY	produces "no answer"; the
	I know no answer.	theme is thus reestablished.
	LEAR	
Lear here directly, albeit	Will you, with those infirmities she owes,	
incorrectly, characterizes	Unfriended, new-adopted to our hate,	
Cordelia as his antagonist.	Dowered with our curse and strangered with our oath,	
	Take her or leave her?	
	BURGUNDY	
	Pardon me, royal sir,	
	Election makes not up in such conditions.	
	LEAR	
	Then leave her, sir, for, by the power that made me	
	I tell you all her wealth.—	
	[To FRANCE]	
	For you, great king,	
	I would not from your love make such a stray	
	To match you where I hate. Therefore beseech you	
	T' avert your liking a more worthier way	Shakespeare's capitalization of
	Than on a wretch whom Nature is ashamed	"Nature" indicates Lear's own
	Almost t' acknowledge hers.	deification of it/her, implying
	FRANCE	the regent's pagan beliefs.
	This is most strange,	
In his rapid succession of	That she whom even but now was your best object,	
"t," "m," and "f" sounds,	The argument of your praise, balm of your age,	
France speaks with much	The best, the dearest, should in this trice of time	
consonance.	Commit a thing so monstrous to dismantle	
	So many folds of favor. Sure her offense	
	Must be of such unnatural degree	
	That monsters it, or your forevouched affection	
	Fall into taint; which to believe of her	

	Must be a faith that reason without miracle Should never plant in me. **CORDELIA** 　　*[To LEAR]* I yet beseech your Majesty—	
Cordelia's syntax ("If for I want…") is archaic.	If for I want that glib and oily art To speak and purpose not, since what I well intend I'll do't before I speak— that you make known It is no vicious blot, murder, or foulness, No unchaste action or dishonored step That hath deprived me of your grace and favor, But even for want of that for which I am richer: A still-soliciting eye and such a tongue That I am glad I have not, though not to have it Hath lost me in your liking. **LEAR** 　　　　　　　　　Better thou Hadst not been born than not t' have pleased me better.	Cordelia here describes herself as "for want of that for which I am richer," furthering the motif of nothingness by suggesting that characters *with nothing* are somehow richer than characters who *have* (e.g., wealth, plots).
Lear's inversion of "Better … not been … not t' have … better" is an example of chiasmus, the syntactical equivalent of a palindrome. In an aside, France asks a rhetorical question, philosophical in nature. His description of Cordelia is of course a clear metaphor.	**FRANCE** Is it but this—a tardiness in nature Which often leaves the history unspoke That it intends to do?—My lord of Burgundy, What say you to the lady? Love's not love When it is mingled with regard that stands Aloof from th' entire point. Will you have her? She is herself a dowry. **BURGUNDY** 　　*[To LEAR]*　　Royal king, Give but that portion which yourself proposed, And here I take Cordelia by the hand, Duchess of Burgundy. **LEAR** Nothing. I have sworn. I am firm. **BURGUNDY** 　　　　　　　　　　　　*[To CORDELIA]* I am sorry, then, you have so lost a father That you must lose a husband. **CORDELIA** 　　　　　　　　Peace be with Burgundy. Since that respect and fortunes are his love, I shall not be his wife.	Again the word "nothing" arises as Lear's offer. Burgundy's response to Cordelia indicates that not only will "nothing … come of nothing," but also that nothingness leads to the loss of what one already has.

Using anaphora with his repetition of "most," France here describes Cordelia using a series of successive paradoxes.
 	
France's apostrophe to the "gods" recalls Kent's earlier references to plural gods, in contrast to Lear's naming of several deities individually; this may be circumstantial, but in a sense France is thus religiously allied with Kent against Lear.
 	
Using feminine rhyme, Lear ends this rhyming couplet with "begone" and "benison."
 	
Cordelia's parting couplet rhymes and is written in perfect iambic pentameter, thus qualifying as a traditional heroic couplet.
	FRANCE
	  Fairest Cordelia, that art most rich, being poor;
	  Most choice, forsaken; and most loved, despised,
	  Thee and thy virtues here I seize upon,
	  Be it lawful I take up what's cast away.
	  Gods, gods! 'Tis strange that from their cold'st neglect
	  My love should kindle to inflamed respect.—
	  Thy dowerless daughter, king, thrown to my chance,
	  Is queen of us, of ours, and our fair France.
	  Not all the dukes of wat'rish Burgundy
	  Can buy this unprized precious maid of me.—
	  Bid them farewell, Cordelia, though unkind.
	  Thou losest here a better where to find.
	LEAR
	  Thou hast her, France. Let her be thine, for we
	  Have no such daughter, nor shall ever see
	  That face of hers again.
	                            [To CORDELIA]
	              Therefore begone
	  Without our grace, our love, our benison.—
	  Come, noble Burgundy.
	
	      [Flourish. Exit all but FRANCE, CORDELIA,
	                  GONERIL, and REGAN]
	
	FRANCE
	  Bid farewell to your sisters.
	CORDELIA
	  The jewels of our father, with washed eyes
	  Cordelia leaves you. I know you what you are,
	  And like a sister am most loath to call
	  Your faults as they are named. Love well our father.
	  To your professèd bosoms I commit him;
	  But yet, alas, stood I within his grace,
	  I would prefer him to a better place.
	  So farewell to you both.
	REGAN
	  Prescribe not us our duty.
	GONERIL
	                Let your study
	  Be to content your lord, who hath received you
		France here resumes the paradox that to be poor in some sense is to be rich; this point may allude indirectly to the Biblical idea (in contrast to the characters' paganism) of the last being first.
		
		France here rhymes internally "buy" and "unprized," as well as "here" and "where."
		
		Cordelia confronts her sisters, using direct—albeit vague—characterization of them.

Appendix A: Notations on King Lear's Literary Devices

	At Fortune's alms. You have obedience scanted / And well are worth the want that you have wanted. **CORDELIA** / Time shall unfold what plighted cunning hides, / Who covers faults at last with shame derides. / Well may you prosper. **FRANCE** / Come, my fair Cordelia. *[Exit FRANCE and CORDELIA]*	Goneril and Cordelia trade rhyming couplets, picking up the pace and/or heating the tone of dialogic delivery.
Goneril's "changes ... age is" qualifies as internal feminine rhyme. Goneril and Regan describe their father using direct characterization. Regan's supposal of "unconstant" behavior is an example of foreshadowing.	**GONERIL** / Sister, it is not little I have to say of what most nearly appertains to us both. I think our father will hence tonight. **REGAN** / That's most certain, and with you; next month with us. **GONERIL** / You see how full of changes his age is; the observation we have made of it hath not been little. He always loved our sister most, and with what poor judgment he hath now cast her off appears too grossly. **REGAN** / 'Tis the infirmity of his age. Yet he hath ever but slenderly known himself. **GONERIL** / The best and soundest of his time hath been but rash. Then must we look from his age to receive not alone the imperfections of long-engraffed condition, but therewithal the unruly waywardness that infirm and choleric years bring with them. **REGAN** / Such unconstant starts are we like to have from him as this of Kent's banishment. **GONERIL** / There is further compliment of leave-taking between France and him. Pray you, let us sit together. If our father carry authority with such disposition as he bears, this last surrender of his will but offend us. **REGAN** / We shall further think of it. **GONERIL** / We must do something, and i' th' heat.	Upon Cordelia's departure, Goneril and Regan speak to each other in prose, which both establishes an allusive comparison between themselves and Gloucester (i.e., earlier) and indicates the informality, and thus suspiciousness, of their conversation. Wholly, Regan and Cordelia's conversation establishes their own characters firmly and foreshadows their imminent betrayal of Lear "i' th' heat" (i.e., quickly).

[They exit.]

SCENE 2

[Enter EDMUND]

Edmund speaks to himself here in a quite famous soliloquy, written for the most part in iambic blank verse.	Edmund apostrophizes deified "Nature," characterizing himself as a pagan and a believer in the victory of the strong over the weak.
He uses rhetorical questions to imply bitter incredulity.	
Edmund's use of "brand" establishes an implied metaphor between bastards and animals.	The clipped repetition of "base" and "bastard" communicates Edmund's infuriated tone.
Edmund here apostrophizes Edgar.	
He once again reverts, in his apostrophe, to the deific, albeit in the form of plural gods, in contrast to the earlier "Nature."	This soliloquy, and in it Edmund's communication of his plot to hoodwink Gloucester and his motivation for doing so, serves as the parallel plot's inciting incident.

EDMUND
Thou, Nature, art my goddess. To thy law
My services are bound. Wherefore should I
Stand in the plague of custom, and permit
The curiosity of nations to deprive me
For that I am some twelve or fourteen moonshines
Lag of a brother? Why "bastard"? Wherefore "base"?
When my dimensions are as well compact,
My mind as generous and my shape as true
As honest madam's issue? Why brand they us
With "base," with "baseness," "bastardy," "base," "base,"
Who, in the lusty stealth of nature, take
More composition and fierce quality
Than doth within a dull, stale, tired bed
Go to th' creating a whole tribe of fops
Got 'tween asleep and wake? Well then,
Legitimate Edgar, I must have your land.
Our father's love is to the bastard Edmund
As to th' legitimate. Fine word, "legitimate."
Well, my legitimate, if this letter speed
And my invention thrive, Edmund the base
Shall top th' legitimate. I grow, I prosper.
Now, gods, stand up for bastards!

[Enter GLOUCESTER]

GLOUCESTER
Kent banished thus? And France in choler parted?
And the King gone tonight, prescribed his power,
Confined to exhibition? All this done
Upon the gad?—Edmund, how now? What news?

EDMUND
So please your Lordship, none.

[Putting the letter in his pocket]

When he enters, Gloucester asks himself disbelievingly rhetorical questions in an iambic pentameter (i.e., blank verse) aside, but reverts to prose upon speaking with Edmund.

Appendix A: Notations on King Lear's Literary Devices

	GLOUCESTER Why so earnestly seek you to put up that letter? **EDMUND** I know no news, my lord. **GLOUCESTER** What paper were you reading? **EDMUND** Nothing, my lord. **GLOUCESTER** No? What needed then that terrible dispatch of it into your pocket? The quality of nothing hath not such need to hide itself. Let's see. Come, if it be nothing, I shall not need spectacles. **EDMUND** I beseech you, sir, pardon me. It is a letter from my brother that I have not all o'erread; and for so much as I have perused, I find it not fit for your o'erlooking. **GLOUCESTER** Give me the letter, sir. **EDMUND** I shall offend either to detain or give it. The contents, as in part I understand them, are to blame. **GLOUCESTER** Let's see, let's see.	The "nothing" refrain again arises, this time in the drama's parallel plot.
The secondary plot's complication arises with the commencement of Edmund's insidious plot.		Shakespeare reasserts Kent's earlier proposition that physical sight is misleading; nevertheless, Gloucester insists, "Let's see, let's see."

References

Adelman, J. (1992). *Suffocating mothers: Fantasies of maternal origin in Shakespeare's plays,* Hamlet *to* The Tempest. New York, NY: Routledge.

Auden, W. H. (1962). Musée de Beaux Arts. In O. Williams & E. Honig (Eds.), *The mentor book of major American poets* (p. 507). New York, NY: The New American Library. (Original work written 1938)

Blake, W. (1979a). Proverbs of hell. In M. L. Johnson & J. E. Grant (Eds.), *Blake's poetry and designs* (pp. 89–91). New York, NY: Norton. (Original work written 1790)

Blake, W. (1979b). The Tyger. In M. L. Johnson & J. E. Grant (Eds.), *Blake's poetry and designs* (pp. 29–30). New York, NY: Norton. (Original work published 1794)

Blau, S. (2003). *The literature workshop.* Portsmouth, NH: Heinemann.

Bloom, H. (1998). *Shakespeare: The invention of the human.* New York, NY: Riverhead Books.

Boose, L. E. (2008). The father and the bride in Shakespeare. In G. Ioppolo (Ed.), *King Lear: A Norton critical edition* (pp. 194–209). New York, NY: Norton. (Original work published 1982)

Booth, S. (1987). On the greatness of *King Lear.* In H. Bloom (Ed.), *Modern critical interpretations: William Shakespeare's* King Lear (pp. 57–70). New York, NY: Chelsea House Publishers. (Original work published 1983)

Boyce, C. (1990). *Shakespeare A to Z: The essential reference to his plays, his poems, his life and times, and more.* New York, NY: Laurel.

Bradley, A. C. (1904). *Shakespearean tragedy: Lectures on* Hamlet, Othello, King Lear, Macbeth. London, England: Macmillan.

Brook, P. (1968). *The empty space*. New York, NY: Atheneum.

Cavell, S. (2002). *Must we mean what we say?: A book of essays* (2nd ed.). New York, NY: Cambridge University Press.

Chaucer, G. (1987). The Miller's tale. In L. D. Benson (Ed.), *The Riverside Chaucer* (3rd ed., pp. 68–77). Boston, MA: Houghton Mifflin. (Original work written circa 1387)

Coleridge, S. T. (1973a). Kubla Khan. In H. Bloom & L. Trilling (Eds.), *Romantic poetry and prose* (pp. 254–257). New York, NY: Oxford University Press. (Original work written 1798)

Coleridge, S. T. (1973b). The rime of the ancient mariner. In H. Bloom & L. Trilling (Eds.), *Romantic poetry and prose* (pp. 238–254). New York, NY: Oxford University Press. (Original work written 1798)

College Board. (2007). *English language and composition, English literature and composition: Course description*. Retrieved from http://apcentral.collegeboard.com/apc/public/repository/52272_apenglocked5_30_4309.pdf

Dickens, C. (1981). *A tale of two cities*. New York, NY: Bantam Books. (Original work published 1859)

Dollimore, J. (1984). *Radical tragedy: Religion, ideology, and power in the drama of Shakespeare and his contemporaries*. New York, NY: Prentice Hall/Harvester Wheatsheaf.

Effinger, S. (2011). *Titles from open response questions: Adapted from an original list by Norma J. Wilkerson*. Retrieved from http://homepage.mac.com/mseffie/AP/APtitles.html

Everett, B. (1960). The new *King Lear*. *Critical Quarterly, 2*, 325–339.

Frost, R. (1969). Bereft. In E. C. Lathem (Ed.), *The poetry of Robert Frost* (p. 251). New York, NY: Holt, Rinehart and Winston. (Original work published 1928)

Frost, R. (1969). Birches. In E. C. Lathem (Ed.), *The poetry of Robert Frost* (pp. 121–122). New York, NY: Holt, Rinehart and Winston. (Original work published 1916)

Frost, R. (1969). Fire and ice. In E. C. Lathem (Ed.), *The poetry of Robert Frost* (p. 220). New York, NY: Holt, Rinehart and Winston. (Original work published 1923)

Frost, R. (1969). Gathering leaves. In E. C. Lathem (Ed.), *The poetry of Robert Frost* (pp. 234–235). New York, NY: Holt, Rinehart and Winston. (Original work published 1923)

Frost, R. (1969). Hyla brook. In E. C. Lathem (Ed.), *The poetry of Robert Frost* (p. 119). New York, NY: Holt, Rinehart and Winston. (Original work published 1916)

Frost, R. (1969). Nothing gold can stay. In E. C. Lathem (Ed.), *The poetry of Robert Frost* (pp. 222–223). New York, NY: Holt, Rinehart and Winston. (Original work published 1923)

Frost, R. (1969). An old man's winter night. In E. C. Lathem (Ed.), *The poetry of Robert Frost* (p. 108). New York, NY: Holt, Rinehart and Winston. (Original work published 1916)

Frost, R. (1969). The onset. In E. C. Lathem (Ed.), *The poetry of Robert Frost* (p. 226). New York, NY: Holt, Rinehart and Winston. (Original work published 1923)

Frost, R. (1969). Reluctance. In E. C. Lathem (Ed.), *The poetry of Robert Frost* (pp. 29–30). New York, NY: Holt, Rinehart and Winston. (Original work published 1913)

Frost, R. (1969). Storm fear. In E. C. Lathem (Ed.), *The poetry of Robert Frost* (pp. 9–10). New York, NY: Holt, Rinehart and Winston. (Original work published 1913)

Frye, N. (1986). *Northrop Frye on Shakespeare* (R. Sandler, Ed.). New Haven, CT: Yale University Press.

Gallagher, K. (2004). *Deeper reading: Comprehending challenging texts, 4–12*. Portland, ME: Stenhouse Publishers.

Goddard, H. C. (1951). *The meaning of Shakespeare* (Vol. 2). Chicago, IL: University of Chicago Press.

Golding, W. (2006). *Lord of the flies*. New York, NY: Penguin. (Original work published 1954)

Hardy, T. (1901). In Tenebris–II. *Poets' Corner*. Retrieved from http://www.theotherpages.org/poems/hardy01.html

Heinemann, M. (2008). "Demystifying the mystery of state": King Lear and the world upside down. In G. Ioppolo (Ed.), *King Lear: A Norton critical edition*. New York, NY: Norton. (Original work published 1992)

Holinshed, R. (1587). *Chronicles of England, Scotland, and Ireland*. Retrieved from http://www.english.ox.ac.uk/holinshed

James I. (2008). *Basilikon Doron [the King's gift]: or His Majesties instructions to his dearest sonne, Henry the Prince*. In G. Ioppolo (Ed.), *King Lear: A Norton critical edition* (p. 157). New York, NY: Norton. (Original work written 1603)

Johnson, S. (2008). Notes on *King Lear*. In G. Ioppolo (Ed.), *King Lear: A Norton critical edition* (pp. 170–172). New York, NY: Norton. (Original work published 1765)

Kott, J. (2008). *Shakespeare our contemporary* (trans. Boleslaw Taborski). In G. Ioppolo (Ed.), King Lear: A Norton critical edition (pp. 177–179). New York, NY: Norton. (Original work published 1964)

Lamb, C. (1818). On the tragedies of Shakespeare. In C. Lamb (Ed.), *The works of Charles Lamb in two volumes* (Vol. 2, pp. 25–26). London, England: C. and J. Ollier.

Lampert, B. (2003). In response to a colleague's description of *Lear* as pathetic. *Möbius, the Poetry Magazine, 18*(2), 2.

Lever, J. W. (1987). *The tragedy of state: A study of Jacobean drama*. London, England: Routledge, Kegan, & Paul.

National Council of Teachers of English & International Reading Association. (1996). *Standards of learning for the English language arts*. Urbana, IL: Author.

Novy, M. (1984). *Love's argument: Gender relations in Shakespeare*. Chapel Hill: University of North Carolina Press.

Reimann, A. (1979). Memories and a vision and what can emerge from them: Notes on *Lear* (S. Spencer, trans.). In *Lear* (libretto accompanying operatic audio recording, pp. 9–18). Hamburg, Germany: Polydor International GmbH.

Reimann, A. (Composer), & Albrecht, G. (Conductor). (1979). *Lear* [Operatic audio recording]. Hamburg, Germany: Polydor International GmbH.

Seuss, D. (1960). *Green eggs and ham*. New York, NY: Random House.

Shakespeare, W. (1970). *Hamlet* (W. Farnham, Ed.). New York, NY: Penguin. (Original work written 1600)

Shakespeare, W. (1971). *Julius Caesar* (S. F. Johnson, Ed.). New York, NY: Penguin. (Original work written 1599)

Shakespeare, W. (1993). *King Lear* (B. A. Mowat & P. Werstine, Eds.). New York, NY: Washington Square Press. (Original work written 1603)

Shakespeare, W. (1971). *Macbeth* (A. Harbage, Ed.). New York, NY: Penguin. (Original work written 1606)

Shakespeare, W. (1992). *Romeo and Juliet* (B. A. Mowat & P. Werstine, Eds.). Washington, DC: Folger Shakespeare Library. (Original work written 1594)

Shakespeare, W. (1997). Sonnet 18. In H. Vendler (Ed.), *The art of Shakespeare's sonnets* (p. 119). Cambridge, MA: Harvard University Press. (Original work published 1609)

Shakespeare, W. (1971). *The winter's tale* (B. Maxwell, Ed.). New York, NY: Penguin. (Original work written 1611)

Tate, N. *The history of King Lear: Reviv'd with alterations* (J. Lynch, Ed.). Retrieved from http://ethnicity.rutgers.edu/~jlynch/Texts/tatelear.html (Original work produced 1681)

VanTassel-Baska, J. (1986). Effective curriculum and instructional models for the gifted. *Gifted Child Quarterly, 30*, 164–169.

Williams, W. C. (2000). Landscape with the fall of Icarus. In C. Nelson (Ed.), *Anthology of modern American poetry* (pp. 200–201). New York, NY: Oxford University Press. (Original work published 1962)

Willson, D. H. (1972). *A history of England* (2nd ed.). Hinsdale, IL: Dryden Press.

Resources for Further Study

Abbott, E. A. (1972). *A Shakespearian grammar* (Rev. ed.). New York, NY: Haskell House. (Original work published 1870)

Baskin, B. H., & Harris, K. H. (1980). *Books for the gifted child*. New York, NY: Bowker.

Bentley, G. E. (1961). *Shakespeare: A biographical handbook*. New Haven, CT: Yale University Press.

Bergeron, D. M., & Sousa, G. U. (1975). A guide to resources: Tragedies. In *Shakespeare: A study and research guide* (pp. 64–81). New York, NY: St. Martin's.

Berlioz, H. (Composer), & Janowski, M. (Conductor). (2010). *Le roi Lear* [Symphonic audio recording]. Germany: PentaTone Music.

Brown, J. R. (Ed.). (2001). *Oxford illustrated history of theatre*. New York, NY: Oxford University Press.

Center for Gifted Education. (1998). *Guide to teaching a language arts curriculum for high ability learners*. Dubuque, IA: Kendall/Hunt.

Clark, S. (1997). *The Shakespeare dictionary*. Lincolnwood, IL: NTC Publishing Group.

Coe, C. N. (1963). *Demi-devils: The character of Shakespeare's villains*. New York, NY: Bookman Associates.

Davis, G. A., Rimm, S. B., & Siegle, D. (2010). *Education of the gifted and talented* (6th ed.). Englewood Cliffs, NJ: Prentice Hall.

Drakakis, J. (Ed.). (2002). *Alternative Shakespeares*. New York, NY: Routledge.

Dutton, R. (1989). *William Shakespeare: A literary life*. New York, NY: St. Martin's Press.

Greg, W. W. (1939/1940). The date of King Lear and Shakespeare's use of earlier versions of the story. *The Library, 4,* 377–400.

Gurr, A. (2004). *Playgoing in Shakespeare's London* (3rd ed.). Cambridge, UK: Cambridge University Press.

Harrison, G. B. (1991). *Introducing Shakespeare* (4th ed.). London: Penguin Books.

Houppert, J. W. (1978). Love and death in *King Lear.* In E. Quinn (Ed.), *How to read Shakespearean tragedy* (pp. 179–228). New York, NY: Harper and Row.

Jazayery, M. A., & Law, R. A. (1953). Three texts of *King Lear*: Their differences. *Texas studies in English, 32,* 14–24.

Lace, W. W. (2005). *Elizabethan England.* San Diego, CA: Lucent Books.

Levith, M. J. (1978). *What's in Shakespeare's names.* Hamden, CT: Archon Books.

Mack, M. (2010). *King Lear in our time.* New York, NY: Routledge. (Original work published 1966)

McMurtry, J. (1989). *Understanding Shakespeare's England: A companion for the American reader.* Hamden, CT: Archon Books.

Morley, J., & James, J. (1994). *Shakespeare's theater.* New York, NY: Peter Bedrick Books.

Muir, K. (2008). *The sources of Shakespeare's plays.* New York, NY: Routledge.

Noble, R. S. H. (1935). King Lear. In *Shakespeare's Biblical knowledge and use of the Book of Common Prayer.* New York, NY: Society for Promoting Christian Knowledge.

Onions, C. T. (1986). *A Shakespeare glossary* (3rd ed.). Oxford, England: Oxford University Press.

Paul, R. (1992). *Critical thinking: What every person needs to survive in a rapidly changing world.* Rohnert Park, CA: Foundation for Critical Thinking.

Parker, B. M. (1979). *The Folger Shakespeare filmography.* Washington, DC: Folger Shakespeare Library.

Parrott, T. M. (1953). 'Gods' or 'gods' in *King Lear,* V.iii.17. *Shakespeare Quarterly, 4,* 427–432.

Ray, R. H. (1986). *Approaches to teaching Shakespeare's King Lear.* New York, NY: The Modern Language Association of America.

Singman, J. L. (1995). *Daily life in Elizabethan England.* Westport, CT: Greenwood Press.

Smith, R. M. (1946). *King Lear* and the Merlin tradition. *Modern Language Quarterly, 7,* 153–174.

Stone, P. W. K. (1979). *The textual history of King Lear.* London, England: Scholar's Press.

Vendler, H. (1999). *The art of Shakespeare's sonnets.* Cambridge, MA: Harvard University Press.

Wells, S. (Ed.). (1986). *The Cambridge companion to Shakespeare studies.* Cambridge, England: Cambridge University Press.

Adaptations of *King Lear* on Film

Birkett, M., & Skot-Hansen, M. (Producers), & Brook, P. (Director). (1971). *King Lear* [Motion picture]. United Kingdom: Filmways International Ltd.

Brook, P. (Director). (1953). *Omnibus: King Lear* [Televised motion picture]. United States: CBS.

Furukawa, K., et al. (Producers), & Kurosawa, A. (Director). (1985). *Ran* [Motion picture]. Japan: Nippon Herald Films.

Kozintsev, G. (Director). (1971). *King Lear* [Motion picture]. Soviet Union: Lenfilm.

Learoyd, B. (Production designer), & Morley, R. (Director). (1948). *King Lear* [Motion picture]. United Kingdom: British Broadcasting Company.

Plowright, D. (Producer), & Elliott, M. (Director). (1983). *King Lear* [Motion picture]. United Kingdom: Granada Television.

Price, R., & Picheta, A. (Producers), & Nunn, T. (Director). (2008). *Great performances: King Lear* [Televised motion picture]. United Kingdom: The Performance Company.

Author's Note: An additional film version of *King Lear* is currently in production; at the time of this book's writing, it was set to be released in 2012, starring Al Pacino and directed by Michael Radford.

Internet Resources

Alchin, L. K. (2005). *Elizabethan era: Elizabethan theatre.* Retrieved from http://www.elizabethan-era.org.uk/elizabethan-theatre.htm

Bellinger, M. F. (1927). Elizabethan playhouses, actors, and audiences. *A short history of the theatre*, 207–213. New York, NY: Henry Holt and Company. Retrieved from http://www.theatrehistory.com/british/bellinger001.html

Bruegel, P. (1558). *Landscape with the fall of Icarus.* Retrieved from http://www.topofart.com/images/artists/Pieter_the_Elder_Bruegel/paintings/bruegel012.jpg

Cambridge University Press. (2007). *An introduction to Shakespeare's life and times: Seminar introduction.* Retrieved from http://www.fathom.com/course/28701903/index.html

Folger Shakespeare Library. (2007). *Lesson plans archive.* Retrieved from http://www.folger.edu/eduLesPlanArch.cfm

Folger Shakespeare Library. (2007). *Teaching resources.* Retrieved from http://www.folger.edu/template.cfm?cid=618

Hern, L. A. (2011). *A teacher's guide to the Signet Classic edition of William Shakespeare's* King Lear. Retrieved from http://us.penguingroup.com/static/pdf/teachersguides/kinglear.pdf

Historic U. K. (2011). *Prehistoric England: 4000 BC–43 AD.* Retrieved from http://www.historic-uk.com/HistoryUK/England-History/PrehistoricEngland.htm

Lange, D. (1936). *Destitute pea pickers in California. Mother of seven children. Age thirty-two. Nipomo, California.* Retrieved from http://memory.loc.gov/service/pnp/cph/3b40000/3b41000/3b41800/3b41800r.jpg

Larque, T. (2001). *Shakespeare and his critics: A lecture on Elizabethan theatre.* Retrieved from http://shakespearean.org.uk/elizthea1.htm

New Internet Shakespeare Editions. (2007). *Sites on Shakespeare and the Renaissance.* Retrieved from http://internetshakespeare.uvic.ca/Annex/links/index.html

Powell, M. J. (2001). *Prehistoric sites in England.* Retrieved from http://homepage.ntlworld.com/mjpowell/Photo_Archive/England/England_2.htm

Pryor, F. (2011). *BBC history overview: From Neolithic to Bronze Age, 8000–800 BC.* Retrieved from http://www.bbc.co.uk/history/ancient/british_prehistory/overview_british_prehistory_01.shtml

Public Broadcasting Service. (2007). *In search of Shakespeare.* Retrieved from http://www.pbs.org/shakespeare

Public Broadcasting Service. (1995–2007). *The Shakespeare mystery: Who, in fact, was he?* Retrieved from http://www.pbs.org/wgbh/pages/frontline/shakespeare/index.html

Rusche, H. (2007). *Shakespeare illustrated.* Retrieved from http://www.english.emory.edu/classes/Shakespeare_Illustrated/Shakespeare.html

Shakespeare Oxford Society. (1995–2007). *A beginner's guide to the Shakespeare authorship problem.* Retrieved from http://www.shakespeare-oxford.com/?p=35

ThinkQuest Team. (2000). *Literature: Elizabethan theatre.* Retrieved from http://library.thinkquest.org/C006522/literature/eliztheatre.php

Web English Teacher. (2010). *William Shakespeare,* King Lear: *Lesson plans and other teaching resources.* Retrieved from http://www.webenglishteacher.com/kinglear.html

William Shakespeare info: Site map. (2007). Retrieved from http://www.william-shakespeare.info/site-map.htm

Wyeth, A. (1948). *Christina's world.* Retrieved from http://www.moma.org/collection/browse_results.php?object_id=78455

About the Author

R. Brigham Lampert, dual-certified in English and Gifted Education, is one of fewer than 50 teachers endorsed by the Virginia Department of Education as a Teacher as Leader. Also a National Board Certified Teacher, Lampert has been nominated for several national commendations, including a 2008 Nobel Educator of Distinction selection by the National Society of High School Scholars and a 2006 Disney Teacher Award. He is currently pursuing his Ed.D. at The College of William and Mary, where he was awarded a scholarship for Excellence in Gifted Education and where he earned his M.Ed. He received his B.A. in English from Haverford College.

Lampert has additionally authored *Advanced Placement Classroom: Romeo and Juliet* and *Perfect 800: SAT Verbal*, both available from Prufrock Press, original poems in various national journals, and six Shakespearean titles in The College of William and Mary's Center for Gifted Education's *Navigator* series, as well as coauthored and edited three updated editions of the center's award-winning literature units for gifted learners. Additionally trained as a building administrator, Lampert chairs the English department at Jamestown High School in Williamsburg, VA.

Common Core State Standards Alignment

Grade Level	Common Core State Standards
Grade 7 ELA-Literacy	RL.7.1 Cite several pieces of textual evidence to support analysis of what the text says explicitly as well as inferences drawn from the text.
	RL.7.2 Determine a theme or central idea of a text and analyze its development over the course of the text; provide an objective summary of the text.
	RL.7.3 Analyze how particular elements of a story or drama interact (e.g., how setting shapes the characters or plot).
	RL.7.4 Determine the meaning of words and phrases as they are used in a text, including figurative and connotative meanings; analyze the impact of rhymes and other repetitions of sounds (e.g., alliteration) on a specific verse or stanza of a poem or section of a story or drama.
	RL.7.5 Analyze how a drama's or poem's form or structure (e.g., soliloquy, sonnet) contributes to its meaning
	RL.7.6 Analyze how an author develops and contrasts the points of view of different characters or narrators in a text.
	RL.7.7 Compare and contrast a written story, drama, or poem to its audio, filmed, staged, or multimedia version, analyzing the effects of techniques unique to each medium (e.g., lighting, sound, color, or camera focus and angles in a film).
	W.7.2 Write informative/explanatory texts to examine a topic and convey ideas, concepts, and information through the selection, organization, and analysis of relevant content.
	W.7.9 Draw evidence from literary or informational texts to support analysis, reflection, and research.

Grade Level	Common Core State Standards
Grade 7 ELA-Literacy, *continued*	SL.7.1 Engage effectively in a range of collaborative discussions (one-on-one, in groups, and teacher-led) with diverse partners on grade 7 topics, texts, and issues, building on others' ideas and expressing their own clearly.
	SL.7.4 Present claims and findings, emphasizing salient points in a focused, coherent manner with pertinent descriptions, facts, details, and examples; use appropriate eye contact, adequate volume, and clear pronunciation.
	L.7.5 Demonstrate understanding of figurative language, word relationships, and nuances in word meanings.
Grade 8 ELA-Literacy	RL.8.1 Cite the textual evidence that most strongly supports an analysis of what the text says explicitly as well as inferences drawn from the text.
	RL.8.2 Determine a theme or central idea of a text and analyze its development over the course of the text, including its relationship to the characters, setting, and plot; provide an objective summary of the text.
	RL.8.3 Analyze how particular lines of dialogue or incidents in a story or drama propel the action, reveal aspects of a character, or provoke a decision.
	RL.8.4 Determine the meaning of words and phrases as they are used in a text, including figurative and connotative meanings; analyze the impact of specific word choices on meaning and tone, including analogies or allusions to other texts.
	RL.8.6 Analyze how differences in the points of view of the characters and the audience or reader (e.g., created through the use of dramatic irony) create such effects as suspense or humor.
	RL.8.7 Analyze the extent to which a filmed or live production of a story or drama stays faithful to or departs from the text or script, evaluating the choices made by the director or actors.
	W.8.2 Write informative/explanatory texts to examine a topic and convey ideas, concepts, and information through the selection, organization, and analysis of relevant content.
	W.8.9 Draw evidence from literary or informational texts to support analysis, reflection, and research.
	SL.8.1 Engage effectively in a range of collaborative discussions (one-on-one, in groups, and teacher-led) with diverse partners on grade 8 topics, texts, and issues, building on others' ideas and expressing their own clearly.
	SL.8.4 Present claims and findings, emphasizing salient points in a focused, coherent manner with relevant evidence, sound valid reasoning, and well-chosen details; use appropriate eye contact, adequate volume, and clear pronunciation.
	L.8.5 Demonstrate understanding of figurative language, word relationships, and nuances in word meanings.

Grade Level	Common Core State Standards
Grade 9-10 ELA-Literacy	RL.9-10.1 Cite strong and thorough textual evidence to support analysis of what the text says explicitly as well as inferences drawn from the text.
	RL.9-10.2 Determine a theme or central idea of a text and analyze in detail its development over the course of the text, including how it emerges and is shaped and refined by specific details; provide an objective summary of the text.
	RL.9-10.3 Analyze how complex characters (e.g., those with multiple or conflicting motivations) develop over the course of a text, interact with other characters, and advance the plot or develop the theme.
	RL.9-10.4 Determine the meaning of words and phrases as they are used in the text, including figurative and connotative meanings; analyze the cumulative impact of specific word choices on meaning and tone (e.g., how the language evokes a sense of time and place; how it sets a formal or informal tone).
	RL.9-10.5 Analyze how an author's choices concerning how to structure a text, order events within it (e.g., parallel plots), and manipulate time (e.g., pacing, flashbacks) create such effects as mystery, tension, or surprise.
	RL.9-10.9 Analyze how an author draws on and transforms source material in a specific work (e.g., how Shakespeare treats a theme or topic from Ovid or the Bible or how a later author draws on a play by Shakespeare).
	W.9-10.2 Write informative/explanatory texts to examine and convey complex ideas, concepts, and information clearly and accurately through the effective selection, organization, and analysis of content.
	W.9-10.9 Draw evidence from literary or informational texts to support analysis, reflection, and research.
	W.9-10.10 Write routinely over extended time frames (time for research, reflection, and revision) and shorter time frames (a single sitting or a day or two) for a range of tasks, purposes, and audiences.
	SL.9-10.1 Initiate and participate effectively in a range of collaborative discussions (one-on-one, in groups, and teacher-led) with diverse partners on grades 9–10 topics, texts, and issues, building on others' ideas and expressing their own clearly and persuasively.
	SL.9-10.6 Adapt speech to a variety of contexts and tasks, demonstrating command of formal English when indicated or appropriate. (See grades 9–10 Language standards 1 and 3 here for specific expectations.)
	L.9-10.5 Demonstrate understanding of figurative language, word relationships, and nuances in word meanings.

Grade Level	Common Core State Standards
Grade 9-10 ELA-Literacy, *continued*	L.9-10.6 Acquire and use accurately general academic and domain-specific words and phrases, sufficient for reading, writing, speaking, and listening at the college and career readiness level; demonstrate independence in gathering vocabulary knowledge when considering a word or phrase important to comprehension or expression.
Grade 11-12 ELA-Literacy	RL.11-12.1 Cite strong and thorough textual evidence to support analysis of what the text says explicitly as well as inferences drawn from the text, including determining where the text leaves matters uncertain.
	RL.11-12.2 Determine two or more themes or central ideas of a text and analyze their development over the course of the text, including how they interact and build on one another to produce a complex account; provide an objective summary of the text.
	RL.11-12.3 Analyze the impact of the author's choices regarding how to develop and relate elements of a story or drama (e.g., where a story is set, how the action is ordered, how the characters are introduced and developed).
	RL.11-12.4 Determine the meaning of words and phrases as they are used in the text, including figurative and connotative meanings; analyze the impact of specific word choices on meaning and tone, including words with multiple meanings or language that is particularly fresh, engaging, or beautiful. (Include Shakespeare as well as other authors.)
	RL.11-12.5 Analyze how an author's choices concerning how to structure specific parts of a text (e.g., the choice of where to begin or end a story, the choice to provide a comedic or tragic resolution) contribute to its overall structure and meaning as well as its aesthetic impact.
	RL.11-12.6 Analyze a case in which grasping a point of view requires distinguishing what is directly stated in a text from what is really meant (e.g., satire, sarcasm, irony, or understatement).
	RL.11-12.7 Analyze multiple interpretations of a story, drama, or poem (e.g., recorded or live production of a play or recorded novel or poetry), evaluating how each version interprets the source text. (Include at least one play by Shakespeare and one play by an American dramatist.)
	RL.11-12.10 By the end of grade 11, read and comprehend literature, including stories, dramas, and poems, in the grades 11-CCR text complexity band proficiently, with scaffolding as needed at the high end of the range. By the end of grade 12, read and comprehend literature, including stories, dramas, and poems, at the high end of the grades 11-CCR text complexity band independently and proficiently.

Grade Level	Common Core State Standards
Grade 11-12 ELA-Literacy, *continued*	W.11-12.2 Write informative/explanatory texts to examine and convey complex ideas, concepts, and information clearly and accurately through the effective selection, organization, and analysis of content.
	W.11-12.9 Draw evidence from literary or informational texts to support analysis, reflection, and research.
	W.11-12.10 Write routinely over extended time frames (time for research, reflection, and revision) and shorter time frames (a single sitting or a day or two) for a range of tasks, purposes, and audiences.
	SL.11-12.1 Initiate and participate effectively in a range of collaborative discussions (one-on-one, in groups, and teacher-led) with diverse partners on grades 11–12 topics, texts, and issues, building on others' ideas and expressing their own clearly and persuasively.
	SL.11-12.6 Adapt speech to a variety of contexts and tasks, demonstrating a command of formal English when indicated or appropriate. (See grades 11–12 Language standards 1 and 3 here for specific expectations.)
	L.11-12.5 Demonstrate understanding of figurative language, word relationships, and nuances in word meanings.
	L.11-12.6 Acquire and use accurately general academic and domain-specific words and phrases, sufficient for reading, writing, speaking, and listening at the college and career readiness level; demonstrate independence in gathering vocabulary knowledge when considering a word or phrase important to comprehension or expression.

For Product Safety Concerns and Information please contact our EU representative GPSR@taylorandfrancis.com
Taylor & Francis Verlag GmbH, Kaufingerstraße 24, 80331 München, Germany

www.ingramcontent.com/pod-product-compliance
Lightning Source LLC
Chambersburg PA
CBHW080409300426
44113CB00015B/2457